Reading Espionage Fiction

Reading Espionage Fiction

Narrative, Conflict and Commitment from World War I to the Contemporary Era

Martin Griffin

EDINBURGH
University Press

Edinburgh University Press is one of the leading university presses in the UK. We publish academic books and journals in our selected subject areas across the humanities and social sciences, combining cutting-edge scholarship with high editorial and production values to produce academic works of lasting importance. For more information visit our website: edinburghuniversitypress.com

© Martin Griffin 2024, 2025

Edinburgh University Press Ltd
13 Infirmary Street
Edinburgh EH1 1LT

First published in hardback by Edinburgh University Press 2025

Typeset in 11/13pt Adobe Sabon
by Manila Typesetting Company

A CIP record for this book is available from the British Library

ISBN 978 1 3995 2079 9 (hardback)
ISBN 978 1 3995 2080 5 (paperback)
ISBN 978 1 3995 2081 2 (webready PDF)
ISBN 978 1 3995 2082 9 (epub)

The right of Martin Griffin to be identified as the author of this work has been asserted in accordance with the Copyright, Designs and Patents Act 1988, and the Copyright and Related Rights Regulations 2003 (SI No. 2498).

Contents

Acknowledgements	vi
Introduction: Revisiting Ramón Mercader, 1966	1
1. The Maugham Paradigm: Performing English Identity amid the Surges of History	15
2. The Past as Prologue: Antifascism and the Prophetic Mode in Ambler and MacNeice	34
3. "We'll Meet Again": War, Memories, and Loss in MacInnes and Garve	53
4. John le Carré and the Jews	71
5. The American Uncertainty: Genre and Borders in Charles McCarry and Don DeLillo	93
6. Race and Intelligence: African-Americans and the Secret Life	113
7. The Soldier's Song: Britain's Irish War in Gerald Seymour's Trilogy	135
8. Espionage Fiction and the Lost Adversary: Carlyle and Mathison	157
Works Cited	177
Index	184

Acknowledgements

Chapter 1 on Somerset Maugham appeared first in *Partial Answers: Journal of Literature and the History of Ideas*, vol. 21, no. 1, January 2023, pp. 71–89. The author is grateful to the editors for permission to reprint it here.

The author also would also like to thank David Higham Associates Ltd., representing the Estate of Louis MacNeice, for permission to quote the lines from *Autumn Journal* in Chapter 2.

The origins of this book go back a long time and are as much the result of innumerable conversations and discussions over the decades as they are of the literary texts themselves. Indeed, it is only relatively recently that the academic study of espionage fiction has acquired enough credibility that one can now speak of a critical conversation on its history, its relationship to other literary genres, and its role in our political culture.

Edinburgh University Press has played a role in these larger developments, and I was fortunate to find an enthusiastic and engaged editor in Jackie Jones; the whole team at EUP has been a pleasure to work with, and no academic author could ask for more.

On a more individual note, alphabetical order has at least one advantage: a level playing field without ranking as to length or depth of contribution. To that extent, the following have all influenced, in various ways, what came to be *Reading Espionage Fiction*: Brad Bannon, Amy Billone, Matthew Blanshei, Dieter Brünn, Noga Emanuel, Dave Gatewood, Sarah Gellner, Michael Griffin, Thelma Griffin, Ann Marie Halpenny, James Hewitson, Mary Honan, Phyllis Lassner, Mike Parker, Vincent Pecora, Yvonne Pelletier, and Danny Thompson.

Special mention for close reading and targeted advice for particular chapters goes to Yvonne Pelletier and James Hewitson for Chapter 3, Mary Honan for Chapter 4, Brad Bannon for Chapter 5, Maggie Warren for Chapter 6 and Catherine Grech for the bibliography.

My upper-division undergraduate course on espionage fiction at the University of Tennessee, Knoxville, a few years ago brought forth some challenging questions from students, which made me think about aspects of the topic I hadn't taken note of before.

The enthusiastic collaboration of two student researchers at UTK, my undergraduate research assistant, Heather R. Doyle, and my graduate research assistant, Maggie Warren, compelled me to think more clearly about the project. In particular, Maggie Warren's eagle eye for a fuzzy argument and her intuitive sense of what the book was actually about made her contribution particularly valuable.

The former and the current heads of the English Department at UTK, Allen Dunn and Misty Anderson, have both been a source of academic solidarity and, sometimes, patience.

One cannot rank indispensability, but even more indispensable was Phyllis Lassner for her generous encouragement in directing me toward EUP and, apart from the example of her own work, for many fascinating email exchanges on espionage fiction, crime fiction, and the relationship of these genres to the political history of the long twentieth century.

And last not least, Catherine (whose sensible advice for this section was "Just thank everyone you know!") has always been there to remind me that (a) I wanted to write this book and therefore (b) should actually do so and finish it. And so it was with her unstinting support and encouragement that I did, indeed, complete the last deletions and insertions on the manuscript one summer afternoon, enabling me to write as a concluding note:

Sauble Beach, Ontario, June 2023

Introduction: Revisiting Ramón Mercader, 1966

Three lines of thinking flowed, over many years, into the readings and arguments in this study. The first line is a deep interest in the nature of plot and plotting, and the impetus to probe a little more into why the architecture of plot tends to be assigned a lower ranking than that of character or of the fabric of the writing. The tendency seems mistaken, as story can have its own dynamics and indeed pleasures, and espionage fiction offers a complex experience of plot which is, I would argue, both distinctive and important for understanding the way these novels, as well as one narrative poem and one television drama, embody their particular readings of the world. The second is the proposition that the narrative of intelligence work can be, and has clearly been, one of the most sensitive instruments for reading the map of political struggle, international conflict, and the philosophical and ideological choices offered and taken, by individuals and groups, during the long and dangerous twentieth century. The third, and one that underpins the first two, is the desire to read the various texts as primarily literary works without becoming overly entangled in arguments over genre. Genre as a concept can play multiple roles in critical approaches to fiction, but not all of them healthy: genre is a category that espionage fiction has both helped create and also, in an obvious sense, become trapped within. The goal may be somewhat optimistic, but I have chosen several novels, one narrative poem, and one television drama not only to cover the period of more than a century but also to bring works with different levels of cultural prestige into conversation with each other, with a view to relativizing genre constraints and querying inflexible rankings of literary quality.[1]

One path to registering such a query goes by way of a novel in translation and the noticeable difference between its style and that of espionage fiction in the Anglophone realm. The extensive use of free indirect discourse in Jorge Semprun's novel *La deuxième mort de Ramón Mercader*, published in 1969, suggests that this mode of narration performs a different function in other European literatures from its role in English.[2] A Spaniard by birth, Jorge Semprun wrote mainly in French during his long career that took in novels, film scripts, and autobiographical works.[3] Translated in 1973, *The Second Death of Ramón Mercader* is an espionage story of a high degree of complexity framed in a long historical perspective from Spain in the 1930s to Amsterdam in 1966. The name in the title will be familiar to many readers but perhaps not as much as it would have been fifty years ago. Semprun uses the name of the Soviet undercover agent who infiltrated the household in Mexico City of Leon Trotsky, a leader of the Russian Revolution who became a refugee from the Soviet Union. Trotsky was regarded by Josef Stalin and the Kremlin as a dangerous renegade and a potential leader of disaffected communists and the anti-Stalinist left worldwide. On August 20, 1940, Mercader murdered Trotsky at his home with an ice-pick. He was tried in Mexico and served twenty years in prison. In 1960 he was released and sent to Cuba; he eventually settled in Czechoslovakia.

Beginning with the literary modernism of the early twentieth century, free indirect discourse—that mode of narration that mimics the pattern of subjective individual thought without the apparent mediation of a narrative framing—has manifested itself in the Anglophone realm as a more advanced and demanding style of narrative. It has the effect of both speeding up and slowing down the reader's perception of time, often bumping the story from point to point in the kind of associative movement we recognize as our own subjective tumbling of disorganized thoughts and impressions, but also creating the verbal equivalent of a film changing suddenly from normal speed to a slow-motion scene in which thinking or action appears to take an almost painfully lengthy time to be completed. Authors in a range of literatures, from Woolf, Joyce, and Faulkner to Zola, Roth, and Kafka, fashioned a more uncompromising version of free indirect discourse into a marker of modern fiction and, to a certain extent, a signal of the difficulty of the work that the reader might want to consider.

Yet, although the technique spread far beyond the few central figures of literary modernism in different languages, it remains a fairly uncontroversial observation that ostensibly more challenging narrative techniques were avoided by authors of popular fiction. And that fact lends a particular flavor to the translation of *The Second Death of Ramón Mercader*. Semprun's novel is a shifting and oblique account of a man calling himself by the same name who arrives in Amsterdam and whose actions draw the attention of both the CIA and the East German intelligence service. The story moves back and forth across time to link the contemporary Amsterdam of the 1960s, the embittered violence of the Spanish Civil War, and the Stalinist purges in the Soviet Union and Eastern Europe. Semprun's Ramón Mercader seems to be either an ideological twin of the original Mercader or someone deliberately using his name to attract attention from intelligence agencies, driven by some obscure agenda of his own.

With a story that roves across history and the subjective experiences of various characters, the novel is also notable for the way in which the narration moves somewhat unexpectedly from standard third-person to extended dialogue to subjectively remembered dialogue to perspectives rendered in such a way as to leave the reader uncertain as to the source or context of the language on the page.[4] A representative example is from an early chapter in which an otherwise unidentified character—he could be Mercader, or he could be the implied author Jorge Semprun—visits a Spanish restaurant one evening in Amsterdam, hidden in an alley, and finds himself thinking about Spanish immigrants looking for a feeling of home, and listening to the flow of idiomatic working-class Spanish all around him. The menu on the wall is represented schematically within the text, and the narrator notes what he would have ordered, had he been there. He meditates on the ability of the Spanish language to capture words from other languages and turn them to its own purposes, and hears a group of male customers arguing vehemently, and somewhat disappointingly, about commercial sex. Clearly an educated man of left-of-center views, he notes regretfully that one might have hoped for "these workmen to have been discussing recent working-class efforts to obtain better pay and freedom to join trade unions; but, alas, the dispute was solely about florins and thighs" (116). The dialogue between the men follows, in Spanish with the English translation in brackets. The narration of chapter 9 draws metafictional attention to itself as a fictional account, and yet renders in a powerful manner central themes and elements from the wider story: Spain in the twentieth century; a thoughtful individual on a confidential mission and with clearly expressed food preferences; the neutrality and reserve of Amsterdam juxtaposed with the political passions of modern European history, now frozen into the Cold War.

One could say that *The Second Death of Ramón Mercader* is an espionage novel that can avail of a different range of literary forms, and noticeably a model (perhaps French, perhaps also Spanish) that regulates the distinctions between popular fiction and so-called literary fiction with a somewhat different measure from that applied in Anglophone cultures.[5] In Semprun's novel, the narrative voices are less clearly defined, the plot lines are more obscure, and the implied values are somewhat more left-wing and cosmopolitan than has been common in either British or American fiction. The dynamics of the novel function, to put it another way, more on a poetic and associative principle than on a sequential and logically connected one. When Peter Boxall, for example, concludes in *The Value of the Novel* that the crucial development in fiction from the modernist period on has been from a realist notion of narrative stance "towards a kind of writing which consistently exposed its own artificiality, its own emptiness of self and of voice," it seems clear that he is referring to a canon of modern and postmodern works that are, simply by virtue of their canonicity, protected from any implication that they also belong to a popular genre.[6] The assumption that his analysis does not include, say, the fiction of John le Carré is so axiomatic that he does not have to make any mention of these literary borders and lines of control. A novel like Semprun's would, in a sense, be almost unreadable, or at least be a striking anomaly, for the intellectual and cultural framework Boxall is working within. *Ramón Mercader* is an espionage fiction that came into being within a less rigid matrix of genre distinctions that allowed its language and narrative organization to present a certain amount of difficulty—with the result that one reads it with the realization that it would likely not have emerged as it is from the British or American tradition. It is, in some obvious ways, a modernist or perhaps postmodernist work in a genre that, in the Anglophone context, is often regarded as a something to be avoided—precisely because such a move would court the danger of being denied literary credibility. It would not be associated, as one theorist of popular literature has noted, with "creativity . . . individuality, origin, and essence."[7]

Despite the ambivalent resistance within the Anglophone branch to being freed from genre as well as to being constrained by it, one can, nonetheless, find a range of interesting issues of narrative strategy for espionage fiction in the English language. In part, that is exactly what *Reading Espionage Fiction* concerns itself with: how authors from Maugham and Ambler to McCarry and Seymour have used highly conventional narrative modes, but also utilized opportunities to reshape character and give plot a new valency. The goal has been to create a storytelling mode that can operate on the level of historical and political reality as well as that of human emotion and interpersonal relationships: to make, as Allen Hepburn expresses it "political subjectivity . . . a mysterious, if thrilling, set of contradictions."[8] In that way, not only *The Second Death of Ramón Mercader* but Helen MacInnes's *I and My True Love* and Gerald Seymour's *The Journeyman Tailor* (to take two examples, discussed in Chapters 3 and 7 respectively) demand to be taken as literary art, rather than exercises in masked documentary or mechanical plot construction. To that extent, this book can be taken as an experiment in thinking beyond genre but without ignoring its legacy and affordances. It is not, of course, as if there are no genres, but a certain problem arises if one particular mode of fiction is seen as having a status that derives from having been already liberated from the label. Then "genre fiction" becomes a term that not only indicates a certain range of story and character but also moves both the individual work and its creative field downward in the table of cultural credibility.[9] To have been spared the genre fiction identifier is to be, as one might put it today, privileged. With the combinations of texts in chapters as well as in this book as a whole, therefore, I hope to at least complicate aspects of that ranking system.

plot, character, history

The question of plot is a complex one, as it involves two separate levels that tend to be confused with each other. The first is the Aristotelian proposition that the interaction of character and action creates the plot, and plot is by implication the temporal unfolding of a series of actions within a unified frame. The second is the interpretive valuation that the reader establishes to guide their reception of the components of any literary or dramatic narrative. Opening his exploration of the inherited status of Aristotelian literary theory for modern fiction, J. Hillis Miller notes succinctly that "Aristotle gives primacy to the plot ('mythos') in a tragedy. It takes priority over all of the other elements of a tragedy, for example, character ('ethos') and diction ('lexis')."[10] The relationship of plot to other elements of the work, namely character and language, or person and poetry, has become over time a much more complex and contested area. It is undeniable that the relationship between action and meaning has proven to be somewhat problematic in the age of the novel, as there has been a cultural shift (and possibly more than one) in the status granted to the various components of fiction.

The long-standing hierarchy, at least since the early twentieth century, has been one in which the status assigned to plot is lower on the scale than its sister elements. This is not simply a technical issue, of course, as it has many visible and invisible consequences, not least of which is a tendency to view too much interest in plot as an indicator of an immature or unsophisticated reading of a text, with the implication that the lack of maturity and sophistication might be a deficit in the person of the reader herself. Likewise, the construction of complex or multivalent plot structures can itself be read as an indicator of a bent toward popular fictional forms, potentially a kind of involuntary pressure toward a lower ranking.

In the case of espionage fiction, however, plot is often the aspect of a work that carries significant weight and is the locus of the imaginative core of a story. Peter Brooks's remark that we can view "the reading of plot as a form of desire" that energizes the basic act of reading itself applies to espionage fiction with particular sharpness.[11] Brooks goes on to say that narrative is one of the large categories that we think within, and plot "is its thread of design and its active shaping force, the product of our refusal to allow temporality to be meaningless, our stubborn insistence on making meaning in the world and in our lives."[12] One might add that it is difficult to impossible to read some novels in any productive way without understanding the plot or, equally important, understanding that it is plot as much as character or narrative form that activates the emotional charge of the narrative. The very act of devoting attention to the plot should not endanger the project of taking a novel seriously as a work of fiction in its own right.

There is a further difficulty here: as Miller has argued in a different context, "Literature, particularly story-telling in literature ... seems to have something essentially to do with the sharing of secrets."[13] The narrative is itself an act of secrecy and disclosure, or different configurations of those two things acting in a simple or complex relationship to each other. As the espionage story will often involve the plotting of an act as a premise, the plot within the plot structures the narrative dynamic which may, in turn, involve the restriction of information with the ethical and observational position of the reader located on the side of those maintaining secrecy.

This phenomenon may sit a little uneasily with some who feel more of a discomfort with the act of plotting. As the British novel gradually achieved its status as the primary literary form to represent in a realistic mode the outer and inner lives of the middle classes (in the broadest sense, distinguishing them from both aristocracy and the working class), plotting was often a sign of the morally or ethically suspect character or entity.[14] The exposure of plotting is often, in the traditional novel, associated with the restoration of appropriate and presentable relations between individuals and communities. This is, in the espionage story, neither so simple nor necessarily the case. Indeed, the successful plot may leave an ambiguous situation behind it, or pose an ethical problem that is recognized but never addressed, or if addressed never resolved. Hence the construction of the fictional plot may, perhaps unintentionally, be morally contaminated by the nature of the plot within that work of fiction. Traditional realist fiction is set up to resolve any such collision of values, but espionage fiction is not.

The revaluation of plot has been, even more recently, given more heft by a similar revival of critical interest in the nature of character. As Toril Moi argues in her essay "Rethinking Character," there is something faintly absurd, even disconcerting, about the fact that we continue to exchange accusations that the one or the other reader is treating characters in a work of fiction as if they were real, even when everyone appears to agree that no critic actually believes they are.[15] Clearly, questions regarding the ontological status of fictional persons point to a somewhat sensitive issue that appears to be still active. This is of particular importance for many espionage narratives, especially those with a strong investment in ideological conviction and conflict. To be specific: without an active realization of character in such a way as to make concrete the ideas and emotions of loyalty and commitment in human life, not only spy fiction but almost any political fiction that seeks to represent how and why people make choices based on experiences, beliefs, and future hopes could not be written. In the texts I explore in this book, character can be manifest in many different modes and framings, but at a certain basic level, the clash of ideas is never simply an abstract jousting of intellectual options but rather the acting-out—with consequences— of stances and choices within the individual and in the wider social and political arena in which they find themselves.

This is not to claim that characters in espionage fiction are, or have to be, excessively realistic. The "draw of character," Rita Felski notes, "has far less to do with realism than with qualities of vividness and distinctiveness."[16] The ability that readers have to understand why a person in a narrative makes a dissenting political choice or carries out an ethically ambiguous act is never founded merely on a one-dimensional identification with that person or a set of shared ideological positions. It is much more a function of the vitality and effect of character in its complex interaction with abstract conviction that can create a bond of (to use Felski's terms) allegiance and empathy: not so much uncritical identification but rather a complex understanding of how a choice may be a wrong choice made by a sympathetic character, or more problematically a choice one would empathize with made by someone in the story for whom one feels little or no warmth.

The inescapability of plot and character, or the architecture and psycho-social verisimilitude, respectively, of a narrative is therefore for those and similar reasons something of a foundational proposition for *Reading Espionage Fiction*, and I hope that that fact itself will be more of an invitation than an impediment to readers of the book. In certain cases, for example Andrew Garve's *The Ashes of Loda* and Charles McCarry's *The Miernik Dossier*, the intricacies of the unfolding plot mesh with the evocation of place and the movements of focalization among both narrative voice and character in such a way as to make the combination the primary vehicle for transmitting the emotional and ethical values of the novel, and ethical judgments are inevitably part of espionage fiction because these fictions, unlike crime novels, are about the search for truth rather than for justice.[17] The story cannot be assumed, or assumed to be merely a tool deployed for a larger aesthetic purpose, and I elaborate on the detail of the plot where it is warranted. One of the remarkable achievements of these and other fictions is to leave the story resonating in the consciousness—the memory of the work is often the memory of the human interaction with plot, an interaction which incidentally guarantees no celebratory or inspirational outcome. Espionage narratives can be the type, perhaps surprisingly, to best resist the tendency, as Martha Nussbaum frames it, to ignore "the mystery and complexity within each life, in its puzzlement and pain about its choices, in its attempt to grapple with the mysterious and awful fact of its own mortality."[18] The awkward dance among equally demanding loyalties has been the most powerful subject for its stories.

chapters

Reading Espionage Fiction begins with a return to the spy story of the early twentieth century, not to Conrad, Erskine Childers, or Kipling but rather to W. Somerset Maugham. Maugham's short stories, published individually in the early 1920s and then in 1928 in a collection entitled *Ashenden; or The British Agent*, are the topic of the first full-length chapter. Set mostly in neutral Switzerland in World War I, Maugham's fiction not only introduces some classic genre elements of the spy story but also complicates and confuses those beginnings by delivering downbeat and sometimes frustratingly undramatic endings to the narratives. The politics of the Ashenden stories are set so far back from the surface of the action as to be almost invisible. When they do appear, as in the story "Mr. Harrington's Washing," they are so bleakly plain as to be like a traffic accident one cannot look away from.

In the second chapter I examine the antifascist writing of the 1930s and focus on two publications that appeared in early 1939, a few months before the outbreak of war in Europe: Louis MacNeice's narrative poem *Autumn Journal* and Eric Ambler's *A Coffin for Dimitrios*. In devoting attention to a poetic work as well as a novel, I take up the implications of Michael Denning's influential study of espionage fiction, in particular his proposition that with regard to the 1930s there are "reasons for treating . . . popular front anti-fascism as essentially an aesthetic position."[19] I argue that antifascism was a widely-shared conviction and, significantly, extended across the cultural landscape from modern poetry to the international thriller, and that this political urgency generates similarities of perspective that collapse the distance from high to lower cultural forms, and also open the door to what I call a prophetic mode in these narratives.

In Chapter 3 the theme is transitioning from World War II to the Cold War, which was not only, of course, a matter of determining one's political loyalties and commitments: it could also involve the cementing or sundering of personal, familial, and intimate relationships. Not only could allies become enemies, but friends and romantic lovers could become ideological opponents, each driven by strongly antagonistic values. In Helen MacInnes's *I and My True Love* (1953), the legacy of wartime comradeship and a common purpose is put under unbearable strain by the new political and strategic realities both in Europe and in Washington. In Andrew Garve's *The Ashes of Loda* (1964), the consequences of deception and a long-term covert operation to penetrate British scientific and industrial circles come to destroy identity and trust at the most intimate center of family relations. Long before the notion that the personal is political became an unavoidable realization, MacInnes and Garve explored the most vulnerable places of existence where the revelation of the truth may be a more overwhelming challenge than the maintenance of the lie.

The next chapter deals with an important aspect of the novels of John le Carré, by far one of the most influential authors of espionage fiction and the writer whose work has determined crucial elements of the genre as it has developed over the past half-century. In this chapter, I argue that le Carré was unusual among British authors of the 1960s, when he began his career, in grasping the importance of the Jewish experience of the depredations of modernity in its most nihilistic and destructive form, the Nazi genocide. His early novels often feature a significant character, not usually the protagonist, whose Jewish identity is built into the nature of the choices they make, in one case (Liz Gold in *The Spy Who Came In from the Cold*) without direct intention but in others with some element of personal choice. I go on to suggest that le Carré's later novel *The Little Drummer Girl* reverses, to an extent, the paradigm of Jewish sacrifice for a somewhat fuzzily conceived greater good. In this work, it is the institutions of the state of Israel, no longer the isolated individual or community, that form the center of decision, and it is a gentile who is selected to be the bearer of secrets and the subject who accepts risk.

Spy fiction authors have had ambitions, but literary fiction has not been shy about helping itself to genre conventions at certain times. The jigsaw-like and non-omniscient composition of Charles McCarry's *The Miernik Dossier* (1973) and the postmodern mystery structure of Don DeLillo's *The Names* (1982), both discussed in Chapter 5, offer themselves as examples of narratives that approach genre boundaries as flexible or even porous divisions. Alert to the twentieth-century ambivalence regarding conspiracy, these two novels play with the fact that conspiratorial resolutions may leave both characters and readers with either too much certainty for reassurance or too little to relieve frustration. In exercises that mirror each other, both McCarry and DeLillo approach the task of fictional invention with different ambitions, but with areas of overlap that suggest that writers of what came to be known as literary fiction have been at moments intrigued and attracted by what the tropes of spy fiction could offer. The question of whether a narrative act can be evaluated on the basis of which end of the spectrum of literary credibility it comes from is significant for the reading of DeLillo and McCarry. They both bring a strong and creative sense of dialogue to their respective fictions, too, with McCarry's ability to portray the conversational interactions of a multinational group of colleagues, ostensible friends, and individuals with different agendas, and DeLillo as the author who, as one critic observed, "catches and transcribes American voices as no other writer can."[20]

The following chapter examines the role played by African-American writers in extending the range of the espionage story, looking in particular at Samuel Greenlee's novel *The Spook Who Sat by the Door* and John A. Williams's *The Man Who Cried I Am*. The experience reflected in these works is one that suggests that, at least for a period and to an extent, black life in the United States is in an existentialist sense a narrative of covert activity and dissembling. The experience of black Americans both under slavery and after was often suffused with tension and the need for heightened alertness associated with covert action. It was not only escaped slaves who moved across the landscape like operatives in enemy territory, but even a century after Emancipation, "passing" as white could still be a fraught but in some cases promising option that enabled an escape into a different life. I also read short stories by Richard Wright as establishing, in the era of the Depression and the realm of left political activism, a powerful trope of the need for protective cover and cover stories in African-American experience.

In the seventh chapter, entitled "The Soldier's Song" (taking the English title of the Irish national anthem "Amhrán na bhFiann"), I examine how the thirty-year Northern Ireland conflict is represented in the three novels that Gerald Seymour wrote between 1975 and 1992, *Harry's Game*, *Field of Blood*, and *The Journeyman Tailor*. The relative paucity of spy fiction set during the war in Northern Ireland—which in real life had a significant covert operations and intelligence dimension, as well as the IRA's bombing campaign in British cities—can be seen as arising from the confusion over whether Ulster was a place at home in the United Kingdom, or abroad. The tentative suspicion that Belfast and Derry were in some way "domestic" locations made it a little difficult to open up a literary genre more attuned to a narrative of global ideological struggle as well as spatial distance. Gerald Seymour was, at the time, somewhat of an exception in the way he approached the social, cultural, and political dimensions of the "Troubles," as they came to be known.

The final chapter looks at the nature and style of espionage fiction as it has changed after the end of the Cold War and, in particular, how it has managed to adapt to the situation of the so-called war on terror and the global threat of Islamist violence facing both established Muslim states and an increasingly paranoid West (and, as a result of the war in Chechnya, Russia too) led by a United States no longer in the position of unchallenged authority it had held a quarter-century earlier. The end of the Cold War and the growing conflict with extremism after 9/11 have posed some intriguing problems for espionage authors. The paradigm has clearly shifted in one area: the growth of a religious rather than a secular belief system, and the way it casts into relief the fact that both Western democracy and Soviet communism were intellectual legacies of the Enlightenment. At the same time, women were becoming a more accepted and even welcomed presence in the intelligence agencies.

The gender assumptions of espionage fiction, inevitably, had to shift as a result of these changes in recruitment policy. I discuss *At Risk* (2006), the first novel by a former director-general of the British Security Service, Stella Rimington. Not the first writer of espionage fiction with some professional experience of intelligence work, Rimington created a younger protagonist, Liz Carlyle, working as an MI5 officer in the post-9/11 world. Rimington's novel complicates the more stereotypical narrative of a terrorist conspiracy with one that takes into account that there can be rational reasons for violence, that a disaffection with modern British life can find an escape route through religious fanaticism, and that assumptions about gender are more misleading than illuminating. The better-known *Homeland*, the television drama centered on the so-called "war on terror," is dominated by a talented but unpredictable CIA officer, Carrie Mathison, who struggles to negotiate a post-Cold War global political environment.[21] *Homeland* ran for eight seasons between 2011 and 2020 and, at its best, made viewers think about how the ideological struggle against a religiously inspired adversary (to an extent, at least) might be different from the dominating twentieth-century struggle between the Soviet Union and the West, where the question was more about the management of political modernity than a contest between a confident liberal secularism and an ironclad belief in sacred truths. Despite its several flaws, *Homeland* was remarkably prescient about a couple of significant political events in our time, including both the increasing tensions between the United States and Russia—although it ended in 2020, before the Russian invasion of Ukraine—and the chaotic American retreat from Afghanistan in 2021, and it raised some uncomfortable and, as I see it, still unresolved questions.

Notes

1. A model for this would be Allan Hepburn's inspired but also dispassionate reading of Robert Ludlum's *The Bourne Identity* at the beginning of his study *Intrigue* (3–10). Hepburn's ability to steer a productive line between narratological and aesthetic perspectives established a new pathway for criticism and scholarship on espionage fiction.
2. There is a spectrum rather than a precisely bounded category for free indirect discourse. At one end it approaches stream-of-consciousness, while at the other it reaches back into experiments with character and narrative perspective in Victorian fiction. In Semprun's text, it appears with different levels of mediation, from defined characters with interior thoughts to ambiguous second-person narration as if the author were in conversation with the reader. The extensive use of this technique makes even more noticeable the absence of this kind of writing in Anglophone espionage novels.
3. Jorge Semprun is probably best known for his work with the Greek film director Costa-Gavras, most notably for writing the 1969 documentary-style political thriller *Z*, as well as memoirs of his incarceration in Buchenwald concentration camp during World War II and his time as an undercover political organizer in Franco's Spain. He was a member of the Spanish Communist Party from 1942 until he was expelled in 1964. He held the post of minister for culture in the Socialist Party government from 1988 to 1991.
4. Although Semprun writes in a narrative mode seldom encountered in Anglophone espionage fiction, many authors have experimented with different styles that appear more conventional but nonetheless transmit specific effects; in my final chapter, for example, I note the use by Stella Rimington of what Dorrit Cohn in *Transparent Minds* calls "narrated monologue."
5. For a more recent example, the remarkable trilogy entitled *Your Face Tomorrow*, by the Spanish author Javier Marías, published in English between 2005 and 2009, offers some evidence of this being a significant feature of Spanish fiction. With its ambitious but assured journey among family memoir, historical memory, espionage story, and marital drama, it integrates subjective interior narration and contemporary social realism untroubled by queries as to genre identity or literary credibility.
6. Boxall, *The Value of the Novel*, 28.
7. Gelder, *Popular Literature*, 13.
8. Hepburn, *Intrigue*, 5.
9. In an interview from 2017 Walter Mosley describes an amusing, if also frustrating, incident at a literary conference at which his publisher introduced him to another writer. The other author persistently asked

Mosley if he was the "crime novelist," to which Mosley kept replying, "Yes, the novelist" ("The Art of Fiction," 267). One wonders whether the somewhat boneheaded attempt to categorize a fellow author as belonging to a subordinate creative rank is particularly common in other national literary cultures too.

10. Miller, *Reading Narrative*, 8.
11. Brooks, *Reading for the Plot*, 37; see Brooks's wider discussion on this in the chapter entitled "Narrative Desire."
12. Brooks, *Reading for the Plot*, 323.
13. Miller, *Other*s, 139. The remark appears in Miller's essay on Conrad's short story "The Secret Sharer" (137–69), which has a strong narrative thread of hiding and discovery.
14. As Wendy Veronica Xin has noted in an essay intentionally echoing Peter Brooks' earlier book, "Plots are often the secret expressions of secret ambitions," "Reading for the Plotters," 94.
15. Moi, "Rethinking Character," 29.
16. Felski, "Identifying with Characters," 28.
17. A proposition that both Allan Hepburn and Conor McCarthy echo, although from slightly different perspectives; see *Intrigue*, 19, and *Outlaws and Spies*, 121, respectively. McCarthy's reading of espionage fiction is framed within a wider exploration of the legal history of the outlaw, which opens up some new and interesting questions.
18. Nussbaum, *Poetic Justice*, 23.
19. Denning, *Cover Stories*, 65.
20. Tanner, *The American Mystery*, 213.
21. As an indication of its importance, in 2015 *Homeland* became the subject of a dedicated issue of *Cinema Journal*, vol. 54, no. 4 (Summer 2015).

Chapter 1

The Maugham Paradigm: Performing English Identity amid the Surges of History

In the Ashenden stories by W. Somerset Maugham, the question of national character seems never to be far below the surface. Against the landscape of war, but in a protected corner in a neutral country, a background hum of Englishness in style and posture can offer a reader the sense of home as something like a portable national attitude. If one only adopts the right tone with the staff, there will be some corner of a foreign hotel lobby that is forever England. And yet, as Terry Eagleton once observed, any nationalist project is inevitably overshadowed by irony.[1] Eagleton meant the rebellious nationalism of the colonial underdog, one should note, but the kind of diffuse national ideology of imperial power that does not even understand itself as such cannot deflect the metaphysics of irony either. Thus the oblique gaze in these fictions of "the British Agent" suggests that insecurity and uncertainty established themselves early in the genre's history, alongside and within the representation of decisive action in the national interest. Indeed, Maugham can lay claim to being the author who introduced irony in a deeper sense to the espionage story: not only the occasional flashes of self-deprecating wit found in his predecessors but a more tragic mode of narrative that sets effort and consequence in a conflictual relationship to each other. The gap between the pressure of the mission and the potential for confusion or even failure is reflected in the required dissimulation on Ashenden's part that is both a tactical calculation and a personal style.[2]

If Rudyard Kipling's 1901 novel *Kim* represents one model or prototype for the espionage tale as a branch of fiction; and if John Buchan's novels *The Thirty-Nine Steps* (1915) and *Greenmantle*

(1916) represent another; then Somerset Maugham's series of interlocking short stories, published between 1919 and 1923 and collected as the volume *Ashenden; or The British Agent* in 1928, embodies yet a third sketch for how this small workshop of narrative art might be identified and evaluated. If *Kim* portrays intelligence work as taking place in a kind of romantic ethnic and racial liminality that has as its aim and justification the security of a British Empire that possesses not only authority but even a leaven of what we might now call diversity, and if Buchan's narratives set out the more inwardly oriented nationalism that sees the threat to the United Kingdom within a European continental power struggle, then *Ashenden* might be the originating fiction that sets out the secret life as both an existential decision born of whimsy, and without doubt also an intellectual challenge not quite like any other.[3] Maugham's Ashenden stories can also be seen in their progression through the years of the Great War, however, as a gradual hollowing-out of the assumption of centrality for British national ideology in the modern world.

The fortunes of these three authors in the canon formation of the twentieth century for British literature are worth viewing in juxtaposition. In the case of Rudyard Kipling, his presence within a range of popular and sub-popular modes kept him from disappearing. The survival of the "Barrack-Room Ballads" with their laconic ironies inspired writers as far away from Kipling's circumstances as Bertolt Brecht, who transformed the Kipling ballad into the dramatic songs that accompanied a new kind of theater in Weimar Germany. Disney's animated movie adaptation of Kipling's *The Jungle Book*, released in 1967, was particularly significant in drawing attention to his writings for children. From a different perspective, a new if somewhat skeptical interest in Kipling's work emerged in postcolonial studies and also helped his return, even if the bearers of that discussion inclined to frame Kipling as a kind of imperial popularizer, while occasionally conceding a class-resentment point about the way in which the people who fought for and secured the British Empire were not those who profited most by it.[4]

The case of John Buchan is somewhat less compelling, mainly because Buchan works within such a thin segment of narrative art in his novels. The best-known of these, *The Thirty-Nine Steps*, has achieved a permanent niche in British popular fiction, assisted by the film adaptations from 1935, 1959, and 1978. Buchan's limited abilities with characterization and conservative if not reactionary attitudes, however, often sit uneasily alongside the narrative's relaxed style and moments of dry humor, reproduced faithfully in Alfred

Hitchcock's 1935 movie adaptation, *The 39 Steps*, in particular. In contrast to Kipling, however, Buchan scholarship has a less visible profile, possibly the result of a more defensive ethnic nationalism present in *Greenmantle* with its premise of a Teutonic-Islamic threat to the rule of the Anglophone powers.[5] To that extent, Kipling's *Kim* is committed in a paternalistic but distinctive way to a view of the world that does not demand a test of cultural purity as the key requirement for service to a diverse community: the empire needs all kinds of people to do its secret work, precisely because it throws its cloak of protection over all kinds of people. Kipling's orientalism has few friends these days, as one might expect, even if his sociological perspective is somewhat more generous than Buchan's. As Harish Trivadi has remarked, "condemned already in his own lifetime, he now has no right of appeal to a postcolonial court."[6]

W. Somerset Maugham poses an intriguing question of canon selection and formation also. Emerging from medical study into the world of London theater, Maugham's early career as a dramatist brought him a great deal of success and put him, for a time, in the company of George Bernard Shaw, at least as far as productivity and popularity were concerned. His early forays into fiction, beginning with the 1897 realist novella *Liza of Lambeth*, reveal a strong affinity with naturalist texts appearing in the United States in the same era, such as Stephen Crane's *Maggie: A Girl of the Streets* (1893) and Theodore Dreiser's *Sister Carrie* (1901). Fiction eventually took over from drama as the main focus of his writing. The two novels *Of Human Bondage* (1915) and *The Moon and Sixpence* (1919) were both commercially and critically successful, and Maugham's later short stories—especially the rendering of the English in the Far East on the fringes of the British Empire—became synonymous with a late-imperial languor that was both attractive and yet also a signal of decline.

In many respects, Maugham became a kind of transitional artist, his work a halfway station between the traditional novelists who continued to work within the mostly coherent structures of the Victorians and the modernist authors such as D. H. Lawrence, Aldous Huxley, and—at a couple of removes—Virginia Woolf.[7] This was, ultimately, not of benefit to him or his reputation. There grew from the 1940s onward a sense that Maugham was both a domesticating and domesticated writer, and this assessment, which was in some ways a mischaracterization, echoed the critique of the "Midcult" phenomenon which originated with Theodor W. Adorno's analysis of the culture industry and was memorably expressed by the American critic Dwight Macdonald in his famous 1960 essay.[8] The indictment is well-rehearsed: middlebrow literature and drama copy the tones and thematic explorations from serious writing that demands attention and effort, and deploy them in more accessible works that give the consumer a feeling of engagement with a more complex art than is truly the case. Middlebrow literature is a simulacrum of actual literature worthy of the name, so to speak. It domesticates a more challenging and risky experiment so that the sensation of depth is offered, but not the depth itself, which might make more demands on a reader than they would wish to entertain.

Somerset Maugham's homosexuality also appears not to have worked significantly to his advantage in more recent critical times. Despite a good two decades of Queer Theory and a more open intellectual and scholarly attitude to the popular or mainstream aesthetic since the advent of cultural studies, the author does not appear to have regained his admission to the ranks of major British fiction and the relative security of the canonical reserve.[9] Indeed, while one might have thought that Maugham's escape from academic legitimacy would help, as a kind of consolation prize, his acceptance as the progenitor of espionage fiction suitably prepared for the twentieth century, in fact the Ashenden stories ended up shelved along with the rest of his reputation. This is essentially a critical misperception of the strength of these narratives, and also of one of the founders' generation of espionage authors who explored some of the bright spots and dark places of the genre.[10]

These short stories will reveal to even a superficial reading that they contain both some of the primary tropes of the genre and also examples of the most original, if not grotesque, narrative developments that one can imagine, ones that seem to not so much take the spy story to new places as to push it into side streets and cul-de-sacs that show both its potential and its embarrassing limitations. Several of the narratives, especially "His Excellency" and "Sanatorium," seem to deliberately circumvent the basic engineering of the espionage genre and offer the reader a kind of displaced enjoyment, a consolation prize that becomes active only if one shrugs off, as it were, the readerly expectation of a certain kind of story, and certain model of resolution.[11]

In a way, therefore, W. Somerset Maugham is both an intellectually queer presence in the literary history of espionage fiction and the critically marginalized author of a seminal text that demands to be found and insists on being re-read. The protagonist, known only by his last name Ashenden, engages with his agents, with enemy forces, and, in "Mr. Harrington's Washing," with the combined force of American confidence and naïveté as it unfolded at the beginning of the twentieth century and moved to intervene in the world. The relative absence of Maugham's stories in both the popular and the academic conception of the beginnings of the genre of spy fiction means not only the marginalization of these texts to the benefit of, say, Kipling's or Buchan's but the loss of these strange but also painfully logical narratives which shaped, whether in a positive or a negative sense, some of the choices made by forthcoming generations of espionage authors. It is perhaps surprising that one who did, very briefly, pick up Maugham's legacy was Ian Fleming.[12]

Maugham delivered some remarkable initial sketches of now familiar tropes of the genre, beginning with Ashenden's recruitment by a middle-aged army officer, who appears to have some war-related responsibilities and to assume that Ashenden's history as a successful author of popular plays might make him a useful intelligence officer. Ashenden is invited to discuss such an offer of employment, and goes to meet him in a nondescript house in a no longer fashionable part of London. The house seems deserted with a FOR SALE sign in the garden, but when he rings the bell a soldier opens the door immediately, and Ashenden is brought to meet the officer, or R, as the head of the intelligence service is known. R. is slightly disconcerted by Ashenden's revelation that dramatists have been inventing the kind of human interaction that can emerge from covert operations for decades, so it is more a case of life catching up with art, but he nonetheless eventually offers him employment in the British intelligence service with assignment to Geneva (10).

The query R. poses to terminate their discussion is possibly the first literary representation of something that has now, over the years and decades, faded to little more than a cliché but is nonetheless important to keep in mind for Maugham's narratives and for the wider cultural resonance of the spy story: the casual request for, and equally casual declaration of, unwavering commitment. "There's just one thing I think you ought to know before you take on this job. And don't forget it. If you do well you'll get no thanks and if you get into trouble you'll get no help. Does that suit you?"

Ashenden replies, "Perfectly," and R. says, "Then I'll wish you good afternoon" (11).

The larger part of the *Ashenden* collection takes place in neutral Switzerland or, in the penultimate story, in Russia, with the final piece, "Sanatorium," being set in England and not involving espionage at all. The period (again, except for "Sanatorium") is the middle years of World War I, from 1915 to 1917. The setting of Geneva is pervaded with the tension of the war going on a few score, at most a few hundred, miles away. The neutrality of the Swiss provides a cheerless but comfortable location for the intelligence activities of the belligerent nations, with the local authorities attempting to surveil and interdict anything that might compromise their position. As Joseph Conrad had already rendered in *Under Western Eyes* (1911), the most highly charged and radical political visions and perspectives could be nurtured within the well-functioning civic stability of the Swiss Confederation and, in particular, its main francophone city.[13]

The question of neutrality itself obtrudes into the narrative stratagem that Maugham deploys in *Ashenden*. The tone of the stories in the collection is one of controlled and even suppressed emotion on the part of the narrator and, by extension, the protagonist who is the focalizing center of the narration. Indeed, Maugham was prescient in seeing that a certain style of narration would be required to reveal that nerve and a calm demeanor were the most important tools in espionage. But the question inevitably arises as to whether the possession of unruffled aplomb is a class thing, a national thing, or just a professional thing. Is Ashenden able to manage and indeed deftly turn complicated situations to his advantage because he comes from a particular English background that has given him the "soft" skills ideal for his new job, or because a certain kind of approach is embedded as a broader-based cultural norm in England and not reacting or showing panic is part of an applied practice, or because he is simply learning to be an intelligence operative? The individual stories reveal, in some respects, more about the internalized assumptions of national personality than they do about rational social or political drives behind the particular, sometimes fateful, choices that individual members of those nations make. That patriotism can become a complicated thing in the conflicts of modernity is a significant premise for the Ashenden project.[14]

This sometimes obscure interweaving of personal, ideological, and national loyalties—in some cases almost constituting an agon—is at the heart of two stories, "Miss King" and "The Traitor." Both narratives involve Ashenden being forced to experience the gap between functional aspects of an individual and any coherent theory about that individual. In other words, any given human being is more like a permanent negotiation among forces within their inner self than a resolved and internally logical entity. Out of such an unconscious negotiation can come a decision, for example, to betray one's own country. Against the background of a destructive war between

Britain and Germany, the threat of infiltration was, if often paranoid, not without substance, and the fictional discovery and neutralizing of such threats became, as Wesley K. Wark has observed, a type of "counter-history" that shadows the professional historians' work and operates as a kind of cultural balance to reality.[15]

In the first story, the titular Miss King is an elderly Englishwoman who has spent most of her life as a governess-chaperone to an Egyptian aristocratic family and their two daughters, never having seen her homeland since she left it many decades earlier. Ashenden is intrigued by her and also by several other guests in the hotel in Geneva, including an Austrian baroness with British antecedents and a German, Count von Holzminden, whom he knew in England before the war and who, he suspects, is also engaged in intelligence work. Ashenden and von Holzminden make no gesture of recognition on either side, although it is obvious that both men sense the irony of the situation they find themselves in. Ashenden makes an attempt to cultivate Miss King's acquaintance, to which she responds with a chilly dismissal. After a somewhat confusing evening playing bridge with the baroness and two Egyptians, during which Ashenden senses that they are making some kind of play to see where he stands politically in respect of Britain's control of Egypt, he finds himself called to Miss King's room by the assistant manager of the hotel. There, a local doctor informs him that Miss King has fallen very ill, and is in a coma of sorts. While she was still conscious, she asked to see Ashenden.

For his part, Ashenden considers the idea that she has intuited that he is in fact with British intelligence, and that something emerging from her long and lonely life away from her own country might be pushing her to contact him, possibly concerning some political intelligence about Egyptian affairs she may have acquired—a sensitive area of British interests during the war.[16] Sitting by her bedside through the night in Geneva, he speculates that "patriotism made one do odd things" (41), although it remains unclear whether, for the narrator, patriotism is some kind of spontaneous feeling or more of an internalized value system that reacts in crisis moments in the manner of a learned discipline. The story ends with Miss King waking up and struggling to speak, managing to express one word, "England," before she collapses into a final spasm and dies.

Ashenden is left, as the reader is likewise, with no guide as to the meaning of that last word. It may have been a final declaration of belonging and return, or something more ambivalent, even hostile. The narrator remains at the conclusion in the dark as to whether it was Miss King's intention to, for example, deliberately invoke the name England, for Ashenden's ears, as a kind of two-syllable curse, the thing that she had rejected or had rejected her for most of her life. Is the name of her country, uttered on her deathbed, an affirmation, a declaration of affection, or some kind of terminal utterance to banish something from her spirit, from her body even, that has been the source of her suffering over the years? The signifier "England" becomes loaded with contradictory meanings, haunted by uncertainty.

A later story in the collection, "The Traitor," carries some echoes of the theme of "Miss King," and it also ends with the death of the titular character. "The Traitor" is, however, very different in terms of both plot and the significance of the conclusion. In this narrative Ashenden is confronted with a case that leaves a noticeable ethical chill in its wake. If the grey ambiguities of intelligence work are embodied in the failure to establish anything resembling a fact about Miss King's motives for her final, enigmatic declaration, then some of the unforgiving wartime consequences of covert operations are reflected in the delivery of Grantley Caypor, the "traitor," from Switzerland back to the British authorities, for his (we come to understand) speedy trial and execution.

In his approach to Caypor and his German wife, Ashenden uses all his talents of dissembling and the maintenance of a detached but affable demeanor. In this particular narrative, however, Ashenden is also revealed as being somewhat disturbed by the degree to which he is accepted into the intimate circle of Caypor and his wife, who become more complex persons than he would really like them to be. In his conversations with Caypor, who is wanted by Ashenden's chief R. because he was the proximate cause of the capture and execution of a young Spaniard working for London, he hears him declare his patriotism, and argue that if it wasn't for his marriage—which he of course had entered before war broke out—he would be devoting his efforts to a British and Allied victory. What is striking is that Ashenden comes to believe that Caypor is telling the truth, that in some way he is a combination of mismatched ideologies and loyalties, all of which have some purchase on his actions in the present. Only by remembering the fate of the young Spaniard, an agent of British Intelligence, can Ashenden maintain his focus on the operation at hand. This mission is, put simply, to develop a belief on Caypor's part that Ashenden, who has admitted that he works for the Censorship Department in London, has absolutely no suspicions about Caypor's connections to German intelligence and can be trusted with helping Caypor return to England alone and potentially even gain entry to government service. The success of the operation is that he eventually trusts Ashenden's bona fides, accepts the letter of recommendation that Ashenden writes for him, and voluntarily sets out on the journey to his homeland.

The process of winning Caypor's trust also takes in winning that of his wife, the German woman who is deprived of a first name and known for the length of the narrative only as Mrs. Caypor. She is a figure that presents Ashenden with a certain challenge, and as a consequence the readers too, and that challenge unfolds to add a question on perspective and loyalty that may or may not have been Maugham's intention in constructing this particular narrative. The challenge for Ashenden is to communicate an understanding of her internalized feelings while not denying—which would be highly suspicious—that, as an Englishman, he cannot openly assent to them as they are not only opinions about culture but beliefs about national virtue and superiority. The challenge for the audience, on the other hand, is to assess whether Ashenden's analysis of Mrs. Caypor's German cultural nationalism is something like a trustworthy evaluation or whether the narrative is opening up yet another space for doubt. It is possible that Ashenden's quiet conviction of the excellence of England is an ideological three-card trick for which we are driven to look at Mrs. Caypor's tunnel vision with a kind of distaste while Ashenden's assumption of British virtue passes muster because it is never openly expressed. It is part of the background equation of reality, whereas Mrs. Caypor's German cultural snobbery cannot but make itself inelegantly obvious.[17] She is one of the more memorable literary representations of the essential difference between the German concept of *Kultur*, which not only carries the spectrum of meaning that the English equivalent does, but also evokes a complex feeling of superiority in which a social identity of organic depth has greater resources than a system of civilizational order. For the tradition of German nationalist and idealist thinking, the inner resilience of the ostensibly more powerful nations, France in particular, was based on an analytic reading of the world that was superficially rooted in a language of abstraction and constitutional theory. In this view Germany, although apparently behind the historical curve of development, had in fact a more resilient and instinctive strength that would prove itself in the longer run.

For Mrs. Caypor, the assumption is that Ashenden, as an Englishman, is partly closer to the German way of thinking but hobbled by the lack of a real, culturally rooted identity. Nonetheless, the English still have, Mrs. Caypor says in head-shaking mock disbelief, a capacity for poetry (140). After an exchange about the English failures in music in particular, Ashenden considers that while the wife's hostility to him is genuine and barely concealed, her relationship with her English husband is one marked by a deep, mutual love. He is conscious, and not for the only time in the course of these stories, of being an observer to an emotional power brought into being by two other human beings. In this way, I would suggest, the author and dramatist in Ashenden finds himself unexpectedly in a position to view the Caypors as sympathetic figures, a perspective that eclipses that of the mission-centered intelligence officer for a passing moment.

The moment is brief, however. Ashenden, continuing to act the part of a man called Somerville, on leave from the British war ministry's censorship unit, gradually draws Caypor into the position where he assumes that his espionage work for Germany remains unknown and thinks he has manipulated Ashenden into providing a letter of recommendation that will smooth his entry into government service when he returns to England. Caypor leaves, but eventually his letters to his wife (containing, Ashenden assumes, intelligence product to be forwarded to the German government) come to a sudden halt. Around the same time, Ashenden receives an oblique message from his chief R. to the effect that Caypor has already been arrested, tried for espionage, and executed. Eventually, observed by Ashenden, Mrs. Caypor realizes that something has gone very wrong with the plan, that her husband has been caught and is possibly dead, and she collapses into despair in the Lucerne post office. Although the dutiful observer to the very end, watching Mrs. Caypor's increasing desperation, Ashenden is nevertheless brought to shiver, imagining the scene as Caypor is led out from his prison cell to stand in front of the firing squad. In the first global war of modernity, espionage and treason are still judged by the inexorable measures of local loyalty.[18]

If certain assumptions about British national identity and patriotism are undermined by the Caypors, then in the third story the intersecting of national stereotypes and the complex politics of the modern world take that entropic process to a more extreme point. In "Mr. Harrington's Washing," personal eccentricity comes to stand for national tendencies that, in turn, drive the ideological commitments that societies embrace or reject. In contrast to the quiet order that largely forms the backdrop of his mission in neutral Switzerland, Ashenden's assignment is now in the most tense, most challenging location possible: Russia in revolution during the early fall of 1917, toward the end of the Kerensky provisional government's time in office. Ashenden's new assignment is to use all his contacts, and to find new ones that can be persuaded or bought, to help prevent Russia from making a separate peace with Germany. The Allies are worried that the effect of ending Russia's role as the major continental empire lined up against the Central Powers will be, first of all, to free German forces in the east and permit them to be deployed on the Western Front, where France and Britain are waiting for the United States, newly a belligerent, to send forces to Europe. The Bolsheviks' promise to negotiate a separate peace treaty with Germany is finding a considerable echo in the population at large, and especially among the millions of enlisted men in the Russian army.[19]

Ashenden's mission is to undermine or reverse these developments, and his journey across Russia from Vladivostok on the Pacific to St. Petersburg gives him time to consider his plan and to meditate on how to handle Anastasia Alexandrovna Leonidov. She is a former lover of Ashenden's from earlier years in London, and the story describes an intense connection between him and Anastasia, who is married already, and the younger and somewhat more impressionable author. As he remembers it, there had been in that prewar era a kind of wave that rose and crested and receded: a wave of fascination for all things Russian—politics, literature, theater, and dance. The implication is that this was something of a hip fashion statement, a way that the British (or a minority of them, at least) found to connect with a type of political and cultural energy that was denied to them, living as they did in a country that eschewed, at least ostensibly, any connection between politics and culture and looked askance at an uncompromising passion for ideas. In any event, Anastasia suggests a trip to France for herself and Ashenden, to test whether they could ever live together, and adds that the problem of her currently active marriage is likely to be solved by her husband committing suicide when he discovers that she loves Ashenden more than him. Ashenden manages to escape this possibly fatal melodrama only by fleeing across the Atlantic.[20]

In the crisis year of 1917, however, Ashenden's trip across Russia is notable for the acquaintance he makes on the train: Mr. John Quincy Harrington, a businessman from Philadelphia on his way to explore commercial opportunities with the Kerensky government.[21] Ashenden's peculiar destiny is to be forced into ten days of close company in the train sleeping compartment with this very determined and in some ways commanding American. Refusing to compromise in any way with the bureaucratic chaos and casual unreliability of the Russian entities he has to deal with, Harrington becomes both a lesson and an endurance test for the Englishman: a lesson, because the implications of Harrington's perspective and demeanor are that the United States' view of how to approach the world will be, as time goes on, something like Mr. Harrington's writ large; and an endurance test, because many of his notions of culture and education are precisely that American mixture of highbrow selectivity and pedagogical virtue guaranteed to get on other Anglophones' nerves. His habit of reading aloud and discussing every topic the chosen text brings up drives Ashenden to near despair, and yet Harrington is also a generous, thoughtful, and helpful travel acquaintance, in some ways the best type of individual you could find yourself sharing a compartment with on the Trans-Siberian Express: "He did everything in the world for him but stop talking" (199).

This narrative about an American traveler in Russia in 1917 not only foreshadows something of the cultural map of the Cold War, of course, but also sketches out a certain British perspective on the experience of US idealism abroad, a perspective that regards the phenomenon as myopic and dangerous both to the American and to others within his field of action, allies as well as opponents. Maugham's early reading of the transatlantic dynamic will be replicated and fleshed out later in the twentieth century, achieving particular resonance in, for example, John le Carré's description of the relationship between George Smiley and the CIA London station chief Martello in the Karla trilogy, or the standoff between General Jack D. Ripper and RAF Group Captain Lionel Mandrake in Stanley Kubrick's 1964 movie *Dr. Strangelove*.[22]

Ashenden's divided response to Harrington, at one moment gratitude and not a little admiration, at the next a patronizing skepticism easily sliding into complete frustration, is given a higher charge by the unexpected and burgeoning friendship between the American and Anastasia Alexandrovna. Although he tries not to reveal it, Ashenden is a little hurt when his previous lover, with whom he had an obviously intense relationship, shows herself to be mildly interested to see him, but nothing more, and furthermore is clearly developing an interest in a recent acquaintance whom he, Ashenden, regards as lacking in certain accomplishments—for example, a sense of the ridiculous. In a curious foreshadowing of the international configuration of a later era, the Britisher looks on as the Russian and the American fail to understand each other in everything except their mild dismissal of him.

Indeed, the conceptual frameworks through which the three central figures in "Mr. Harrington's Washing" view events and determine their next moves show obvious traces of their respective nations of origin. For Harrington, the removal of medieval Tsarist rule in Russia looks like a move toward Western democracy and free markets, which he wants to open up for his company back in Philadelphia. Anastasia Alexandrovna is aware of the capacity of her people to make a sudden historical swerve and change the nature of the country and of its relationship with the world, even perhaps at a significant cost to Russia itself. Ashenden is the representative of the centuries-old British strategy of trying to balance the continental European powers against each other in such a way as to prevent one of them becoming so powerful as to threaten the rest of Europe and then Britain. All three characters fail in one way or another.

The strength of the national traits that describe, if not caricature, Ashenden, Harrington, and Leonidov is, if nothing else, a narrative tribute to those notions of culture and identity set out at the beginning of the nineteenth century by Johann Gottfried Herder. Although sometimes mocked in political discourse for what are often oversimplified renditions of his theory delivered by others, Herder has tended to be proven right by history: the way a group of people evaluate the world is as much dependent upon intuitive and interior pressures deriving from long-standing cultural experience as it is upon externally obtained ideas. In many respects Herder's arguments are no different from the more economically expressed declarations of (mostly) ethno-national separateness that marked the subsequent disintegration of European continental empires, the Russian included. It is, in essence, not so much concepts or ideas that compel the three main actors in this story to see the world the way they do but rather culture. Ashenden, Leonidov, and Harrington are less individual actors at this level; rather, they are more suitably described as vectors of the particularities of English, Russian, and American intuitions and their respective frameworks for expressing these.[23] This is not to say that they cannot or do not register ideas, but rather that how they respond to that perception happens somewhere below the level of individual awareness.

Mr. Harrington cannot see past the surface events and responses in his dealings with the Kerensky government and its various would-be profiteers and hangers-on. He assumes a basic legitimacy as regards the local structure of political power and thus makes the mistake of taking what people say for a consistent statement of position that will be adhered to if he meets them again tomorrow. Harrington's bourgeois behavioral drive leads him to believe that "business" on the transatlantic model, with its faith in contract law and a set of unspoken ethics regarding undertakings and accountabilities, is something other than a set of ideological assumptions. A slightly different way of describing Harrington's approach to Russia would be to regard him not so much as the hapless Western businessman, scared and out of his depth—indeed, he maintains his balance and refuses to be panicked—but rather as the Whig theorist of history. Unlike Ashenden, Harrington sees a kind of inescapable teleology in political transformation, one leading to orderly public administration and a liberal economy: for him, there is only one road for Russia to take, now that it has succeeded in throwing off its oppressive monarchical and aristocratic inheritance, and that is the one pointing in the direction of Philadelphia, site of the birth of a secular republican constitution that sought to balance and integrate freedom, government, and law. That a society might take a different path, perhaps in some ways involuntarily, would not be a notion that made sense to him.

Neither Ashenden as a more cynical observer nor Anastasia as a Russian patriot make the optimistic assumptions that their American friend does. In the tragic final phase of the narrative, picking up one's clean laundry is both a plot element and a metaphor, and costs Harrington his life. He goes with Anastasia to retrieve his washing, but when they arrive, it is still packed as it was the day before and has not been touched. Harrington suggests to her that he "preferred coloured people" (227) to Russians at this stage: for a white American of the Jim Crow era a deadly racist insult to deliver, of course. During their attempt to return to the hotel, Anastasia Alexandrova and Harrington lose each other in the crowd at a street demonstration that ends in shooting. As he has not returned to the hotel, she and Ashenden head out into the city to search for him. They find him lying in the street in a pool of blood, but still with his hand "clenched tight on the parcel that contained four shirts, two union suits, a pair of pyjamas, and four collars. Mr. Harrington had not let his washing go" (228).

The story concludes on a note of satirical pathos: Harrington's stereotypically American obsession with hygiene and laundry services proves to be the burden that, fatally, slows him down. Not able to read the Russian room, as it were, he moves through revolutionary Petrograd with a set of filters that he seems determined not to remove, or even to recognize as filters. But Ashenden and even Antastasia achieve something like affection and even respect for him.

In the latter's case, Harrington seems to exert an oddly platonic (for his part) attraction on this woman, and in a way they seem to understand each other on a level that Ashenden, slightly miffed, cannot gain access to. There is even something Russian, something risk-loving and uncompromising, in Harrington's approach to the world, and Anastasia Alexandrovna recognizes it for what it is. This sudden bipolar charge serves to connect the unyielding American highbrow and the passionate Russian intellectual, leaving the cautious and calculating Englishman outside the charmed arena. Stereotypes of national identity, indeed, but curiously appropriate for the historical moment this narrative seeks to express. At the third phase of Maugham's surgical exposure of British national exceptionalism, therefore, the observer slot is the one that Ashenden finds himself steered unwillingly toward. Frustrated by friendship from an American who lacks cultural savvy and rejected by a Russian passion that has little time for English nostalgia, Ashenden's mission seems to be curtailed, as London's desire for global management is defeated by the scale of the events of 1917 and the revolutionary dynamic they have released. Or perhaps "decentered" is the better term. Through the various stages of the Ashenden narrative, the kind of casually expressed but internally committed belief in the nation that provides the cultural frame for the protagonist's initial recruitment and overseas assignment slips gradually out of focus. From the enigmatic deathbed performance of Miss King's invocation of "England" through the strange national hybridity of the Caypors' marriage to the humiliating sidelining of Ashenden's mission to St. Petersburg, what had once simply assumed significance must now struggle to be noticed amid the surges of history.

Notes

1. Eagleton, "Nationalism," 23.
2. The long historical connection between dissimulation and irony is noted by Fernandez and Huber in their introduction to *Irony in Action* (5); they go on to discuss the disconnect between "inner" and "outer" realms of communication and understanding (11–12) that would seem to embody the practice of covert action in the field.
3. Working on this book in early 2021, just after the United Kingdom's final withdrawal from the European Union, could not but provoke some thoughts about how, a century on, the ideological differences among Kipling, Buchan, and Maugham seem to have had an afterlife

in the various attitudes toward Britain's role in, and relationship with, the European Union. If Kipling's commitment to empire represents the romantic and nostalgic side of the 2016–20 Brexit campaign, then Buchan's Hannay might represent the more suspicious and authoritarian side of English nationalism, with its strain of ethnic distaste for the foreign. And perhaps Maugham's own preference to be an Englishman abroad might suggest that he would be at least pragmatic in his choice and favor Britain remaining part of the European project?

4. A striking example can be found in Kipling's "Tommy" (1890), in which the refrain in particular targets the hypocritical snobbery of shifting civilian attitudes toward the common soldier. The poem concludes "For it's Tommy this an' Tommy that, an' 'Chuck him out, the brute!' / But it's 'Saviour of 'is country,' when the guns begin to shoot. / Yes it's Tommy this, an' Tommy that, an' anything you please; / But Tommy ain't a bloomin' fool—you bet that Tommy sees!"

5. Kate MacDonald makes a strong case for Buchan, however, in her introduction to the Oxford University Press edition of *Greenmantle* (1993), describing it as a "wonderfully plausible novel" (viii) and also reminding the reader that Buchan, similarly to Maugham, spent much of the war in intelligence and diplomatic work.

6. Trivadi, "Reading Kipling in India," 196. Recent scholarship tends to divide over this issue. Thus Bart Moore-Gilbert argues for a positive framing of the multicultural nature of India in *Kim* ("Kipling and Postcolonial Literature," 158), while Jon Thompson is highly skeptical of the claim that Kipling shows the reader the interaction of cultures (*Fiction, Crime, and Empire*, 89).

7. Maugham would have probably regarded his own position as holding the line against the kind of modernist literary aesthetic he regarded as moving in the wrong direction, as his suspicious and somewhat class-based dislike of D. H. Lawrence and his writing reveals; see Myers, *Somerset Maugham*, 156–59 for comments on this relationship, such as it was, with Lawrence, and also on Lawrence's dismissive review of *Ashenden*.

8. Dwight Macdonald does in fact directly reference Maugham in "Masscult and Midcult" but in notably ambiguous terms. It seems as if he is including him in the tradition of authors who had one basic premise and stuck with it more or less successfully throughout their careers (26), but he seems to also imply that he shares Maugham's criticism of precisely that aspect of literary culture. In some ways, Maugham might be regarded as standing in for Macdonald's admission in the same essay of "the limitations of my Anglophilia" (64).

9. It has not been the case so far, but it is certainly possible that Maugham could enjoy rehabilitation via a new focus coming from LGBTQ literary studies. His status as an "imperial" author has worked against him, however.

10. Earlier histories of espionage fiction were often defensive or jocular about their subject and ambivalent about the value of the genre, and tended to sacrifice depth on the altar of comprehensiveness. Even with the arrival of more sophisticated studies, Somerset Maugham is granted a few paragraphs (generously calculated) in books many years apart, for example in Cawelti and Rosenberg, *The Spy Story* (45–46) and Snyder, *The Art of Indirection* (62–63). To be fair, although Snyder devotes only a short passage to Maugham, he identifies crucial narrative moves in *Ashenden*, in particular the use of a motif suggesting intelligence reporting as a kind of creative equivalent to fiction writing. This connects Maugham to Graham Greene's *Our Man in Havana*, and Greene to John le Carré and *The Tailor of Panama*.
11. Brett F. Woods, for example, notes that Maugham may have realized that he had "set a new standard in the evolution of the spy novel" (*Neutral Ground*, 38) and for that reason never returned to the genre, preferring to leave *Ashenden* as a solitary but distinctive achievement.
12. A striking example is the *Ashenden* piece "His Excellency" and its distinct echo in Ian Fleming's short story "Quantum of Solace" (1959). James Bond, on a mission in the Bahamas, is invited to dinner at the governor's residence and finds himself seated next to a woman whose conversation bores him. He later hears an account of her life from the governor (but without knowing that the subject is the woman he has just met) that surprises him and makes him realize how much he has misjudged her. This homage to Maugham on Fleming's part unfolds as a somewhat different narrative from Maugham's, but it does occupy a type of sub-genre niche in which the British intelligence officer is temporarily removed from his operational milieu to hear a story about a non-professional matter that eventually forces him to rethink some of his assumptions.
13. The English narrator of *Under Western Eyes* describes the city as that "respectable and passionless abode of democratic liberty, the serious-minded town of dreary hotels, rendering the same indifferent hospitality to tourists of all nations and to international conspirators of every shade" (271).
14. See, for example, Antonino Palumbo and Alan Scott's analysis of the "outward-looking" patriotism favored by Max Weber and the "inward-looking" variety endorsed by Emile Durkheim in their essay on these two philosophers, German and French respectively, and their thinking on patriotism and the state in the years before and during World War I. Palumbo and Scott also discuss the longer-term implications of each model, in particular the emphasis on either international prestige in a competitive world as a basis for community pride or, alternatively, a sense of national principles that uphold individual moral worth as a primary value ("Weber, Durkheim, and the Sociology of the Modern State," 383–87).

15. Wark, "Introduction," 3. The detail of Wark's argument is more nuanced, and he suggests that the "counter-discourse" (3) of espionage fiction can have both utopian and dystopian variants: it is not always an attempt to deflect from historical fact by offering a romantic or heroic narrative for public consumption. It can also be an effort at a higher level of authenticity. In Maugham's case, one can say that the errors and blind alleys of intelligence work portrayed in *Ashenden* are a counter-history that embraces rather than departs from psychological realism. Interestingly, Wark also takes up Dominick La Capra's arguments for a more generous and flexible critical evaluation of fiction that combines insights from both history and literary studies.
16. Egypt had been a British Protectorate since 1882 with the ruler, the Khedive, owing nominal fealty to the Ottoman sovereign. In 1914 Khedive Abbas II had declared for the Ottoman Empire, which was the ally of the Central Powers, and he was subsequently removed by the British, who appointed his brother Hussein in his place. During World War I Egypt became a Sultanate, but nationalist resentment of British authority was growing steadily, culminating in the uprising of March 1919.
17. The fact that narrator, text, and (in this case) reader are all operating within an Anglophone frame cannot help but create a structural disadvantage for Mrs. Caypor's arguments.
18. One should not conflate Ashenden with the narrative voice of the stories, but at the end of "The Traitor" there is at least the intimation of a merging of narrator's and protagonist's ethical stances, struck as they are by the pathos of events while nonetheless believing in their necessity. See Robert Calder's biography *Willie* for a description of the kind of generational and also class-inflected patriotism that Maugham was impelled by (128); he was something of a (sexual) outsider, but not ambivalent in his commitment to the nation in wartime.
19. For a detailed account of how the political turmoil and the armed forces interacted in 1916–17, see, for instance, Michael Melancon's study of revolutionary activists' success in turning the enlisted men (and some officers) against the Tsarist government, *The Socialist Revolutionaries* (115–27; 256–64; and passim).
20. In his article "Tsars and Commissars," Keith Neilson argues that Maugham has a second-order aim in relating the story of Ashenden's former romance in a somewhat arch and humorous style: to undermine the overpowering clichés about Russia and the Russian people that were encountered everywhere in England in the early years of the century.
21. Although the classic stereotype is that of an American businessman hoping to connect with the liberal democrats in the new Russia, US commercial interests in Russia existed long before the overthrow of the monarchy, and prestigious foreign companies maintained offices,

factories, and sales forces and had been comfortably embedded in the Tsarist structure of power. For an intriguing example of how modern American business operations, relatively unproblematic at home, could trigger paranoia and nationalist suspicions in Russia, see Sawyer, "Manufacturing Germans."

22. Christopher Hitchens's wide-ranging and entertaining study *Blood, Class, and Empire* contains several worthwhile and historically grounded observations on the tensions and complexities of the "Special Relationship" (see, in particular, 332–39 for comments on how these played out between the American and British intelligence services after World War II). The relationship between James Bond and his Central Intelligence Agency (CIA) liaison Felix Leiter deserves a mention, too, although it is a much more comradely dynamic in Fleming's fiction.

23. As F. M. Barnard notes, "Language in particular . . . plays a pivotal role in Herder's anatomy of political culture in its broadest sense" (*Herder on Nationality*, 150), and also "an important bridge between individual self-enactment and the enactment of the self-constituting nation" (182). One can imagine the inner landscape of the three main characters' political thinking as having a large area of overlay between individual self and national "self," whether British, Russian, or American.

Chapter 2

The Past as Prologue: Antifascism and the Prophetic Mode in Ambler and MacNeice

The relationship between literary form and antifascism in an era in which writing on the one side and political and ideological positioning on the other were both important is, in some distinct sense, a fateful one. Between the wars—a phrase that at once signifies an historical era and conjures up a nostalgic cultural memory in black-and-white newsreel mode—a range of fiction, non-fiction, poetry, drama, and screenplays was produced that can be regarded in retrospect as both diagnostic and premonitory. That is, these texts often combine an analytic reading of their immediate social and political environments with an uncanny certainty about the future outbreak of World War II. The term "intermodernism" has been coined to identify more clearly the era, beginning roughly in the late 1920s, during which complex interactions between traditional and modernist literary and cultural forms took place—often, as Kristen Bluemel has noted, challenging and undermining the standard division into "supposedly known periods of modernism and postmodernism" (5). If, as Bluemel observes, intermodernism is crucially "both period and style" (5), then one can approach authors such as Louis MacNeice and Eric Ambler under that rubric, with a sense of their overlapping perceptions of political crisis, their interest in bending both elite and popular literary forms toward new objectives, and their willingness to explore political dynamics beyond rigid ideological schemata.

Eric Ambler published his fifth novel *A Coffin for Dimitrios* in 1939 (the original title, *The Mask of Dimitrios*, is still valid for some British editions), which has made its own contribution to that combination of analysis and foreseeing, and also inevitably to a set of stereotypes that were not necessarily so stereotypical at the time of composition. Indeed, the role of types as such in Ambler's novel is less to provide easily recognizable figures to enable the reader to make fast judgments as to the moral equation of the story, than to show that consequential misjudgments can be made by characters within the narrative itself. The protagonist, Charles Latimer, is himself prone to making assessments of other characters that are later challenged when they reveal things he has not expected to find. Indeed, an aspect of the narrative structure of *A Coffin for Dimitrios* is the gradual undermining of Near Eastern and European stereotypes—the shifting manifestations of the persistent and puzzling Mr. Peters being a notable example—despite their ostensible usefulness as a map by which to negotiate the world. Peters, for his part, has the stereotypical aura of the feminized Levantine businessman much deployed for comic or semi-comic purposes in British and American fiction and film.[1]

There is without doubt a volatile and crisis-ridden Europe to negotiate in *A Coffin for Dimitrios*, as its protagonist travels across the unhappy continent of the late 1930s. In the course of the novel, Latimer, a British crime-fiction author and former academic with some time on his hands, attempts to look behind the curtain in locations stretching from Salonika to Paris; he hears evidence of past violence ranging from a sordid murder plot in which two criminals, one Greek Orthodox and the other Muslim, join together to kill a Jewish merchant, to the organizing of a military coup in Bulgaria; he tries to grasp the relationship between simple crimes of greed and political ideology; and his moral universe is subjected to a sustained inner transformation from the opening with its cheerful conversation at a cocktail party in a villa in Istanbul to the ending as the French train enters a tunnel and the reader understands that Latimer is not going back to England. *A Coffin for Dimitrios* as a work of fiction reads the fragility of European political systems, especially those of central and southeastern Europe, as if diagnosing a nervous disease in a patient.[2]

In his narrative poem *Autumn Journal*, also published in early 1939, Louis MacNeice is walking a similar line to Eric Ambler, but approaches it from the opposite side of the literary marketplace. While Ambler is taking the risk that the average reader of spy thrillers might be put off by the significant presence of local historical information and politics-laden dialogue in *A Coffin for Dimitrios* (the dinner conversation explaining the Stambuliski Affair between Latimer and Marukakis in Sofia [77–81] would be an obvious example), MacNeice is also experimenting with returning the second-generation British modernist aesthetic to a vernacular cultural context, one influenced by—among other things—movies and music of the day, and constructing a poetic speaker who not only is the voice of a conscious authorial experience but can also adopt the accessible style of a character narrator in a popular fiction. Indeed, Ambler's protagonist for his part might well be a displaced figure from MacNeice's poem, his continental journey into politics and conspiracy mirroring the *Autumn Journal* speaker's domestic travels across the geographical space and social fabric of the British Isles. Both journeys also probe inwardly, into the protagonists' own circumstances, cultural values, and social and political preferences.

It is one of the markers of the era that many works from the interwar years, especially the late 1930s, appear to be certain that a major conflict, some cataclysmic international disruption, is approaching, and that its arrival is doubtful only as to the exact date. This sense of urgency informs what I would call the prophetic gambit of both these texts, as they take the risk of invoking the almost-inevitability of war in Europe: *Autumn Journal* and *A Coffin for Dimitrios* balance and even in some ways query each other in respect of their sense of the present and future danger. Each text practices its vocation expertly within the constraints of literary genre and cultural resonance, but also tests the bars and even steps outside the given line: in the one case, the entertaining departure into narrative verse and occasionally comic doggerel on the part of a poet identified with the era's conception of modern poetry as a difficult and arcane art;[3] in the other, the work of popular fiction which demands that the reader's attention be focused on the obscure political history of southeastern and central Europe during the two decades that followed World War I and the Versailles Treaty.

Both Charles Latimer in *A Coffin for Dimitrios* and the poetic speaker of *Autumn Journal* (whom for ease of reference I will interchangeably call the "the *Autumn Journal* speaker" or "MacNeice's narrator") are educated citizens of the United Kingdom, with Latimer the more distinctively English voice in contrast to the *Autumn Journal* speaker, who confesses his Northern Irish Presbyterian origins in the angry rhetoric of stanza xvi, reflecting the complicated identities, Irish and English, embraced by Louis MacNeice and visibly evident in his own biography.[4] The two protagonists seem to be around the same age, in their middle thirties, and are both single, although the *Autumn Journal* speaker is looking back on a past relationship or marriage of several years. They both have college or university degrees, Latimer having written an economics textbook and, under a pseudonym, a number of successful detective novels, and the *Autumn Journal* speaker shaped by his degree in Classics from Oxford.

When we look at these two texts from 1939, both *Autumn Journal* and *A Coffin for Dimitrios* reveal a common conviction that sets up a convergence of perspectives. In both works, which are aimed to some extent at very different audiences, we find a near-absolute conviction that war is inevitable and even imminent. This iron certitude is, perhaps, in one way born of politics and political loyalties, but in another shares in a deeper, more intuitive sense of how a specific historical reality will turn toward violence and darkness and how one can respond to this reality as an individual with both political and ethical choices to make. Neither Latimer nor the *Autumn Journal* speaker leaves any doubt as to the necessity of formulating an individual point of view in relation to contemporary events, and, as Michael Denning notes, "the centrality of point of view marks the dominance of an ethical mode of thought."[5]

Both Ambler's and MacNeice's texts occupy positions that would, of course, normally be distinct and at quite some distance from each other in the cultural ranking order, but nonetheless they exhibit some notable parallels: both *Autumn Journal* and *Dimitrios* are set in a highly specific historical period, the last few months of 1938; both are dominated by an antifascist perspective; both authors are convinced that another European war is coming; and in each work they take risks that would reveal them as hyperbolic doom-sayers if the future were to turn out differently. They gamble with the prophetic voice, in other words.[6] Indeed, the first-person narratives of both these texts are themselves nothing new, but in the manner of their engagement with their particular time in history they declare a presence and stake a claim.

It is, however, still worth asking the question: How could they be so certain? A surefooted analytic reading of events, an awareness of the true intentions of Nazi Germany and of other right-wing sympathizer governments, watching the panicked dithering of democratic polities: all these can be legitimate explanations. But something remains unexplored, as I see it, in the landscape of guesswork and prophecy from the years before the outbreak of world war. At one remove, it begins to look as if they foresaw with some accuracy simply because we know now that they were right. But people have confidently predicted both conflict and disruption as well as the absence of conflict and disruption at many points since then, and have been often embarrassingly wide of the target.[7]

Although I use the term prophecy interchangeably with prediction in connection with Ambler and MacNeice, there is the consideration that prediction is a more mechanical procedure—ultimately a sufficiently advanced artificial intelligence could predict with accuracy if provided with enough data. "Prophecy" seems to be more appropriate, not because of any religious or mystical beliefs on the part of either Ambler's Latimer or MacNeice's speaker, but because it seems to involve, inevitably, some measure of value judgment (perhaps even community values), of risk, of something other than detachment.[8] A prophetic statement might prove in a strict historical sense to be mistaken, but might even gain credibility on some other grounds, for example for the aesthetic power of the vision itself.[9] The prophetic moves in *Autumn Journal* and *A Coffin for Dimitrios* might, speculatively, have survived a counterfactual history in which the war did not come, or if it did come, arrived in a different way. In that sense one could speak of an aesthetic of urgency, of cultural crisis management, perhaps, in which qualities such as elegance and humor become less stylistic options and more an extra layer of national security and risk reduction, reflected by the new technology of radar stations along the English coast or the "narrow wands of blue" in MacNeice's poem that describe the beams of the anti-aircraft searchlights scouring the night sky over London (23).

The memorable opening stanza of *Autumn Journal* juxtaposes the slow end of the summer of 1938 and a quiet domestic routine with modern military technology and aviation, conjuring up Hampshire and the south coast of England as both relaxed and yet in a certain waiting posture:

> . . . the spinster sitting in a deck-chair picking up stitches
>   Not raising her eyes to the noise of the 'planes that pass
> Northward from Lee-on-Solent. Macrocarpa and cypress
>   And roses on a rustic trellis and mulberry tree
> And bacon and eggs in a silver dish for breakfast (3)

The question of why the "spinster" does not react to the sound of the aircraft coming and going from the air base hovers over the lines.[10] Is it a detachment from the political volatility in Europe? Or perhaps a comfortable certainty that Britain is suitably protected by its armed services? It could be some combination of both, but it is also interesting that the poetic speaker, from the very beginning, takes an intelligence agent's interest in both armaments and public morale. The MacNeice narrator is not a professional, but he understands what to look for.

A sense of crisis pervades *Autumn Journal*, and the nature of the crisis is gradually exposed and tightened as the sequence of twenty-four stanzas proceeds to its conclusion. *Autumn Journal* is, at the distance of over eighty years, an iconic product of those political and literary circles in Britain in which a second-generation poetic modernism jostled with a left-wing and individually dissenting vision of the state of the nation and the world. Such a pigeon-holing of the poem does no level of justice, of course, to MacNeice's rendering of a complex struggle in the speaker's mind over the possibility of, and the legitimacy of, a left-progressive response to the political challenges at home and abroad. The language is in large part realistic and conversational, and the most effective use MacNeice makes of the doggerel style is often to bring a commonplace observation or an everyday social image to a kind of aphoristic and skeptical conclusion, as in the lines on social distinctions in education:

> But the classical student is bred to the purple, his training in syntax
>   Is also a training in thought
> And even in morals; if called to the bar or the barracks
>   He will always do what he ought. (42)

The *Autumn Journal* speaker is delivering an obviously less than admiring evaluation of the privileged upper-middle class graduate whose studies have prepared him for a profession as well as to be an officer in wartime, but has not encouraged much of what we would now call critical thinking. But the rhyme on "thought"/"ought" offers a moment of verbal comedy, the brief entertainment balancing the weight of the political judgment. Likewise, in his satirical dismissal of the legacy his Oxford education, he finds himself caught between the need for categories and the English distaste for abstractions:

> They don't want any more philosopher-kings in England,
>   There ain't no universals in this man's town. (44)

and can't decide whether this perspective is to be condemned or admired.

Echoing the mobile narrator of *A Coffin for Dimitrios*, the speaker of *Autumn Journal* meditates on his travels through European countries, revealing the interplay of an outsider's gaze and an intuitive sympathy with political struggles far from the smug privacy and apparently unshakeable stability of English life. In at least one case, that of Greece, Ambler's and MacNeice's texts converge in invoking aspects of that nation's history, culture, and sensibility in ways that are both personally relevant and historically compelling, as if subtly confirming each other's perspective by emphasizing their difference: for Charles Latimer, the perspective is the political violence of recent history, the massacre of ethnic Greek refugees by Turkish forces at the beginning of the 1920s;[11] for MacNeice's narrator, it is the ironies of an idealized classical world delivered by England's socially stratified educational system.

The central movement of *Autumn Journal* is the speaker's return to London as the summer is coming to a close. The season's slow change is described in Edenic terms as a kind of English paradise of unhurried ease. Other locations radiate around the points of the compass from London, which is both an active present and one of the key sites of memory for the speaker as he recalls his now terminated marriage and the emotional imprint it has left on him. The journeys in real existing time and the journeys into memory take in Oxford, Birmingham where he had his first teaching job, and Ireland, which is the topic of stanza xvi on the larger implications of militant Irish nationalism, including the parodic echo of heroic names in William Butler Yeats's poem "Easter 1916":

> The bombs in the turnip sack, the sniper from the room
>   Griffith, Connolly, Collins, where have they brought us?
> Ourselves alone! Let the round tower stand aloof
>   In a world of bursting mortar! (53)

Other threads of both past and current history draw his gaze toward Spain, where the left-wing Spanish Republic is crumbling now under the pressure of conservative nationalist forces, assisted by the stronger fascist powers of Europe, Germany and Italy.

Over the course of the poem, the *Autumn Journal* speaker meditates with ever more intensity on the possibility of war in Europe. Hitler's voice on the radio brings thoughts of war "Buzzing around us as from hidden insects," a sound that is simply a feature of the environment but could become a sudden threat (14). In stanza vii, workers are cutting down trees in Primrose Hill Park in northwest London as the site is needed for anti-aircraft defenses

>   The guns will take the view
> And searchlights probe the heavens for bacilli
>   With narrow wands of blue. (23)

Similarly, the fall rain fills the "raw clay trenches" that now disfigure all of London's public parks (29).

There are moments in the course of the poem when a vernacular or comic image works to move it closer to a type of satirical ballad or even doggerel than the sophisticated meditations and paradoxes encountered elsewhere in the text: in stanza xviii, for example:

> Yes, the earlier days had their music,
>   We have some still today,
> But the orchestra is due for the bonfire
>   If things go on this way. (62)

This ability to move in and out of an elevated poetic register and into a popular and more casually conversational verse style is also suggestive of a kind of convergence of cultures. For MacNeice in the 1930s, modernism had been a liberating arrival, but as a poet he was always open to deploying more traditional forms, although as in W. H. Auden's verse the traditional forms are subject to tensions that come from the very fact of being admitted into modern poetry as one option among others: they have to earn their place, so to speak, and in some ways the power of rhyming and metrical patterns comes from the shadow of *vers libre* that hovers over them. In *Autumn Journal*, MacNeice treats the rhymed quatrains of his poem with more generosity, giving them in effect aesthetic command over the entire project. In the sometimes lyrical, sometimes somber language of the *Autumn Journal*, and in its witty social realism, one can perhaps see a foreshadowing of the convergence of national cultural formations during the approaching wartime years, when classes normally living separate lives were made suddenly more aware of each other's existence.[12]

At the beginning of *A Coffin for Dimitrios*, the protagonist Charles Latimer has at one point been plunged into a depressed mood by having to read, for academic purposes, Nazi political theorist Alfred Rosenberg's *The Myth of the Twentieth Century*.[13] Later, in Bulgaria, he hears the details of how the forces of conservative reaction put the brakes on important social reforms with the Stambuliski Affair of 1923.[14] At one point, and in a way that cannot help but strike the contemporary reader, the narrator describes the launching of the Turkish massacre of Greek and Armenian refugees in Smyrna in 1922 with the sentence "The holocaust began" (37).[15] That the social order in Europe is disintegrating is clear to Latimer's Sofia contact, the journalist Marukakis, who suggests that Latimer knows it too, and the phrase "future war" is deliberately emphasized in their conversation (83).

Robert Lance Snyder's reading of the complete body of fiction in his *Eric Ambler's Novels: Critiquing Modernity* (2020) has opened up several works to a new level of critical scrutiny, including *A Coffin for Dimitrios*. Snyder emphasizes that the narrative structure of this novel frames a search for explanatory solutions which are ultimately not there to be found. The narrative is potentially "a parable of the compulsive need to find a secret meaning in fiction."[16] The reader assumes what Latimer assumes, that a resolution of the story will provide both dramatic and contextual clarification. Over the course of the novel, the figure of Dimitrios, already dead but possibly not at all, becomes the negative icon of a civilizational shift echoing William Butler Yeats's timely and ominous question in his 1920 poem "The Second Coming": "what rough beast, its hour come round at last, / Slouches toward Bethlehem to be born?"[17] And yet, as his journey comes to a climax, it remains an unresolved question whether Dimitrios and his career are no more than "an opportunistic criminal" or indeed a man "whose history mirrors the miasmic politics of Europe at the time."[18]

The vector along which *A Coffin for Dimitrios* moves is quite distinctively different from that of *Autumn Journal*, therefore, despite the overlapping political concerns. Superficially but significantly, instead of a return to the England after the summer of 1938, Charles Latimer's journey is one of depth as well as movement on a map. While traveling slowly from Turkey through Greece, Bulgaria, and Switzerland to Paris, Latimer finds himself sliding deeper into the political and criminal enigma represented by the presumably deceased criminal.[19] Either the sense of a temporary meditative safety which England represents for the *Autumn Journal* speaker is not there for him or he refuses it, as the last passage of the novel indicates clearly that Latimer is not on the way to Calais, the Channel ferry, and home but rather on a train approaching the city of Belfort, on the French side of the border with Switzerland. He is heading southeast toward Athens and, speculatively, to reconnection with Marukakis, who has offered the possibility of a skiing trip in Bulgaria during the winter. The letter from Marukakis is couched in his dispassionate, ironic style, and their friendly relationship signals, in a more political and metaphorical reading of the train entering the tunnel at the end of the novel, a movement toward confronting the dangers of fascism and war rather than away from them. If MacNeice is exploring, in *Autumn Journal*, the possibility of a resource of Englishness providing, for a skeptical left-winger, a perhaps unexpected quality of resistance to the forces on the European continent gathering for assault, then Eric Ambler seems far less convinced of any such promise. Taking the implications of the novel's ending as a signal pointing to his assessment of what the future holds, Charles Latimer prefers to put his faith in the weary but courageous realism of Marukakis and other foreign observers who have no great trust in the assumed virtues of national resilience or civic responsibility.[20]

The conversational but rhetorically intense quatrains that give *Autumn Journal* its distinctive poetic identity are highly traditional, drawing on English popular ballads and narrative verse more generally and aiming for an accessible musical prosody rather than using poetic form, in the modernist approach, to create a level of difficulty that stymies casual reading.[21] In fact, despite the sophistication of its political references and arguments, MacNeice's text is replete with witty asides, popular cultural references, and satirical images of social phenomena, and would itself be clearly an artifact of popular literary culture if it had only been published a generation or two earlier, before the genre of poetry itself became associated with the modernist avant-garde, or at least with a reading practice demanding a high level of intellectual investment. British and American poetry of the previous century had a broader and more diverse audience than became the norm after the modernist transformations of the early twentieth century. It seems thus arguable that *Autumn Journal*'s closest predecessors can be located in, for example, James Russell Lowell's satirical sequence *The Biglow Papers*, a caustic review of the political and social condition of the United States in the late 1840s, or, despite their political conservatism, in Rudyard Kipling's "Barrack-Room Ballads" from the 1890s, rather than any obvious model from the modernist poetic revolution.[22]

One cannot overlook the fact, either, that one particular characteristic seems to connect the protagonists of both texts: their distant and problematic relationship to women. In *Autumn Journal*, the poetic narrator is mourning the loss of a marriage, in one reading an evocation of MacNeice's relationship with his former wife Mary Katzman, who like the unnamed woman in the poem has left Britain for America. This experience is not given a great deal of prominence in the course of the poem, but forms one corner of the triangle of personal, political, and cultural concerns that dovetail to frame the thinking of *Autumn Journal*. To say that the speaker is somehow disabled or numbed by the experience of this dimension of this life having come to an end might be an overstatement, but the evocation of a certain, although possibly productive, loneliness is inextricable from the emotional landscape of MacNeice's poem. There is a distinct irony in the way *Autumn Journal* satirizes the comforting past-directed routines of the middle classes, their deep investment in particular long-standing attitudes and behaviors, while the speaker is obviously struggling with his own nostalgia for his lost romantic and sexual happiness. Like Latimer traveling east but at the same time thinking wistfully of a return to his civilized detective stories, he feels himself impelled to take a stance, perhaps even commit a political action, but is also haunted by the memory of a more carefree past.

In *A Coffin for Dimitrios* Charles Latimer appears, in contrast, to have no romantic or sexual interests, present or past. No indication is given in the narrative, either directly or obliquely, that he has ever had a relationship, or been married, or that he is interested in sex even in a casual way, in the context of a relatively young, single man traveling through Europe. There is also, one should clarify, no implication in the story that he is gay or even that he has problems with social interaction generally. The implications of the scene in the nightclub and brothel, including the interview he and the journalist Marukakis conduct with Madame Preveza, however, who has had a long association with Dimitrios in the past, are intriguing. Latimer is disturbed not so much by any latent sexual feelings aroused by Madame Preveza during her conversation with him and Marukakis but by her female emotional vibrancy; he feels like an "austere prig" (97) in the nightclub with its dancing and erotic promise and wishes that the champagne served them had been drinkable; he has also been drawn into the narrative of her former connection with Dimitrios to the extent that he feels "absurdly distressed" (115) when their conversation eventually comes to an end after a couple of hours.

However one might read their attitudes to attraction and desire, Ambler's novel and MacNeice's poem echo each other as contributions to a prophetic vision of 1930s antifascism. To frame *A Coffin for Dimitrios* as a meditation on the nature of political intimidation, while simultaneously reading *Autumn Journal* as something like a downbeat spy novel in verse, reveals that both authors' political views circle around the same critical set of issues and challenges. At times, too, MacNeice's and Ambler's choices as to style and voice echo each other in a manner that raises intriguing thoughts about literary genre and cultural valuation, and without doubt both the novel and the long poem sit historically in the shadow cast by both an oncoming and a historically receding disaster, depending upon where one situates one's implied readerly location.[23]

There are three possible approaches to the question of why we might perceive these texts as having that unmistakable condition of a prophetic stance. These approaches, or conceptual categories, are not mutually exclusive but can appear in different combinations and different levels of emphasis in any given text. I call them, respectively, *retrospective emphasis*, *analytic gravity*, and *historical risk-mitigation*.

The first, retrospective emphasis, emerges from that active and sometimes expectant speculation during the latter half of the 1930s that war, potentially on a large scale, was coming, and in our reading of these works we unconsciously seek out those passages that appear to anticipate this future and invest them with more weight and significance than they really could have contained at the time. The growth over recent decades of the study of cultural memory and the survival on the political left (broadly conceived) of an admiration and affection for the popular antifascist aesthetic of that era provide a number of perspectives, both objective and subjective, for identifying, reading, and validating the idea that a major historical test was under way. The objective angles include a knowledge of European history, our understanding of political ideologies, and a grasp of human relations in modernity; our subjectivity comes into play when we enact the drama of political choice in the 1930s in our imagination, the imagination of those who know how events unfolded: we wonder if we would have made the right decision, the courageous choice, and we endorse a certain partisanship to the benefit of those protagonists who are attempting to negotiate their crisis, or crises, and calculate their possible futures in line with our perception of shared values across time.

In this reading of *A Coffin for Dimitrios* and *Autumn Journal*, we follow the psychic journeys of Charles Latimer and of MacNeice's poetic speaker with a nervous interest, wanting them to emerge safely, and seeing their mental struggles as an early, and perhaps a more innocent, version of ours. The projection of our wished-for innocence can also be, of course, a certain retrospective envy for the historical clarity of the choices they face. With the second category of approach, analytic gravity, I mean that the kind of investigation of character, choice, political ideology, and other phenomena that MacNeice and Ambler advance in the two texts is marked by an inescapable recognition of the Real.[24] The actual existing violence and threat of fascism and reaction stand ready to rupture the symbolic order of the literary text—indeed one can make a good case for Ambler's conscious construction of Dimitrios as the destroyer of symbolic fictional worlds, especially Latimer's very English mystery novels with their intriguing but ultimately rational plots and their reassuring endings.[25] A useful alternative term for this scenario would be "grounded urgency." There is no sense in either *Autumn Journal* or *A Coffin for Dimitrios* that positions are adopted or statements made for rhetorical effect or to fulfill a stereotypical expectation on the part of the reader. It is not only that, as many a cliché would have it, politics is a serious business, and politics in an age of aggressive and totalitarian governments more serious still, but that the play of social and political forces in these two works emphasizes the fragility of the momentary state of affairs on the European stage, and that fact alone makes any speculative proposition a play for high stakes. To that extent, the emotional landscapes of Ambler's novel and MacNeice's narrative poem are such as to suggest that a casually dismissive reading of them would betray that reader as either uncomfortable with, or even hostile to, the vision of a conflict over political values and the desirability of a society that is built on more than a fantasy of power and terror. The gravity of analysis is not a humorless statement of the balance of abstract historical forces but rather a rich poetry of the kind of threat that fascism embodies and the unpredictable nature of resistance.[26] Neither the recklessly curious former professor and crime writer of *A Coffin for Dimitrios* nor the ambivalent and questioning speaker of *Autumn Journal* are an obvious choice for antifascist hero status, but in their different but oddly parallel ways they sketch out a model of how one might deal with an unattractive future that cannot be avoided.

The third and last approach involves the notion of historical risk-mitigation. This has a simpler as well as a more complex dimension, the first being that the perception of the European or global political world in the latter part of the 1930s was so marked, or perhaps "battered" would be more accurate, by the increasing force and scale of events that the risk involved in a predictive or prophetic assertion of oncoming catastrophe had declined, if not to zero, then at least to a very small number. The observable march of history had mitigated the risk of prophesy in 1939 significantly more than even five years earlier. The force of such a prediction of war would, of course, have been precisely as correct in 1933, the year of the Nazi Party's ascent to power, but the historical frame would not have mitigated the risk of being wrong in such a prediction the way it could six years later. To be closest to the moment of disaster offers, ironically, the greatest protection against being wrong.

One might conceive also of a somewhat more complex variant of historical risk-mitigation that would imply something like the following: although one can look at a set of unfolding events and, given some perspective on the unfolding as it has revealed itself over time, make a low-risk prediction as to how near-future events will play out, there is another way in which historical circumstances mitigate risks of error in prediction. For example, a particular aesthetic of fiction, poetry, or drama could work at framing the prophetic gambit in such a way as to have it emerge from deeper currents of historical interaction than merely the events of the day. Here, a kind of aesthetic priming happens:[27] for example, of regret leading to destiny (a past world is slipping away, what is to come is waiting at the crossroads) or of illusion giving way to recognition (we lived with the hope that something would not be, but now it undeniably is). The priming will, if it succeeds, educate and prepare the audience to accept an authenticity, an undoubted seriousness, in a vision of the near future even if it turns out to be mistaken in the real world. Ambler and MacNeice did not, in the end, require this back-up justification, of course, but its presence is perceptible in both *Dimitrios* and *Autumn Journal*. The more implicit shifts in events, the slower movements in history, underwrite these fictions with an extra line of insurance. In other words, while the precise imaginings of these and other writers and artists might potentially have been undermined by actual events in real time, even if the war had not come when it did, their works would have been validated by the implications buried in the march of events anyhow.[28]

The geographies of *Autumn Journal* and *A Coffin for Dimitrios* are, in addition, a foreshadowing of some of the major features of World War II as it eventually unfolded across Europe. Both MacNeice's rendering of the growing presence of civil defense or other quasi-military measures in everyday life, such as the documentary and simultaneously metaphorical presence of the anti-aircraft guns installed in London's public parks, and Ambler's regional political education efforts distributed throughout his novel sketch out in a general way those dimensions of the war that have, over the decades, become not only actual histories but also moments of cultural change that exercise influence on people's thinking down to the contemporary era. In particular, aspects of the two texts speak to the long-standing consensus that the experience of the Blitz (the common Anglophone borrowing of Hitler's *Blitzkrieg*, or lightning war, to designate the bombing of British airfields, cities, and general infrastructure that began in the fall of 1940) boosted a new sense of shared hardship and more egalitarian perspectives that later shaped postwar political reform and the Welfare State.[29]

In Ambler's novel, the political education Latimer receives is a clear premonition of the crucial role of southeastern Europe for the course of the war, where Britain both enabled a communist resistance to Nazi occupation to take control of postwar Yugoslavia and deployed troops to crush a parallel movement in Greece in late 1944 while the war was still in progress. Often cited in leftist and socialist discourse to contest the claim that the Allies were on the side of democracy and self-determination (rather like the situation on the other side of the globe in French Indochina), the patchy record of the United Kingdom in its late imperial maneuvering in Greece and Yugoslavia took place in a political environment vividly evoked in its prewar character in *A Coffin for Dimitrios*.

As the story moves to its conclusion, it becomes obvious not only that Dimitrios and Peters are prepared to use force, lethal if necessary, to achieve their particular goals, but that in a situation of existential survival Charles Latimer is also willing. In the curiously all-masculine world of *A Coffin for Dimitrios* the discovery is that even the most peaceable and civilized individual is capable of unearthing a capacity to fight back. Indeed, the distribution of aggressive tendencies is complicated by Latimer having a kind of self-discipline that Peters, closer to the world of criminality and brute force than Latimer, lacks. Dimitrios's assumption, as he goes into the meeting at the Paris hotel, that his complete lack of scruple will see him emerge inevitably as the victor, mirrors Hitler's conviction that the democratic nations would be unable to summon up the strength to resist the ruthless and unapologetic deployment of force and intimidation in international relations. The hovering accusation of feminine weakness that followed the appeasement strategy of the major European powers in their dealings with Berlin in the 1930s is reflected in the fact that Dimitrios regards Peters and Latimer in the same way, and in some ways his two opponents are subject to fears and self-doubt themselves.

While Dimitrios can be regarded as both the temptation and the consequence of Charles Latimer's willingness to leave the relatively coherent surroundings of his life and his professional success as a writer of crime fiction, in many ways it is the Istanbul police officer Colonel Haki who enables the fateful breach in the symbolic order of the traditional English murder story that brings Latimer to acts of violence. Describing a plot which he has worked out himself—which Haki wants to give to Latimer so that he can write the actual book—he forces Latimer to keep a straight face as the premise is that "the butler did it," already by the 1930s a cliché ripe for parody. But when Haki invites Latimer to view the corpse of Dimitrios, the author realizes that it would be a bad mistake to underestimate the Turkish security man on the basis of his embarrassingly stereotypical notions about detective fiction. But not only does Latimer see a different man from the suave interlocutor at the cocktail party; he also senses that following the trail into Dimitrios's past will be a different experience from anything he has done previously.

There is a certain level of ambiguity in the final paragraphs of the novel, and a certain doubt invades the status of Latimer's intention to write a conventional detective novel again. He seems to regard it as a return to a badly missed normality, one in which the violence remains on the page. But he is also, clearly, not returning to England, as his train is traveling southeast from Paris toward the Swiss border. The obvious answer is that he is heading for Athens, where he plans to write his novel. Nevertheless, in terms of the geographic and political landscape of *A Coffin for Dimitrios*, Latimer is in fact returning to the Balkans, with their unresolved national tensions and conflicts and their capacity to render a kind of preview of the larger, more menacing, European conflagration that will follow.

Both works are concerned with the individual capacity to retain authority over choices that will inevitably be made elsewhere. The violence of Dimitrios is abroad in Europe as much as Hitler's speeches can be broadcast continent-wide over the radio. To recognize that there may be no escape is perhaps an escape of a kind, if only from a world of comfortable illusion. Both academics and writers, MacNeice's narrator in *Autumn Journal* and Charles Latimer in *A Coffin for Dimitrios* become in different ways accidental players whose experiences are cast within a prophesying of encroaching disaster. The *Autumn Journal* speaker is a covert analyst of the political and cultural tensions of British life in 1938 and of his own uncertainty in relation to both his ideological beliefs and his personal and emotional life. He hides himself at times behind the curtain of his poetic wit, and in that sense he is aligned with Charles Latimer, who also undergoes an intense orientation in the deeper relationships between criminal and political violence in Europe. As Latimer comes to understand the nature of the investigation he has entered upon, so does the *Autumn Journal* speaker come to grasp the underlying forces that are at work in Britain and Europe, shaping the future in the last months of 1938. The poetry of Eric Ambler's novel, one could say, meets the narrative of MacNeice's poem as if the fascist threat has woken both authors to look beyond the given boundaries of their literary and intellectual forms. "The bloody frontier," as MacNeice's narrator puts it, "Converges on our beds" (16).

Notes

1. The character of Joel Cairo, memorably played by the Hungarian-Jewish actor Peter Lorre, is one of the iconic performances of this stereotype in John Huston's *The Maltese Falcon* (1941). Anecdotally (and curiously), Peter Lorre was not cast as Mr. Peters, but rather as a version of Charles Latimer called Cornelius Leyden, in the 1944 movie adaptation of *The Mask of Dimitrios* (the role went to Sidney Greenstreet, who had played the suave international fixer Kaspar Gutman in *The Maltese Falcon*). The Eastern European link was further strengthened by the fact that *The Mask of Dimitrios* was directed by Jean Negulesco, who came originally from Romania.
2. For a more detailed background, see especially chapters 5 and 6 of Barbara Jelavich's panoramic *History of the Balkans*, vol. 2.
3. Sometimes, however, MacNeice combines the vernacular with the obscure, as in these lines into which he drops an ancient Persian unit of distance: "The crisis hangs / Over the roofs like a Persian army / And all of Xenophon's Parasangs / Would take us only an inch from danger" (27).
4. The individual stanzas in the Faber edition of *Autumn Journal* are given lower-case Roman numerals.
5. Denning, *Cover Stories*, 83.
6. From our later perspective it seems like a safe gamble. But the late 1930s was also replete with voices declaring that the war was next to impossible, of course.
7. One obvious example is the extent to which as late as 1988 the Soviet Union was assumed to be a stable entity which would survive and perhaps even flourish. This premise was widely shared across the political spectrum.
8. "Prophecy" has most often the air of a religious or at least a mystical frame of reference, but the political force of prophetic visions can sometimes have a destabilizing effect on a ruling establishment or system.
9. The sustained importance of George Orwell's *Nineteen Eighty-Four*, for example, is not undermined by the historical fact that the world of 1984 was not quite as the novel portrayed it (as Orwell himself said, it was neither a prediction of the future nor an ungrounded fantasy, but an exploration of real possibility).
10. Lee-on-Solent was the site of naval aviation training and operations from 1917 to 1996.
11. Ambler must have been aware of Ernest Hemingway's semi-documentary short story from 1930 "On the Quay at Smyrna."
12. In popular memory, the war years were a period when English class divisions were put aside for the cause of national solidarity and eventual victory over the enemy. Angus Calder's *The People's War* (1969) is the classic historical study of wartime social behavior in the United

Kingdom, which attempts to separate the truths from the legends. The term "intermodernism" might well serve also as an historical shorthand for the transformations (actual or only prospective) of the time.

13. Alfred Rosenberg was the official who oversaw cultural policy during the Nazi era; he was tried at Nuremberg and executed in 1946.
14. Alexander Stambuliski was a populist leader of Bulgaria after World War I, with a strong base among the rural peasantry. His reforms ran into significant opposition from the middle classes and the military establishment, however, and he was detested by Macedonian nationalist extremists. He was kidnapped and murdered in a coup in 1923.
15. The choice of the term "holocaust" in 1938 is almost uncanny.
16. Snyder, *Eric Ambler's Novels*, 31.
17. Accessible online at the excellent Poetry Foundation website: https://www.poetryfoundation.org/poems/43290/the-second-coming.
18. Snyder, *Eric Ambler's Novels*, 33.
19. Snyder analogizes Latimer's research as trying to look into "a black box" (*Eric Ambler's Novels*, 33).
20. Although it is not specifically referenced in the novel, confidence that the September 1938 Munich Agreement, signed by Hitler, will be observed is presumably also minimal.
21. See Glyn Maxwell's essay "Turn and Turn Against: The Case of *Autumn Journal*" for a convincing analysis of the prosody of MacNeice's poem, in particular the way in which the rhyme scheme alternates from stanza to stanza and modulates the feeling and perspective as they go back and forth throughout the text.
22. Although the essays in Bluemel's collection *Intermodernism* do not deal with poetry, one could make a reasonable case for important poets of the 1930s and 1940s adapting or even breaking with certain principles of modernism, and for emerging poets who develop new perspectives: MacNeice would in certain respects offer a role model here.
23. Poetic works with an espionage theme are, to put it mildly, rare, but John Hollander's quasi-narrative collection *Reflections on Espionage*, originally published in 1974, is a memorable contribution. One notable aspect of the book is its many references, via codenames, to fellow poets, including the recently deceased W. H. Auden, who is called "Steampump." MacNeice, who had worked with Auden on their collaboration *Letters from Iceland* (1936), died in 1963 but might, I think, have seen elements of *Autumn Journal* in Hollander's dedicated but self-doubting poet-agent hidden behind the cryptonym "Cupcake."
24. I use an upper-case R here to draw (possibly less than faithfully) upon a psychoanalytic category on the Lacanian model: the argument here is that the Real is something akin to history itself, that exists prior to any attempt to render it as a symbolic order in language.
25. Snyder notes that, in essence, *Dimitrios* (both novel title and character) represents an "irreducible mystery"; *Eric Ambler's Novels*, 33.

26. And this might be one reason why one essay takes the leap of declaring that *Autumn Journal* "should be considered one of the key poetic texts of the twentieth century" (Wigginton, *Modernism from the Margins*, 98).
27. "Priming" in linguistic terms means a method of directing an apparently spontaneous association of two different terms; here I mean the capacity to steer the audience's response without that maneuver being necessarily observable.
28. MacNeice and Ambler were, of course, far from the only figures between the wars to sketch out a somber, not to say grim, future for the United Kingdom and European democracy in general. Storm Jameson, for example, published what Elizabeth Maslen describes as "a disturbingly vivid English version of Hitler's second year in office, in the three-month period leading up to the Night of the Long Knives" ("A Cassandra with Clout," 25). There is very likely an important distinction to be made between speculative fictions, even ones extrapolating from existing realities, and what I call the prophetic mode in this chapter, but that is a discussion for another place.
29. See n. 12 above on Calder.

Chapter 3

"We'll Meet Again": War, Memories, and Loss in MacInnes and Garve

"This is a bad night to misquote that again," says the State Department official Martin Clark in Helen MacInnes's *I and My True Love*, in response to another character's misplaced allusion to President Franklin D. Roosevelt's famous remark in his 1933 inaugural address that Americans have nothing to fear but fear itself (295). The brief exchange mirrors the confusions and morbidities of the immediate postwar years and the opening stages of the Cold War, a time that put considerable pressure not only on nations and political ideologies but also on individuals and personal relationships, often even intimate ones. The alliances and collaborative effort of World War II, regarded idealistically by some and cynically by others, had become possible only within the framework of a common enemy, and that enemy had been defeated when the Red Army raised the Soviet flag on the Reichstag in Berlin on April 30, 1945. The defeat of Nazi Germany had been a shared objective, but the vision of what was to come after was not shared in the same way. Even the Western Allies, with somewhat aligned perspectives on the correct path to follow, did not always see eye-to-eye on how, and to what end, the occupation of Germany should be managed. It was therefore unsurprising that, for example, American self-confidence interacted with Russian paranoia to generate an atmosphere of decreasing trust and tightening suspicions. With the division of Germany and Austria into separate occupation zones, what might have been a pragmatic method of restoring public order and resuscitating economic life became something else entirely: a kind of laboratory in which societies and institutions were reshaped to reflect the specific occupying power's ideological and strategic purposes.

Yet to say merely that leaves out a significant complication. As laid out in the London Protocol of 1944, each of the Allied Powers, the United States, the Soviet Union, Britain, and France, enjoyed uncontested sovereign authority in its particular sector of the former German Reich.[1] The situation of central and Eastern European countries was, however, quite different. Josef Stalin was determined to create a protective ring of states with governments sympathetic to, and later obedient to, the communist system and the political and strategic requirements of the Kremlin. Nevertheless these countries, Poland, Czechoslovakia, Hungary, and others, had often resisted the Nazi occupation forces in ways both organized and informal, often had their own left-wing parties going back decades before the war, not just the communists, and had had their own national identities shaped by different experiences over the centuries. In other words, commitments to national autonomy and a distinctive political face to the world often sat alongside a nuanced understanding of the Soviet Union's position, and sometimes even within the local communist party itself.

Czechoslovakia offered a revealing and ultimately tragic version of this process. Over the five years following liberation in 1945, the Communist Party (KSČ) moved from being a partner in the multiparty government to being the dominant force with command over key administrative posts, including the interior ministry. Czechs had been disappointed with the West ever since the Munich crisis of 1938; after the war an orientation toward Russia was not unpopular, and the communists also maintained a show of political openness and willingness to compromise. Non-communist leaders such as Jan Masaryk, the foreign minister and son of the former president Thomas Masaryk, envisioned a Czechoslovakia that might act as a mediator between East and West. With the deaths of Jan Masaryk and President Eduard Beneš (the former having fallen, under mysterious circumstances, from a window in the foreign ministry building in Prague), however, no credible political leadership remained that might have challenged the advances of the KSČ and retained some aspects of a democratic constitutional system.[2] By 1949 any such possibility had vanished, and elements significantly loyal to Stalin and the Moscow line controlled the Czechoslovak state and the direction of the country's foreign policy. The country would no longer be a bridge between the opposing world powers in Europe, but rather an obedient member of the emerging political and military alliance shaped by the needs of the Soviet Union in the Cold War.[3]

Against this background of recent history in Europe, Helen MacInnes set *I and My True Love* in the Washington DC of early

1952, amid the personal and professional uncertainties brought about by the Korean war, the threat of the atomic bomb, and a general air of paranoia that has descended over the city and, by implication, the country. This atmosphere is due in part to the ongoing congressional hearings on both real and purported subversive activities, as well as a hazy sense of unspoken social constraint: meeting certain people or maintaining particular friendships might turn out be inadvisable in respect of one's career, for example. The figures in MacInnes's drama of unity and separation include, at its center, the thirty-year-old Sylvia Pleydell; her older husband, State Department economic analyst Peyton Pleydell; and a representative of the Czechoslovakian embassy, Jan Brovic. During World War II, Brovic was an RAF pilot and later a representative in the United States of the Czech government-in-exile in London. Seven years earlier, in 1945, Sylvia and Jan had become lovers, although she was already married to Peyton. Jan Brovic has returned to Washington and is now, to the surprise of former acquaintances, representing in some capacity the communist government in Prague.

I and My True Love opens with a dinner party at the Pleydells' house in which a range of personalities and attitudes are fencing and jousting across the table: whether the Soviet threat is real or simply a new kind of American paranoia that leads people to behave oddly and accept more government intrusion into their lives; whether the United States can be blamed for the Korean conflict; whether one could meet Jan Brovic now, in the current state of world affairs. In semi-clandestine meetings with both Sylvia and with her young cousin Kate Jerold, visiting from California, Brovic himself reveals that he has both political and personal reasons for meeting Sylvia in particular: ostensibly, to give the communists in Prague the idea that he has now come around, grudgingly at least, to their position by opening up old connections in the Georgetown milieu that could assist in intelligence-gathering. In fact, as he explains, he is planning to help his family leave Czechoslovakia so he is free to make his move. He can then speak freely in the United States against the Czech government (122). His other goal is to find out whether Sylvia still loves him, and if so, to invite her to leave her husband and join him for a future together.

MacInnes places the nature of betrayal and its consequences at the heart of the social ballet of affections and ideas in *I and My True Love*. Sylvia betrayed Peyton with Jan at the end of the war, but Peyton's response to this was a dramatic subterfuge involving a fraudulent medical condition designed to make Sylvia feel intense guilt and abandon any notion of leaving the marriage: also in its own way a distinct type of betrayal. For Brovic, he is pretending to share the KSČ ideology now firmly established in Czechoslovakia, but his intention is to betray the Czechoslovak communists with his plan to organize his family's escape and, once that is successful, come out openly against his government at home; from the Cold War perspective that informs the different emphasis given to assumptions about the world in 1952, this is a virtuous act of betrayal, but nevertheless it involves risk. Dr. Formby, the Pleydells' family doctor, more or less accidentally betrays the history of Peyton's fake illness to Sylvia, which causes her to re-examine the nature of her marriage and the kind of relationship she has with her husband. In the case of Peyton Pleydell's friend and former State Department colleague Minlow, there is a betrayal of confidential information about the provisions of a trade agreement to the Czechs that makes its way into the newspapers, dragging rumors about the Pleydells' marriage in its train. As with every skein of narrative in *I and My True Love*, personal relations and romantic affections are inextricable from the mesh of political and cultural struggles between the communist bloc and the West, whether it is a covert intelligence operation in Washington or open war on the Korean peninsula. In the world of 1952, even Sylvia's careless and self-regarding mother has gotten herself into trouble for joining and sending a donation to an organization that has been revealed as a pro-communist front rather than an independent entity. The certainties of the antifascist struggle have long since been swept from the stage, and now a higher watchfulness rules. Casual membership of groups with feel-good titles and collective gestures at universal brotherhood and understanding can now involve a risk that was not evident in the 1930s or during the war.

Indeed, MacInnes does not leave the political framing of *I and My True Love* at the surface level of the standard Cold War paradigm. Not only is the conflict, whether covert or in plain view, not just between capitalist democracies on the one side and Soviet bureaucratic socialism on the other, but there are other wars under way, perhaps eventually even more significant in their implications. It is obvious that the Georgetown diplomatic and policy community is quite divided over how to deal with the new challenge of Soviet expansionism and the nominally independent but predictably pro-Soviet nations of central and Eastern Europe. The approaches favored around the table at the Pleydells' range from the assertive and combative, expressed by the army engineer Lieutenant Bob Turner, home after serving in Korea and involved in nuclear weapons research, to the cautioning against fear and hasty judgments of Stewart Hallis. "We have to admit that there's a wave of reaction sweeping America," he says, provoking the straight-laced State Department security officer Martin Clark to comment that many present "in 1939 felt a wave of reaction against the Nazis" (46). Hallis dodges the implication with his reply: "Analogies are always dangerous," he counters (46).

On the other side of the Iron Curtain lie the Russian satellite states, most important among them Poland, Hungary, and Czechoslovakia. These uniformly Stalinist governments, the creation of their communist parties in the immediate postwar era, are also subject to their own internal ideological divisions and contested strategies. As Martin Clark points out to Whiteshaw after the publication of the gossip about the breach of security regarding the draft trade agreement, it is not even a simple matter of Prague gaining advance warning in respect of the American side's positions in future negotiations, but rather of the possibility that the more pro-Soviet and hardline members of the KSČ will use the leaked information to identify and purge their more open and less dogmatic colleagues who want productive economic relations with the United States and Western Europe. As in most Warsaw Pact countries, the Czechoslovak party has not only members committed to the Moscow line in its ranks, but also what were often called "national communists."[4] Clark lays out the situation for Whiteshaw:

> "They'll weed out the Czechs who would have welcomed a trade treaty with the West as a chance to limit Russian domination."
> "Titoists?" Whiteshaw asked quickly.
> "You could call them that. Or Czech Communists who'd like to run their own country. And the fact that we were willing to renew a trade treaty will convince the Russians that we were trying to influence the nationalist-Communists." (282–83)[5]

Clark disabuses Whiteshaw of the idea that the nationalist camp in Prague is in any way friendly to the United States or its allies, but emphasizes that "they've lost the rose-tinted glass they used to wear when they looked east" (283). In *I and My True Love*, there are no relationships, between nations or individuals, which remain simple upon closer inspection.

In one curious example, Stewart Hallis is quietly attempting to seduce Kate Jerold. On a sightseeing trip around Washington, Kate finds his air of disenchanted maturity and his casually encyclopedic knowledge to be attractive, describing him as "rather sweet" (102).

Obviously regarding Hallis with some suspicion, Sylvia quotes Kate's own words back to her, with a vaguely bitter tone, saying that that was why she married her husband: "I thought he was rather sweet" (104). At the end of the novel, the suspicion hanging in the air is not only that his interest in Kate is more manipulative than genuine, but that he himself played a role in the sequence of events that leads to the public revelations about the information leak from the State Department as well as the marital difficulties in the Pleydell household. What the narrative is most evasive about, however, is the degree to which *I and My True Love* presents male homosexuality as a significant danger in both personal and political terms.

In one exchange between Bob Turner and Kate Jerold, he implies that Peyton seems to be liked by "some men" (146) and thinks that both Sylvia and Kate are unaware of some fact about him. This echoes an unspoken dimension of Sylvia's earlier remark to Kate in which a certain undertone conveys that her marriage to Peyton involved some fateful error or misjudgment. What that error might be, however, remains somewhat unclear to Kate, although her thoughts on the arrival of Peyton's two friends and colleagues Minlow and Whiteshaw after dinner at the Pleydells' are more focused on their appearance:

> They wore dark flannel suits, narrow-shouldered, tight-legged. Their expensive brown shoes were well polished. Their ankles were neat in tightly-gartered black socks. They had the same way of talking: quiet voices, half-drawled, flatly even. Their one touch of bravado was in the finely checked waistcoats. (52)

Kate describes them to herself as "wildly improbable young men" (53), although it remains unclear exactly which limits of probability they have breached. As they appear toward the end of the novel, some distinctions are made, to the extent that Whiteshaw is attempting to repair the damage that an unthinking Minlow has caused by chatting too freely with representatives of the Czechoslovakian embassy.

What connects Peyton to Hallis as well as to the two younger men is the fact that Minlow and Whiteshaw have no interest in women, and Hallis, while seemingly intrigued by Kate, is unmarried and childless. Peyton is married to Sylvia, but they have no children. Although never explored in detail in the narrative, Peyton and Sylvia's relationship is set against that of Martin and Amy Carter, the latter heavily pregnant with twins. That MacInnes establishes a subset of characters contrasted by the presence and absence of fertility and family is undeniable, but it is threaded through the narrative in such a deft manner that to label *I and My True Love* as a homophobic fiction of its era faces some impediments. Sylvia's meditation on her situation at the beginning of the story reveals her recognition that Peyton has no desire for her but needs her for the social dimension of his State Department career, and that he regards her as something like a prized possession. No specific action of his reveals any particular sexual orientation, however. His behavior may be simply evidence of a narcissistic and manipulative personality. Neither does Minlow or Whiteshaw engage in any particular action or dialogue that might provide evidence of his own particular orientation. The novel succeeds, therefore, in presenting implications of homosexuality that remain in some key respects circumstantial: they hover around and within the narrative at the level of subjective perception and speculation on the part of other characters. The novel seems to articulate a hostility to, or a warning about, male homosexuality without necessarily wanting to slip into a more definitive rhetoric of indictment.[6]

To that extent, the title of *I and My True Love* begins to take on resonances beyond the stereotypical reading of it as signaling the resurrected love affair, after a hiatus of several years, between Sylvia Pleydell and Jan Brovic. If viewed in an ironic frame, it raises the specter of multiple iterations of true love, some perhaps hidden from the reader behind the dominant characters and the movement of the plot. If Sylvia represents something other than a beloved for Peyton, to what or whom is his emotional attachment directed? Is love dependent upon political conviction? The answer from Sylvia might be affirmative, as she admits to Jan that she could never have trusted him if he had genuinely become a communist. Does the title perhaps non-ironically point to the Clarks in their small apartment, with Amy expecting twins, as an example of the warmth of domestic happiness so hard to discern in the wealthier Pleydell household? And the bleak denouement of the story casts without doubt a retrospective chill over what the reader may have taken as a promise of a satisfactory resolution signaled by *I and My True Love*.

That the novel intends to complete a tragic arc is intimated by Kate Jerold when she suddenly feels emotions of "pity and fear" (214) rather than anger when she realizes that Peyton Pleydell knows he has lost Sylvia, and confirmed by Bob Turner, who says to himself that he and Kate are "watching a dead man," (336) as Jan leaves his apartment after a final meeting with them. Not only does the failure of the plan to extract his family from Czechoslovakia mean that Brovic can no longer speak against the communists from the relative safety of the United States, but the fact that they are being watched closely by the security service means that the government in Prague knows that he was never planning to carry out his mission in Washington. He will have to return to Czechoslovakia, where interrogation, prison, and a likely execution await him. For her part, Sylvia's transcontinental railway journey to Kate's family in California, planned as the easiest way of escaping Washington and a potentially brewing scandal, takes a different turn. Reading the news of Jan's departure in a newspaper at the terminal in Oakland, Sylvia decides to get a hotel room in San Francisco and has some idea of finding a job and radically changing her life. Amid the confusion of thoughts and feelings that distract her, however, she appears to step into the street in the path of an oncoming bus. The final passage of *I and My True Love* suggests but does not offer absolute certainty that Sylvia Pleydell, hearing voices as people try to help her, imagines Jan Brovic standing near her as she lies on the sidewalk. The final sentence of the novel reads, "Then she could close her eyes" (378), the narrator concluding the story by leaving a tiny sliver of ambiguity behind.

If Helen MacInnes's model of a fateful mismatch of individual emotional commitment and global ideological conflict is mitigated at least by the authenticity of what draws Sylvia Pleydell and Jan Brovic to believe in each other, Andrew Garve's *The Ashes of Loda* (1964) follows a path to a more complex and traumatic revelation of interpersonal deceit and its double-edged legacy for the present. The complete devastation that World War II brought to Poland, Ukraine, and Russia is both a generator of traumatic memories and a means of burying, distorting, or re-inventing memory for political and ideological purposes. The stability and relative peace of England in the 1960s serves as the refuge—if illusory—from the terror of history, whether recalled truthfully or not, and the principal settings for the story, Moscow and Ukraine, are the places where the memory can be probed and investigated, and potentially revealed to be fraudulent. *The Ashes of Loda* is a narrative of the politics of memory and the conflict between the actual past and the desired past, which in turn can determine the viability of one's future.[7]

The Loda of the title is the fictional name of a Nazi concentration camp in Poland, which first emerges as Marya Raczinsky, the British daughter of a Polish refugee, relates the story of her father Stefan to Tim Quainton, the Moscow-based correspondent of a British newspaper and the novel's narrator. Stefan Raczinsky was, in Marya's account, a young student in Poland, recently married, when the German and, a few weeks later, the Russian invasion came in the autumn of 1939. He lived in Lvov, a city now in eastern Ukraine, which was occupied by the Soviets in their acquisition of what was then Poland.[8] When Hitler broke the non-aggression pact with Stalin by invading the Soviet Union in the summer of 1941, all of Poland came under German occupation and Raczinsky is sent to a series of labor camps, ending up in Loda. In his story, he escapes and briefly joins the Polish resistance, is shot in the leg, but manages to make his way back to Lvov. There he finds his three-year-old daughter again, being looked after by a neighboring family as his wife is now gone and presumed dead, and the two of them travel to Britain, where Raczinsky's scientific qualifications are an advantage in his application for asylum. Marya Raczinsky and Tim Quainton fall in love and Marya introduces Tim to her father, now a successful commercial chemist with a large cosmetics company.

The first indication that something might be wrong occurs when a colleague of Tim's says casually, after Tim has mentioned Marya, that the name Raczinsky rings a vague bell (28). Driven to check whether anything is in the newspaper's reference library, he finds a old clipping from the early 1950s that begins to undermine his relationship with Marya and opens the door to later events in the narrative. The clipping contains a brief report from a Russian newspaper, to the effect that Stefan Raczinsky has been tried and found guilty *in absentia* by a Soviet court for war crimes committed at Loda. The accused had apparently deliberately betrayed an escape plan to the German camp authorities and caused a group of prisoners to be executed immediately. Unsure of what to do, Tim Quainton shows the clipping to Marya Raczinsky the day they had planned to buy an engagement ring, and she reacts by cancelling the shopping trip and querying Tim as to whether he believes the accusations or not. She says that nobody who knows her father could imagine him to be guilty of such a thing. Tim claims he doesn't, but obviously he is not sure.

At a meeting with Tim and Marya at their house, Raczinsky explains that the story is false, and that nobody who knows him believes it has any credibility. He did not want to worry Marya about it when she was much younger, and thus kept quiet about the Russian announcement. He also says that the United Kingdom authorities had given no credence to the story—it could have been an attempt to cast doubt on a Polish scientist and imply that the British employed former Nazi collaborators—and that the Foreign Office had tried to establish further details via diplomatic channels but nothing had been forthcoming. He also points out that the trial could well have been based on sheer mistaken identity, as Stefan

Raczinsky is a fairly common Polish name and there could easily have been more than one imprisoned in a large camp like Loda (34).

Convinced that Tim still harbors some residue of doubt about her father's past, Marya breaks off the almost-engagement, and Tim returns to Moscow after his unexpectedly eventful leave.[9] Once back in the Soviet Union in midwinter, he begins to think that he might be able—especially as he speaks very good Russian—to use some connections to clear up the story once and for all. One somewhat troubling development is that Tim finds the original newspaper from which the clipping in London was taken, so it was genuine to that extent, but curiously enough the story does not appear to have been picked up or highlighted by any other Russian publication. The announcement of the trial and the verdict appears briefly in the news, but then vanishes. The newspaper article mentions two witnesses, however, and he is able to establish that they are both real individuals and can potentially be located. Quainton appeals to Pavlov, his main contact in the Soviet foreign ministry, for some help on what is, for him, an entirely personal matter, and Pavlov obliges by inviting one of the witnesses to Moscow to answer Tim's questions. The narrative of *The Ashes of Loda* pivots around these two interviews, the second one of which Tim Quainton seeks out himself.

The two witnesses, Lutkin and Skaliga, give very different accounts of the events at Loda. Lutkin seems to suggest that he might not have remembered the name correctly, and generally appears uncertain of his facts at twenty years' distance. Skaliga, a recovering alcoholic visited by Quainton in a dismal Moscow apartment complex, is apparently very sure of his recollection, and, like Lutkin, overheard Raczinsky speaking German, a language that both Russians understood. Skaliga suggests, in fact, that Raczinsky could have been German rather than Polish. Tim is taken by surprise when Skaliga not only describes Raczinsky accurately but remembers that he had received a gunshot wound in the knee, causing him to hobble (70). In London, Raczinsky had described the same wound, but told Tim he had been injured while fighting with Polish partisans after escaping from Loda. He realizes that it is suspicious in the extreme that Raczinsky had apparently been in the camp with a leg wound, as normally Germans would have sent a worker who was physically incapacitated to an even more arduous camp where survival was next to impossible, or he might have simply been shot. If Raczinsky had been some kind of informer, however, or even a native German, then the story in the Russian newspaper gains in credibility.

The passages of *The Ashes of Loda* that narrate Tim Quainton's trip, on a freezing Moscow night, to the municipal tenement block to interview Pavel Alexandrovitch Skaliga are some of the most memorable in the novel and work on several levels. There is the evocation of a Moscow of social classes or, at least, distinct levels of privilege. Clearly the neighborhood is anything but prosperous, and the novel's portrayal of the hidden corners of Soviet society has a Dickensian atmosphere, with echoes of the urban naturalist fiction of the late nineteenth century. The nature of the Bolshevik experiment over forty-five years has clearly remade Russian society in significant ways, but the basis of equality seems to be scarcity rather than shared plenty. Skaliga might be a middle-aged blue-collar citizen with a drinking problem in any city in Britain or the United States (although, as he notes somewhat resentfully during the conversation, he once attended university [71]), and his surroundings are far from the Moscow of foreign correspondents and higher officialdom that Tim is familiar with. Beyond the social setting, however, the memories of Loda and the Raczinsky incident take shape in Skaliga's account of things with an eerie accuracy that undermines Tim's belief that there may have been a confusion of identities. Dizzy with vodka and the implications of what has just heard, he leaves the apartment in a state of dismay and physical repulsion, vomiting on the sidewalk before he can make his way home (72).

The second and less ambiguous shock takes place when Tim makes an unofficial trip to Lvov, the formerly Polish city now in Ukraine (less ambiguous in the sense that, despite his seemingly spontaneous confirmation of the Soviet court's indictment of Stefan Raczinsky, Skaliga might still have been misremembering or inventing facts). Raczinsky's nostalgia for the city and his memories of growing up there had made a positive impression on Quainton in London, including his account of playing in a park opposite the family home. Finding the street and the house, Tim knocks on apartment doors and asks anyone he can find if they remember a Raczinsky family as former residents. None can, and all his interlocutors appeal to the war as the reason why nobody is around who could potentially recall the names of earlier tenants. Finally, he comes across an elderly man on the top floor who was there before the war. He can't recall the name Raczinsky, but quite by accident he reveals that the park that Marya's father fondly remembers playing in was not there at that point in time: it had been built at a later date, and he would be too old to recall playing there as a boy. This is the snapping of the final thread that has been, until now, holding up the possibility of

Raczinsky's story being authentic. Tim Quainton is now certain that Stefan Raczinsky is not the person he claims he is, and this realization opens up not only the likelihood that the testimony of the Loda witnesses is credible, but the disturbing thought that he will have to tell Marya of his discoveries about her father, with unpredictable consequences for everyone concerned.

Leaving the broad brush-strokes recounting the first half of *The Ashes of Loda* at that place in the story, one could say that by the time the novel's final act takes place it becomes obvious the degree to which memory has been nurtured, suppressed, or invented. The politics of memory or, more accurately, the politics of memory management have been on display, overtly and covertly, throughout the narrative, even when—or especially when—the actors have a misunderstanding or only a partial understanding of the larger picture. When history and memory are instrumentalized by people and institutions, whole lives can be grounded on a false premise. Sometimes, of course, the motives can be seen as valid, even if only in the eyes of one party, as Tim argues in a somewhat unexpected way to partly justify Stefan's betrayal of his adopted country. Marya asks Tim if he is trying to defend her father. He replies:

> "I'm trying to be fair to him. He was a Russian and a patriot. He was also a Communist. He felt he was virtually at war with the West . . . every man has the right to choose his cause and do the best he can for it." (170)

Stefan Raczinsky's life was a covert mission for the Soviet intelligence service but his love for his daughter was also a part of that life, and the tension between politics and parental affection was clearly, as evident from his long suicide note, an unresolved torment.

Nevertheless, we rely instinctively on some level of truthfulness in others when it comes to constructing a sketch of where we came from. Marya's cry of anger and bewilderment at the end of the novel, "He turned my whole life into a fraud. He made me believe I was Polish when I was Russian. He made me believe in a background I'd never had" (170), is an appeal rooted in the necessity of assuming that persons of trust are indeed trustworthy. Believing her father, as well as believing in her father, means that she is now experiencing every apparently fixed point in her life becoming unmoored. Ironically, her belief that Stefan Raczinsky could not be guilty of the charges laid against him by the Soviet court, that he deliberately betrayed a prisoners' escape plan at Loda, has been borne out. That he is, however, guilty or at least responsible for a completely different set of actions,

actions Marya could never have imagined, was unforeseen. Rather like the Ukrainian city of Lvov that seems to be detached from its history as a part of Poland, Marya has been essentially deprived of memory.

If it were a child being told finally that it has been adopted, or someone discovering an aspect of their background that they had had no idea about, the experience might be integrated in time, as if often is, into someone's life. It might even be, in some circumstances, a gain. In Marya Raczinsky's case, however, it is a psychic loss of considerable proportions. "Heartbreak" might be an accurate term for her condition.

After all the intimations of and maneuvers with memory in the novel—Tim's colleague's vague recollection that sets his journey in motion; the poignant biographical account given by Stefan to Tim in the house in Hampstead; the elusive significance of the report in the Moscow newspaper; the invented and re-invented stories of the two Russian witnesses, Lutkin and Skaliga; the evocation of World War II on the Eastern Front as the destroyer of long-term social memory during Tim's visit to Lvov—all these have played a role in the intelligence operation, playing out over decades, that terminates with a posthumous letter of explanation, and Marya's accusation that her sense of her own identity has been betrayed and violated.[10] The title of the novel suggests, furthermore, that the legacy of Loda (an invention, but clearly standing in for real historical locations) is not only a name that evokes Nazi occupation and a war of annihilation, but divergent ideologies and loyalties even many years after the conflict was over. The arrival of the Cold War meant that a lot of raw history would not be simply available for general review but would be reshaped and deployed in this new struggle. *The Ashes of Loda* is in many ways a prescient novel for its time, as it predicts the wrestling with memory, trauma, and ambiguity that would arrive with more comprehensive and more probing investigations and studies of both the Nazi genocide and the nature of Stalinist rule.

Both MacInnes's *I and My True Love* and Garve's *The Ashes of Loda* frame the significant political divisions of the mid-twentieth century within a narrative of mystery, inquiry, and resolution—no matter how tragic or injurious such a resolution may be—that meets the basic requirements of a popular literary form. In both novels the setting is one that, while probably directly familiar to only a small segment of the readership, has a certain formalized existence within the mind: an existence that is a feature of the cultural repetoire that we walk around with, in our different societies and environments. These geographical locations, Washington DC and Czechoslovakia in the one case and London, Moscow, and Ukraine in the other, are of course in many ways also stereotypes, but in the course of each story the type does not remain simply inert or untouched, but is opened up and enriched, and place and person are given ideological nuance and emotional resonance. This is particularly striking in *The Ashes of Loda*, in which a wide range of Russian characters, the people whom Tim Quainton meets during his attempt to flee the country after the attempt on his life, appear to represent some important aspects of Russian social reality beyond the usual Cold War caricatures. The section of the novel in which he visits the Loda trial witness Skaliga in his room in the shabby apartment in the middle of the Moscow winter, a scene that is both about a complicated past and a frustrating present, on several levels, is particularly memorable for the way it seems to touch a live cable between what was and what is, history and recollection, truth and fiction. The ghosts of World War II in its intensity and savagery on the Eastern Front, of the countries it devastated and the nations it changed, hang in the stuffy room as the two men talk.[11]

What *The Ashes of Loda* does is both restore a human dimension to the abstract entity known as the Soviet Union and give the protagonists and the setting a past that explains their roles and actions in the contemporary time of the novel, the early 1960s. Emerging from the enigma of the title, the truth buried in the ashes, presumably all that now remains of the camp at Loda, involves questions, archives, and interviews, all potentially saying something about an event twenty years earlier. The narrative calls forth a fascination with the past, the nature of memory, and why someone might invent a fiction that ultimately creates trauma and shock within the intimate family circle. To remember correctly can be dangerous, or at least problematic, in certain circumstances, and there is a certain commonly held view that poking around in the past is a somewhat thoughtless and self-indulgent exercise, if not the action of someone who wants to upset other people's lives. The truth at the end of *The Ashes of Loda* is, of course, far from a nostalgic visit to an exhibition of sepia-colored photographs: rather, it causes pain and dislocation, perhaps never to be fully assuaged.

Timothy Synder's *Bloodlands* (2010), an unrelenting study of the impact of fascist and communist dictatorships as felt across Eastern Europe and Russia in the twentieth century, opens up an interesting thematic connection with *The Ashes of Loda*. Snyder's achievement is to have gathered the disparate histories of the afterburn of the German, Austro-Hungarian, and Russian empires as those entities spiraled into sites of nationalist exclusivism and racial paranoia, as well as mass imprisonment, ethnic removals, and murder for the sake of progress, into a larger theoretical model in which the exercise of force without mercy comes to override any other political or ethical tradition.[12] These wars and struggles in the region that stretches from eastern Germany to Russia and from the Baltic to the Black Sea were, among other things, conflicts over memory and what was to be remembered, and what was not. At various times, the Communist Party wanted Russians to not recall the limited individual civil rights of the early twentieth century; the Nazis wanted the Germans to not recall the rule of law even within the powerful Prussian state; radical nationalists wanted various communities in central and Eastern Europe to not recall that they had once lived together for several decades, more or less peaceably, in the demographic patchwork of the Habsburg Reich; and in contrast the Jews and the Roma were meant to recall that they didn't really belong anywhere and nobody liked them very much.

As Snyder argues, the act of commemoration for victims can itself become a search for "the right sort of political remembrance," one which validates a teleology of contemporary nationalism, for instance, or for an advantageous ranking in "the international competition for martyrdom."[13] It is not only authoritarian regimes, or societies that have just emerged from authoritarian rule, that want to manage the guidelines for the work of memory. Democratic and more or less liberal capitalist countries also have sensitive spots, be it the crimes of empire or the selective application of supposedly universal principles, and any public act of remembrance can invite hostility and repercussions. The passionate controversy over the last few years in the United States triggered by efforts to remove statues of Confederate leaders or to rename buildings named after slaveowners has often been the opposite of civil or rational debate.[14] What *The Ashes of Loda* does effectively, and even movingly, is to find a literary format within a broadly popular mode that makes the reader understand that part of the political struggle in Europe, before and during the Cold War, was to massage the collective memory of events and sometimes, as in this novel, private and intimate memory as well.[15]

MacInnes's *I and My True Love* and Garve's *The Ashes of Loda* are narrative fictions that query and undermine the assumption that personal affections and relationships exist in a protected sphere that cannot be invaded by the political struggles or ideological divergences around them. Long before the feminist revolution of the 1970s, in fact, the recognition that "the personal is political" informed stories of the early Cold War in which the alliances of World War II and the antifascist front were either a fading memory or a reality turned sour as the Soviet Bloc nations bunkered in behind the Iron Curtain. For its part, the United States in particular among Western countries created an atmosphere in which deviations from the approved norms, whether political, sexual, or racial or some combination of these, became grounds for accusations of disloyalty or even espionage and subversion.[16] These novels present complex plotting, attention to historical detail, and a willingness to avoid superficially reassuring conclusions. It is easy to forget that the eventual outcome of the Cold War was not known in 1953 or in 1964, and both MacInnes and Garve assumed that the international situation would remain in its then current state for the foreseeable future, with the hope that it would not become even more dangerous. Whatever one can say about the broader literary careers of the two authors dealt with in this chapter, novels such as *I and My True Love* and *The Ashes of Loda* seem, today, strikingly attuned to the psychological and political stresses of the postwar decades and the complicated decisions about loyalty and commitment that individuals made under pressure, often with serious consequences for those close to them. Realists in a basic sense of the term, MacInnes and Garve wrote out of an understanding that the past and the present are actively at work in the human consciousness, on both individual and collective levels, and often make demands on us that we cannot easily meet.

Notes

1. The original London Protocol foresaw occupation zones in Germany and Austria for the United States, Britain, and the Soviet Union only; a French occupation zone was created in an annex to the agreement in summer 1945.
2. For a glimpse of the political realities and power relations on the ground in 1948, see the letter from President Beneš to the leadership of the Communist Party, and their reply, in Judge and Langdon, editors, *The Cold War through Documents*, 54–57.
3. For a detailed account of the Czech experience, see the chapter "Stalin over Prague" in Skilling, *Communism National and International*, 84–105.
4. Broadly, the model of national communism aimed at a socialist transformation of society but also wanted a level of autonomy for individual communist parties rather than uncritical obedience to the Moscow line. Stalin was hostile to nationalist tendencies, and show trials were

held in several countries, most notably Hungary and Czechoslovakia, to indict and often execute people suspected of being open to Western influence or showing too much interest in their own nation's room for independent action.

5. "Titoism" was often used as shorthand for national communism in the postwar era. See Jelavich, *History of the Balkans*, vol. 2, 321–31 for a succinct account of the split between the Soviet Union and Yugoslavia that gave rise to the term.
6. Even a rumor of homosexuality could be a career-ending danger in Washington in the 1950s, but see Signorile, *Queer in America* for an analysis of the situation of gay men in government service, which remained to a large extent unchanged even into the 1990s.
7. Although not particularly visible in most of the texts and authors I deal with in *Reading Espionage Fiction*, the motif of ashes is quite important for the larger vision behind this book. In recent decades, the influence of memory studies has grown and opened up connections to many other fields and sub-fields of study. Drawing literature and drama (and, often, visual arts) into an investigative relationship with history, psychoanalysis, and sociology, memory studies has not only addressed those major traumatic experiences of modernity such as World War I, the Nazi Holocaust, or long-drawn-out colonial wars, but also offered new ways to think about social conflicts of race or gender, environmental threat and damage, and the politics of public monuments and acts of commemoration. Its appearance in the title of a forgotten espionage novel of the early 1960s—one I had read a long time ago and rediscovered on the shelf in the library at the University of California, Los Angeles—convinced me that it might have at least a small role to play in working through the themes and arguments of this book.
8. The city is now generally referred to by its name in Ukrainian, Lviv, but the Russian name Lvov is used throughout the novel.
9. Given the nature of Marya's background and the presence of the recent war in her life, it seems a somewhat peculiar choice of words when Tim thinks to himself that his courtship of Marya must have seemed to her "like a bit of a blitzkrieg" (17).
10. The last sentence of the novel, set off in a paragraph of its own, in which Tim Quainton asserts his conviction that Marya will eventually get over her sense of loss and agree to marry him, makes the impression of a late addition pushed on the author by his editor (speculation, of course, as I have no proof one way or the other). The penultimate paragraph ends on an ambiguous note. Ironically, Tim's statement that he knows now that it will come out right for both of them in the end concludes a narrative which hangs on his being almost convinced of something that turned out not to be exactly the case. Marya also knew she was Polish, of course, which she was not.

11. See Judt, "The Past Is Another Country" for a powerful reading of the trauma of the postwar era.
12. Snyder notes in his conclusion that a remarkable number of people were able to find a justification for participation in mass murder, whether directly or *ex officio*, and both Nazism and Stalinism operated as higher causes to which the individual freely offered their loyalty and obedience. We cannot find these people incomprehensible, he argues, because that would be "to abandon the search for understanding, and thus to abandon history" (*Bloodlands*, 400).
13. Snyder, *Bloodlands*, 402.
14. The removal of statues and place names is often derided as an attempt to deny history in favor of present-day ideas and assumptions. There are genuine positions to be examined fairly here, but to meet any alteration with the counter-argument that it is manipulating history would imply that the square in Berlin that was Adolf-Hitler-Platz from 1933 to 1946 should still be called that today. In fact, in 2014 it underwent a brief restoration of that name because of an error in Google Maps: https://www.cbsnews.com/news/google-apologizes-for-hitler-name-on-maps/ (accessed June 18, 2023).
15. This did not cease entirely with the collapse of the communist system under the political and military dome of the Soviet Union. In the early 1990s visitors touring former Soviet Bloc countries often found a general unwillingness to admit that, for example, the communists had sometimes been the only political force willing to put through some badly needed reforms (reforms that would have been unobjectionable in Western Europe) after the war, or that the communist system had its own gradations and rankings and had even enabled, within limits, a certain amount of upward social mobility.
16. The saving grace is, one should note, that such accusations or even evidence proving the charges did not, generally, involve a long prison sentence or execution as was often the case in Eastern Europe or the Soviet Union. There were exceptions, nonetheless, and the death sentences for Julius and Ethel Rosenberg at their trial for espionage in 1953 is a dramatic example thereof.

Chapter 4

John le Carré and the Jews

To begin with the tragic and move on to the comic would be a traditional approach to dealing with texts in different modes. In this chapter, however, I begin with the comedy and move on to the tragedy or, more accurately, a convergence of tragedies. The comedy surrounding the characters, in particular the protagonist Harry Pendel, in John le Carré's novel *The Tailor of Panama* (1996) and Pendel's role as a recreation or re-embodiment of James Wormold, the reluctant agent in the field in Graham Greene's 1958 novel *Our Man in Havana*, is obviously le Carré's homage to Greene. Greene continues to be adduced as an influence on le Carré or, in past decades, almost as a mentor of his, despite the two authors revealing an obvious divergence in both intention and authorial product—Greene's casual downgrading of certain novels (including *Our Man in Havana*) to the status of "entertainments" as against le Carré's ambition to provide his espionage fictions with literary credibility.[1] For le Carré, Greene was a writer to be admired, and they shared professional experience in intelligence work, but a tendency to group them as a pair appears more akin to a journalistic unwillingness to alter a fixed narrative.[2]

As le Carré and others have noted, there are two more powerful polar influences on his writing: Joseph Conrad's fiction, especially *Under Western Eyes* and *The Secret Agent*, and Rudyard Kipling's *Kim*. Despite the history of reviewers misreading le Carré's relationship with Graham Greene, however, he turns his affection and respect for Greene's darkly comic *Our Man in Havana* into a defining presence in *The Tailor of Panama*. "And what's life if it isn't invention?" Harry Pendel queries rhetorically in one of his many soliloquizing passages, saying out loud what Greene's protagonist James Wormold never would (240).

In any event, *The Tailor of Panama* is both le Carré's only substantial narrative that could be with some justification filed under comedy, and also relatively unusual for its commanding and vivid non-European setting, with perhaps *The Honorable Schoolboy* (1977) offering the only substantial comparison in that regard. That the narrative takes place against the backdrop of the earlier US invasion of Panama in 1989, ostensibly to remove the authoritarian regime of Manuel Noriega in retaliation for his having threatened the security of the Canal Zone, then under the direct administration of Washington, gives the novel a flavor that, in many respects, echoes Graham Greene's choice of Cuba, then ruled by the dictator Fulgencio Batista, for his novel.[3] The two historical and geographical locations of *Our Man in Havana* and *The Tailor of Panama* are not, of course, mirror-images to be placed alongside each other: they do not simply align in terms of period, situation, or character interaction. Nevertheless, there are aspects that, at a deeper level of story and motif, suggest how John le Carré has refurbished and re-vitalized Greene's original while continuing to both admire it and simultaneously hold it at a critical distance.

There is no equivalent in Greene's novel for Louisa, for example, Harry Pendel's engaging and strong-willed wife, nor for Andrew Osnard, the new and corrupt MI6 officer on station at the British embassy in Panama City. *The Tailor of Panama* showcases a much wider range of characters than Greene does in *Our Man in Havana*, and the downbeat, provincial atmosphere of the earlier story gives way to a more panoramic and colorful menu of personae and incident. Where le Carré plays most clearly and effectively with the legacy of *Our Man in Havana* is in the character of Harry Pendel, tailor and inventor of stories, in the Caribbean setting with its occasional evocation of other classic spy stories.[4] Secondly, there is the more subversive implication that intelligence services desire, rather like nations, stories that meet their institutional and cultural requirements. The line between invention and reality can be manipulated surprisingly easily by the source, using his or her creative imagination.[5]

Harry Pendel becomes not so much the moral anchor of his story as, under the gaze of the omniscient narrator, the creative mind whose moral compass is very much that of a popular writer: wanting to deliver, to please his audience. He has several opportunities to do this: in his conversations with his wife, who does not know everything about her husband's history; in the introductory interrogation-conversation with Andrew Osnard; and then, under different degrees of pressure, as he is providing intelligence product to London, and being paid for it. Against the background of the narcissism of Panamanian society and politics, embodied in many of the other characters in the novel, especially Mickie Abraxas, with whom Harry has a complicated history, he often appears to be a man with a grip on reality rather than a fantasist on the loose and heedless of the damage he can cause.

The lever that Andrew Osnard uses to change Harry Pendel's life from something simply problematic (debts he can't pay and a past that he hasn't told his wife about) to something nerve-wracking (taking a lot of money for providing fake intelligence from sources that he has never actually recruited) is the truth of Harry's past. In a series of passes rather like in a bullfight, Osnard invites Harry to let him have the classic story of a Jewish son of London's East End who is taken under the wing of a Savile Row tailor, learns the trade from someone who saw tailoring as not only a craft but an ethical way of life, and somehow ended up in Central America selling handmade suits to a wide array of moneyed clients who have bought the whole deal of English bespoke tailoring as the necessary component of an image of wealth and social status, whether they have that status in fact or just think they ought to.[6] After hearing out the myth, Osnard proceeds to documentary realism, as it were, laying out for Harry Pendel the less than admirable reality behind the Pendel and Braithwaite fiction: his time in Her Majesty's penitentiary, for example, when he took the blame for his Uncle Benny's burning down his own warehouse for the insurance (48); the non-existence of an actual Braithwaite in his past, the invention of that character being simply useful for lending an atmosphere of historical rootedness to the tailoring business and relating anecdotes about the imaginary patron's wisdom to Harry's customers and family (46–47). Finally, there is Harry's lack of an actual basis for a genuine Jewish identity, as he is in fact the illegitimate child of an Irish Catholic housemaid (96).

Thus does Harry Pendel the Jewish tailor of Panama, already in that shape the bearer and recipient of assumptions and stereotypes about Jews and tailors, turn out to be Harry the not-quite-Jewish tailor, who has created his own mythology that not only offers but invites those very assumptions and stereotypes. It is one of the enigmatic achievements of *The Tailor of Panama* that the reader is never quite sure, even at the end of a long novel, whether Harry is a guilty fool who, at the very least, causes the death of one of his closest friends, or a literary artist who, when given the opportunity as well as the generous payment for it, cannot but create, spinning fictions out of the rich interstices of his imagination. If le Carré means his narrative to be, in some way, a kind of indictment-plus-defense of fiction writing, the need to send elegant untruths into the world because other people enjoy them or find them convincing, it is noticeable that he has selected and shaped a character whose principle is, maybe, a dangerous one: "To say the right things at all times, even if the right things were in one place and the truth was in another" (237).

So Harry can cut cloth and tell stories, measure a man's inseam and assess how much of the Braithwaite legend he'd like to hear, and in some ways play the person he is more effectively than actually be him. Osnard, for his part, has convinced his Secret Intelligence Service (SIS) boss Luxmore, a Scotsman who plays at being a Scotsman, that Pendel could potentially be a significant source for a re-established British intelligence presence in Panama. Osnard's own performative efforts have convinced Luxmore that he is a loyal and willing intelligence officer appropriately deferential to the wisdom of his elders. The character interactions in the novel that involve one party performing the role that the other, or others, expect or are paying for culminate in Pendel's supplying more or less completely made-up intelligence on a non-existent Panamanian democratic underground to Osnard and London ("London" being here more of a conspiracy of media barons and corporate interests than Her Majesty's government in the traditional sense of the label).[7]

As *The Tailor of Panama* is obviously paying public literary homage to *Our Man in Havana*, it is worth raising the question as to how these parallels are deployed by le Carré. Is Harry Pendel a recreation of James Wormold for the end of the twentieth century? Pendel is Jewish, but not really. English, but with the residue of an immigrant East End that has long since faded away in reality. He is, like Wormold, given to a certain kind of culturally determined dithering, polite diffidence under pressure. Both are salesmen, Wormold of vacuum cleaners, Pendel of handmade suits. Perhaps most importantly, both conceal a certain quantum of amoral hardness underneath the layer of stoic civility, and this hardness emerges when something they value is seriously under threat: in Wormold's case, his life but also his daughter Milly; in Pendel's case, Osnard's demand that he recruit his wife Louisa for the network turns him into an even more assiduous supplier of fictions, but in his managing of the clearing-up after Mickie Abraxas's suicide Pendel shows his resources, capabilities, and sheer nerve. Both Greene's character and le Carré's character face the uncontrollable consequences of their elaborate schemes, but Harry Pendel at the novel's conclusion is more wracked with guilt than Wormold is as his story comes to its close.

Both men are cast in the first stages of their narratives as to some degree emasculated. This is partly communicated in the form of a quasi-comic juxtaposition between the hesitancy of the British and the assertive and unapologetic masculine domination of the Cuban or Panamanian social scene. Harry Pendel is, as a tailor, in a more delicate position than Wormold as his job involves touching men in semi-intimate ways. Add the requirement of the tailor to crouch down below the belt level when making particular measurements, and it might seem as if every note of subservience has been sounded. It is only the assumed superiority of the Savile Row tailoring mythology that gives Harry a means other than the existence of his children Mark and Hannah to push back against any assumption that he is sexually neuter. Furthermore, the fact that Harry is believed by all (including his family) to be Jewish adds an extra opening for stereotypical projection—precisely the stereotypes that Harry has been working hard to establish in everyone's mind since he arrived in Panama.

Unlike Wormold in *Our Man in Havana*, therefore, le Carré's Harry Pendel is not only the agent who invents first-rate intelligence product to sell; he is also the Jew who isn't a Jew, and also the peaceable and reasonable man who may well have started a small war with his fictions. Perhaps for all its sparkling satire and extended comic performances, from Ambassador Maltby's pirouettes of irony through Louisa Pendel's dry wit to Luxmore's baroque, Dickensian antisemitism, *The Tailor of Panama* is not all that funny at the end, and Harry Pendel cannot escape from that place of tragic suffering to which John le Carré sometimes appears to want to consign his Jewish characters. When Phyllis Lassner in her study *Espionage and Exile* evokes "the cultural history of representing the spy in relation to the injured and historicized Jew," she establishes a basic framework for assessing the way in which le Carré's fictions stage the repeated intersecting of identity and destiny in the modern world.[8] In his characterizations there is an emphasis on the way Jews can be both outsiders and insiders, but often insiders with only temporary residence permitted.

To go back to the roots of the tragic, the primary scene of merely conditional belonging, in his portrayal of Jews means to revisit le Carré's memorable debut novel *Call for the Dead*. Published in 1961, this short novel must be one of the most assured performances delivered by a writer looking to attract some attention with their first effort: not only the opening passages that describe George Smiley, le Carré's most famous and beloved character, in ways that seem to establish his presence for later novels that the author could not really, at that point, have known he was going to write, but also the development of a certain downbeat tone that established distance but did not eradicate empathy is clearly in evidence in the prose. The novel opens with a chapter which is an extended biographical note on Smiley presented within the narrative frame of an early morning taxi ride through London to the Cambridge Circus headquarters of MI6 (known to the initiated as "the Circus" in the Smiley novels), where he is confronted with the news that an official of the Foreign Office, recently interviewed by Smiley, has committed suicide in his home (1–8).

Smiley explains to his superior, Maston, that the news is baffling because Smiley had more or less cleared Fennan of any suspicion of being a security risk: the service had responded to an anonymous letter about Fennan harboring communist loyalties, but Smiley had regarded it as having no credibility. Visiting Fennan's home, still in the early morning, to establish what has happened, Smiley meets Fennan's wife, now widow, Elsa. She is German or Austrian, and a Jewish refugee from an earlier life marked by war, suffering, and loss. She has an odd affect, seeming to regard her husband's suicide with stoical resignation, as if she had always expected something like this in life. Standing in the Fennans' hall as the phone suddenly rings, Smiley is the accidental recipient of an alarm call from the telephone exchange (normal in 1950s Britain) for Fennan, which he requested the previous evening. Thinking about this after he leaves the house, Smiley becomes more certain that Fennan's suicide lacks any obvious motive and that his widow was unconvincing in her account of her husband's last days and hours. Smiley's interactions with Elsa Fennan throughout the novel seem to revolve around disruption and trauma, as her past as a Holocaust survivor (although that term would hardly have been used only fifteen years after the war) reappears in the context of postwar England as an uncomfortable and awkward foreignness, not fitting within a local language of studied neutrality and the suppression of powerful feeling. Furthermore, the possibility of Elsa's foreign presence being not only Jewish but potentially a bearer of communist ideology in the Cold War begins to emerge. She is, in Lassner's words, "a spectral figure" and "the undead embodied memory" of both the Nazi Holocaust itself and, more generally, the fate of Jews to be regarded as outsiders in the nation that simultaneously refuses to accept them within that particular national community.[9]

The reappearance of Dieter Frey, a half-Jewish former student of Smiley's who survived the war, partly because his logistical skills were so important that his papers were conveniently lost by the German authorities, reveals a longer conspiracy at work. Frey had been a significant asset in a loose network of British agents in Nazi Germany that Smiley had been involved in organizing, the latter having recognized his potential when he had been there as a visiting lecturer just before the war. It emerges that Dieter Frey not only survived but went on to commit himself to the German Democratic Republic (GDR), the country that was born out of the Soviet occupation zone of the defeated Reich. Frey had contacted Elsa Fennan and reminded her of their mutual past as people subject to a particular fatal threat but who worked for a better society for all. Elsa permits herself to be recruited by Dieter, and this relationship over time provokes a suspicion in her husband that he does not know how to deal with.

In *Call for the Dead*, the politics of the narrative are cast, strikingly, in terms of friendship, ideology, national cultural norms, and the memory of the war. Although George Smiley's job is that of "intelligence officer" (2), the meanings of the novel are not articulated by the unfolding or discovery of the East German espionage operation so much as by the degree to which characters hold to the commitments of their younger days. Dieter Frey, Smiley's brilliant and passionate antifascist student in late 1930s Germany, is the enemy, the opposition, that he most of all does not want to have. The faint suspicion that Smiley may have abandoned the comradeship of the wartime years more distinctly than Dieter has is foregrounded in the progress of their confrontation: Smiley attacks Frey physically but Dieter refuses to defend himself. With the insouciance of German Romanticism, a tradition which had no small influence on German communism, Dieter Frey puts friendship ahead of cause or nation, and pays the price. The price Smiley pays is to know exactly what has transpired.

The question of national cultural norms is an intriguing one: as noted above, it is Elsa Fennan's background that in some way discomfits her postwar British environment. The memorable final passage of the novel, in which Smiley is flying from London to Zurich to see his wife Ann, involves his facial expression being misinterpreted by a young male fellow passenger. This passenger sees a "tired executive out for a bit of fun," smiling to himself on the plane and assumes he is some kind of management type looking forward to a weekend of illicit sexual enjoyments (157). It seems that the English mind is somehow inevitably going to opt for the narrow vision, the ungenerous reading: no place for Elsa Fennan; perhaps even no place for George Smiley.

If Elsa Fennan is the mature woman who walks with the shadow of her past as a Holocaust survivor, and Dieter Frey is the idealistic communist who nonetheless permits an old comradeship to trump ideological commitment at the end, then Liz Gold and Fiedler in le Carré's third novel *The Spy Who Came In from the Cold* (1963) are very different variations on a Jewish theme. Liz Gold is a young and impetuous Londoner, a member of the Communist Party of Great Britain, and her brief romantic and sexual attachment to former SIS officer Alec Leamas brings her unexpectedly to East Germany and a courtroom meeting with Fiedler, the deputy head of counter-intelligence at the GDR ministry for state security (referred to informally as the Stasi). The complexities of the plot of *The Spy Who Came In from the Cold* are certainly well known to two generations of le Carré's readers (and the 1965 film, directed by Martin Ritt, remains completely faithful to the novel in that respect). To summarize, the covert organizing principle of the story is an operation whose objective is, counter-intuitively, to be discovered and discredited. The British service's intention is that the real purpose of the operation will remain intact if the ostensible purpose is uncovered, but with considerable difficulty. Leamas's willingness to supply the East German Stasi with information on London's networks in the GDR is crucial to the mission, and despite Leamas's request to George Smiley not to involve his former lover, that relationship with Liz Gold leads to her becoming, involuntarily, an extra component in the machinery of the plot.

Liz is portrayed in the novel as an empathetic and kind-hearted young woman who joins the Communist Party mainly because she believes that the party is dedicated to peace in the world and creating a better society for all citizens. Largely alienated by the theory and analysis discussed at Party meetings, and skeptical of comrades she believes are mostly egoists with a liking for the sound of their own voices, Liz is practical enough to complete her Saturday paper sales of the *Daily Worker* by purchasing a few copies herself (134). She is brought together with Alec Leamas, now fired from the service for embezzling funds, in a badly paid job in a specialist private library, and the two become sexually involved with each other. Unaware, of course, of the nature of Leamas's past life and of other things unfolding as she enjoys having a lover—even if he is dismayed when she reveals that she is a communist—Liz is then surprised and hurt by Leamas's sudden disappearance from her life. Receiving an unexpected invitation, via the party, to visit East Germany on an educational trip, she sees Alec again for the first time in weeks in the Stasi tribunal where the operation is coming into its final phase.

The trial of Hans-Dieter Mundt, Fiedler's superior at Stasi counter-intelligence, is part of the web of suspicion that London plans to weave, and then deploy, around the two senior figures in the East German security apparatus. When Liz begins testifying at the trial, she pulls apart the legitimacy of the case that Fiedler has been building as he seeks to prove once and for all that Mundt is a double-agent and British spy. Suddenly the role that Liz has unwittingly played in the game plan is produced: she has received money from obscure sources and she was visited by someone called George who claimed to be a former colleague of Leamas's. With the unraveling of the case that Fiedler has put together with the help of Leamas's crucial information from his time as chief of the SIS's West Berlin section, Fiedler himself falls immediately under suspicion and is arrested. The tribunal switches gears to determine a finding of guilty with Fiedler as the accused, completely exonerating Mundt.

At one moment in *The Spy Who Came In from the Cold*, the narrative implies that both Liz Gold and Fiedler, standing in the courtroom, see each other suddenly as Jews. As she looks at him, "he smiled very slightly, as if in recognition of her race," and it seems quite clear that what is communicated is a sense that they both have become victims once again (187). When Liz is in the Stasi lock-up, although not officially a prisoner, the German woman who takes care of her remarks that "[w]e don't need their kind here" (194). The intuitive assumption that Jews are simply untrustworthy is woven into the popular mind of the GDR, ostensibly a socialist nation that has shucked off the remnants of fascism and ethnic nationalism. The GDR, it becomes clear, has kept some of the forms of Nazi militarism and certain social attitudes that are expressed in a roundabout way, but expressed nonetheless. In stark contrast to Fiedler, Hans-Dieter Mundt is given a history as a member of the Hitler Youth and subsequently a convert to communism in the early days of the Soviet occupation zone, when young people were often seen as capable of being redirected to become, potentially, loyal partisans for a communist rather than a national socialist or capitalist future for Germany. It is clearly the case that, in *The Spy Who Came In from the Cold*, the nature of postwar Germany is seen as a society, in this case specifically its Soviet-created eastern variant, in which a substantial residue of the traditional suspicion of Jews is still there to be drawn on.

In the broader context of his fiction from the 1960s, le Carré did not ignore the West German side of that particular phenomenon, as I discuss later, but it is in this novel that his trope of a tragic arc for Jewish progressive radicalism takes on its most intense expression.[10] When Alec and Liz are in the car together waiting for the signal to cross the Berlin Wall safely, Leamas gives his memorable speech about the nature of spies and the values that direct intelligence work—namely, expediency, and nothing else—and tries to disabuse Liz Gold of any notion that they may allow higher thoughts or feelings to influence their choices. When he explains what Liz has not quite grasped, that the operation was set up in order to protect Mundt from Fiedler, the clever Jew who was his deputy, Liz is shocked in part because she has seen one side of Fiedler but not the other, the animated intellectual but not the ruthless security officer loyal to the mission of the party. But Leamas puts London's plan to her directly when he says that the order was to "kill the Jew" (199).

Leamas's implication in that statement is certainly open to some interpretation. Presumably, he is not suggesting that the Circus decided on a plan to do away with Fiedler simply because he was a Jew. But, in a way, that is not an inaccurate description: they knew that there was an aura of doubt, no matter how nebulous, surrounding Fiedler as a Jewish intellectual in a country, the GDR, that had hardly any Jews any more (which in many ways applied to West Germany too, of course), and London obviously intended to exploit that margin of mistrust. And the mistrust is itself odd, as there is no suggestion that Fiedler has been less than a dedicated servant of the party, in some ways he has been a more consistent fighter for communist ideals than anyone else in his milieu. And yet that mistrust is exactly what was available to be deployed against him, to save the man who is actually a British asset on the Stasi senior leadership floor.

But might "killing the Jew" be a sort of joke that the senior planners at the Circus goofed around with, as a way of disguising from themselves the fact that they were using the German distrust of Jews (a national trait now even stronger because they had recently tried to exterminate them), or is it suggestive of something more unpleasant? Leamas conjures up a historical reference but the impact of the remark is, in relation to Liz Gold's awareness of herself as Jewish, to rub her nose in the fact that London used the surviving residue of Jew-hatred in German society to achieve the expedient result. But the phrasing also implies a kind of casual acceptance of the available mechanism: Germans don't really trust Jews, at heart, not even or especially not after they tried to annihilate them. So communism or no communism, went the thinking at MI6, our best option for protecting Mundt is to raise suspicions regarding Fiedler. Their own prejudices will do the rest, and isn't that just the way of things? Leamas's crude summarizing of the conspiracy is ironic to the extent that the final body count will include, when the action reaches the attempted escape across the Wall, not just the Jew Fiedler but the other Jew Liz Gold, and the non-Jew Alec Leamas.[11]

Control, Smiley, and mission planning would no doubt protest that their intended victim was not Fiedler the Jew but Fiedler the communist security officer. And they would also, no doubt either, assert that their agent was Mundt the senior East German functionary and not Mundt the brutal secret policeman who learned his trade in his younger years in the Nazi system. But the novel does work hard at leaving open the question as to whether the significance of the operation against Fiedler was fully explicable in terms of its Cold War ideological justification.[12] It does seem peculiar that, even if Fiedler was no innocent in any sense of the term, Liz Gold, the other Jew, should be so cruelly turned into collateral damage at the climax of the story. It is not entirely clear from the narrative to what degree London took the possibility of her imprisonment, injury, or even death seriously into account when it involved her against Leamas's specific request in the operation.[13] The suspicion remains that Liz is on the expendable list because, once again, it is not her ethno-religious background but her politics that makes her vulnerable, and that she, the most obviously harmless and unknowing figure in *The Spy Who Came In from the Cold*, has lost all claim to be an innocent participant simply because she once joined the Communist Party of Great Britain.

The questions of Jewish victimhood and the subterranean swirls of polite exclusion surface again in John le Carré's fifth novel *A Small Town in Germany* (1968). The novel is set in both the official and the informal circles of the British embassy in Bonn, then the capital of the Federal Republic of Germany; the character who mirrors the roles that Dieter Frey and Elsa Fennan, and Fiedler and Liz Gold, play in le Carré's first and third novels respectively, and even foreshadows some of Harry Pendel's delicate mix of vulnerability and positivity, is Leo Harting. Harting, a German who spent his teenage years during World War II in Britain, has a vaguely undefined job in the embassy, and is seen by a lot of his colleagues as both knowledgeable and helpful, and also slightly pathetic. The son of mixed Jewish parentage who came as a child refugee to England just before the war, Harting is one of those people who are essentially bi-national while being occasionally regarded as uncomfortably foreign in both their countries, the one they came from and the one they arrived in. In the opening chapter, an unnamed person, in retrospect obviously Harting, is chatting at night with a policeman on a street in Bonn:

> His accent was neither wholly English nor wholly German, but a privately elected no-man's land, picked and set between the two. And he would move it, he seemed to say, a little in either direction, if it chanced to inconvenience the listener. (4)

The difference between Leo Harting and the others, even the tailor of Panama who is so good at observing from the sidelines and inventing where necessary, is that Harting is not physically present in the narrative at all. He has already disappeared from the embassy without trace, and has carried off certain files from the archives that would seriously compromise the United Kingdom's status in its relationship with the West German government. Leo Harting is therefore among the two most significant characters in *A Small Town in Germany*, but has nothing directly to say for himself in the course of the story: the progress of the narrative turns about his absence; his colleagues and acquaintances discuss him from all sides; the official bodies in the embassy and in the German government are feinting with each other about his disappearance; and Alan Turner, the security man from London, has the task of finding him.

The political background to this novel is notably specific. The action takes place in the mid-1960s in West Germany, when the rising Social Democratic Party, Willy Brandt's SPD, was in a so-called "grosse Koalition" or grand coalition with the Christian Democratic Union, the conservative party alliance that had been in power for the eighteen-year history of the Federal Republic. The grand coalition, which was essentially a tool utilized by the SPD to leverage the Christian Democratic Union out of office, had generated a negative reaction especially among liberal and politically aware Germans, who regarded this political arrangement as tending ultimately to deliver political significance and credibility to the more fringe or extremist parties, right or left. If nobody is there to take on the role of a serious parliamentary opposition because the two major parties are now together in government, went the thinking, then unserious and even ominous opposition parties will move into the vacant space.[14]

In the novel, the new political force is called the Movement and embodies a challenge to the stable political system of West Germany. The Movement combines an idealistic appeal to young people and the student left with a deployment of the kind of rhetoric of resentment and betrayal that is often the signal of a right-wing populist or nationalist project at work.[15] The leader of this new political actor, Karfeld, is not a rabble-rouser or demagogue, but a modest and even uninspiring former scientist who touts his own lack of experience in mainstream politics as a qualification rather than a deficit. Those familiar with the era might see a curious mingling of the emergent radical student left and a more assertive nationalist right in le Carré's vision of the political landscape, although such a formation never really existed in reality.[16] In the novel, one implication is that German as well as foreign governments are considering how a potential victory for the Movement might change some well-established assumptions, and they are nervous about this. The chilly federal interior ministry mandarin Ludwig Siebkron, for instance, who suspects correctly that the British are not telling him everything about Leo Harting, is clearly preparing for a new political arrangement in West Germany, and appears to want to bury whatever Harting might have taken with him when he fled. What Harting has with him, material on Karfeld and his actual research during the war, would terminate his claim to have been a young scientist with no history of involvement with the Nazi Party or in crimes against humanity.

In the investigation carried out over a couple of days by Turner, who arrives from London to assess the situation, he is noticeably uninterested in the potential motives for Harting's absconding with the compromising files. As he moves through the brushwood of the embassy's social undercurrents, oblique prejudices, and embarrassing moments like a logger with a small buzz-saw, Turner's direct but effective approach to questioning people produces results. His blunt interrogations turn up likes, dislikes, affairs, affections, and the general impression that Leo Harting was more or less alone in the British embassy in Bonn in thinking that one should perhaps do something about the possibility of an ex-Nazi with a hidden past gaining political power in Germany in a new, more harmless-looking guise.[17]

As seen in le Carré's previous novels, Harting is the next incarnation of the Jew who is forced, in this case by a British government looking to adjust its attitude to a changing wind, to take on the thankless task of reminding everyone what can happen when the populist rebellion against the constitutional order begins to catch fire. The fact that he is not actually fully Jewish is almost a confirmation of his status, as any chance that he might feel less inclined to nurture that one part of his identity has been obliterated by the English social policing that works hard to find people who are a little different and politely let them know of their inadequacy. An awkward and even discomfiting presence at the British embassy, Harting proves by his disappearance along with the stolen files that he never belonged anyway: the Jew tends to "rupture[s] the stable narrative of citizenship."[18] The hunt for the absconder is in no way an attempt to bring him back into the fold and take his concerns seriously. Rather, it is to get to him before the German security people do, because then the problem would be that both the British and the Germans know what is in the documents about Karfeld, and Ludwig Siebkron could point out smugly that it isn't the Germans who have been hiding material on Nazi war crimes.

At the climax of *A Small Town in Germany*, when Turner and embassy officials try to meet Leo at the main railway station in Cologne during a political demonstration by the Movement, he also fails to enter the narrative on his own terms. Seen only in the crowd, and then as a lifeless body on the street, Leo Harting has once again shown the terminal heroism that, in le Carré's vision, his kind are so willing to display, to shame the rest of us.

With its contemporary backdrop of the Israel–Palestine conflict and the absence of the isolated Jew (or the half-Jewish character who is essentially subsumed into that side of their origins), le Carré's *The Little Drummer Girl* (1983) operates with a very different atmosphere from the English and German locations of the previous texts.[19] The question of the individual Jewish motivation and drive to assume wider responsibility in a situation where perhaps there is a choice that could be made disappears to a large extent from *The Little Drummer Girl*. In this narrative, the individual Jew in the Diaspora, especially a Diaspora informed by European antisemitism and genocide, has been replaced by the security and intelligence apparatus of the state of Israel. Nevertheless, some of the threads in this novel are worthy of examination, and there is a case to be made that it fits something of the pattern that the earlier books established. As in several of le Carré's later novels, the precision of the historical moment in which the action of *The Little Drummer Girl* plays out is important, as the story posits a struggle for dominance between opposing sides within the Israeli security structure, one looking for a military solution via an application of force, the other wanting to use intelligence and covert operations assets in as targeted and restrained a manner as possible.

It is worth mentioning that, in contrast to le Carré's previous fictions, *The Little Drummer Girl* is built around a somewhat implausible proposition: namely, that a young, radical, flaky, and decidedly non-Jewish British woman, an aspiring but not very successful actress, would either be offered a mission designed by Israeli intelligence to strike at the international networks of the Palestine Liberation Organization (PLO), or if receiving such an offer, would accept it. What seems a maliciously inventive plot to protect an important agent in *The Spy Who Came In from the Cold* tends to look like something of an absurdist political fantasy when it comes to the counter-intuitive recruitment of Charlie for an Israeli operation to locate and kill a successful PLO bomb-master named Khalil, who is the key operative behind a terror campaign in Europe. And yet there is something compelling about the offer by Martin Kurtz, the senior Mossad officer, to use her skills, as any actor would naturally desire:

> The part we have in view for you combines all your talents, Charlie, human and professional. Your wit. Your excellent memory. Your intelligence. Your courage. But also that extra human quality to which I already referred. Your warmth. We chose you, Charlie. We cast you . . . Everybody in this room has seen your work, everybody admires you. (117)

Charlie's performance becomes, as the novel moves to its climax, better than any she has given before. She has been offered the chance to prove herself in what Kurtz calls the Theater of the Real.[20] She is suddenly pitched into situations, many of them dangerous and potentially fatal, of which she has no real experience to prepare her: the prime example would be her months in the PLO training camp, where she has to prove that her radical dedication to the Palestinian national cause was no mere pose invented to please her lover (in Charlie's cover story, she was the girlfriend of Khalil's deceased younger brother Salim). The psychic strain she is under is considerable, however, and at the end she witnesses Khalil's death as he is shot by Joseph, her Mossad case officer and, eventually, lover. This experience proves too much for her, and she collapses, exhausted both physically and emotionally by the pressure of the role she has been playing so effectively.

In *The Little Drummer Girl* the figure of the virtuous Jew who takes on, willingly or not, the suffering of the world does not appear, although Martin Kurtz embodies a certain kind of ethical thinking that tries to find a larger good for the evil that one has to do. Kurtz would see no particularly good choice available, and while the members of the Mossad team are certainly saying what Charlie wants to hear when they assert that they are working for a fair solution to the Middle East conflict as hard as anyone is, he is the only one present who does not see it merely as an expedient story to get Charlie on board. That she does come on board, and carries out a harrowing mission in which she has to pretend to be the person she was (radical cheerleader for Palestinian rights) in order to become the person she is (an undercover agent working for the Israelis), suggests not only professional talent but also psychological robustness in her that she and many others would have seriously doubted she possessed.

Perhaps there is, twenty years after *The Spy Who Came In from the Cold*, a touch of Liz Gold in Charlie, a clever and attractive young woman who is somewhat adrift, who has a soft heart for suffering, and who finds herself in a much more serious theater of events than she had ever dreamt of. Liz pays the bleak final price, of course, and Charlie does not, which may say something about le Carré's desire not to have *The Little Drummer Girl* repeat the tragedy of collateral damage in the earlier novel, or something about the unlikelihood of a narrative such as this simply disposing of a character in which so much has been invested on different levels. In a standard cliché about Israel, of course, the isolated and persecuted Jew of European history is transformed into the confident defender of the nation, but le Carré does not milk that obvious trope, or not overmuch. Israel is clearly undecided how best to deal with Palestinian violence abroad, and Kurtz's way is only one way, and an elaborate one at that, with few short-term results to show beyond Khalil's death. But it is true that Kurtz reverses or at least triangulates the configuration dominant in le Carré's earlier fiction and manages to convince a gentile to take on a portion of fear and suffering for the Jews herself.[21]

If the "Jewish Question," as originally proposed by Karl Marx in the early 1840s in his debate with Bruno Bauer, was an attempt to deal with the matter of how Jews were to relate to modernity, then obviously the answer over the next century, at least in central and Eastern Europe, was not a happy one.[22] The selection of excluded communities, of which the Jews were the first chosen, did not end with the selection process itself, of course, or even with a pogrom from time to time, but with the process's natural conclusion: genocide.[23] It may of course be a prize that nobody could actually want, but the attempt to solve, or more accurately eradicate, the "Jewish Question" transformed that question into one of the burning themes of the twentieth century, and perhaps the twenty-first also. Burning or not, however, the history of this process did not play out, even after World War II, identically in every country.

In the Britain of the postwar era, the notion that Nazi Germany had been an enemy worth defeating was vaguely connected with the savagery of the regime and its administrative projects of mass murder, but the specific targeting of European Jewry and the trauma of survivors were often either seen as abstract manifestations of German malice, or just downplayed. Obviously, the armed conflict in the British Mandate in Palestine in the late 1940s between the authorities and Jewish nationalist groups also introduced a complication into the picture, one that allowed Jews in the Middle East to be seen as regional troublemakers. There were also some Anglo-Jewish veterans of the war who went to Palestine and joined groups such as Haganah, and who therefore, potentially, could become involved in armed combat against British forces.[24] But the point to be made is that the mainstream culture of the 1950s was one in which World War II was a positive and meaningful history, despite the losses suffered, and the differing (but not necessarily opposing) perspective of British Jews could in that context be regarded as too particular, too emotional, and thus a kind of flaw in the texture of appropriate national attitudes. That culture, and the list of unsayable things pinned up on its mental wall, is the territory on which Elsa Fennan, Liz Gold, and Leo Harting had to live and work, and to try to belong to. When Charlie arrives on stage as a protagonist, much has changed. In the early 1970s the British left became more open to *troisième-mondisme*, a new political vision that saw the marginalized populations of the colonial and postcolonial Third World as the authentic bearers of the revolutionary message, and the mild interest in the collectivist *kibbutz* movement in Israel's early decades gave way to a theory of Israel as a belated colonialist project supported by the United States as part of its plan to lock down the Middle East for its own purposes.[25]

In the initial phase of his career as an author, le Carré was somewhat of an exception among British novelists, and particularly those in genre fiction, in the way he grasped the centrality of the European Jewish experience for the questions of political modernity, national citizenship, and the ideologies of exclusion. Deploying Jewish characters who either implicitly or expressly challenge the provincial and casually inward-looking concerns of British society, le Carré placed them in his fictions to suggest that the transnational intellectual vision of a free individual who is also a welcome member of a community may often confront the English tendency to politely identify and ring-fence the outsider and let them slowly realize their compromised status. Even in the ostensibly exotic location of Central America, the satirical project of *The Tailor of Panama* locates Harry Pendel at the heart of British entertainment history, and makes of its protagonist one third Fagin, one third Harold Pinter, and one third

Sid James: cunning ethnic alien; gifted and subtle dramatist; beloved comic actor.[26]

It is important to see le Carré's contribution, however, as not only identifying the postwar iteration of a Jewish cosmopolitanism that triggered the suspicions of an earlier era. His fiction probes further, revealing that the ideal of a new arrangement of humanity, one in which Jews no longer need to see themselves as a separate group under threat, is far from achieved. When Liz Gold and Fiedler stare at each other across the East Berlin courtroom, suddenly catching each other's gaze, what do they see? Within the frame of the narrative, of course, they are two communists who happen to be Jews, or two Jews who happen to be communists, or both. But I believe le Carré means something more than just that recognition of political identity. They are the easiest pieces on the chessboard to knock over, precisely because they are Jewish. Even Fiedler, the communist in a communist state, discovers that the finger of suspicion hovers more pleasurably over him than it does over Mundt, and the reason for that is something that he cannot but be aware of. The GDR was the creation of the Soviet Union, directed by German communists who had survived the war, but its population had transitioned from Nazism directly into the Soviet-style administrative state, with the occupying power having obedience rather than moral self-examination as its principal goal.

The fact that le Carré's fiction is, at the end, more about a certain theory of Englishness than it is about departures from that norm should not be held against him.[27] Without the theory, these novels would not have their richness and sense of purpose. His willingness, however, to open up the stories to, in particular, those characters who depart from the English norm because of their Jewish identity is something that gives his earlier fiction an extra dimension it otherwise would not possess, and keeps alive the questions it asks, many decades later.

Notes

1. Even a brief glance at Adam Sisman's official biography *John le Carré: The Biography* reveals the reviewers' interminable comparisons with Greene during the 1960s and 1970s.
2. As early as 1965, le Carré expressed his respect for Graham Greene in a BBC Television interview with the influential journalist Malcolm Muggeridge in a program called *Intimations*, saying, "What I love in Greene, in every book he writes, in this sense of a moral search, still

within the content of story. They are solitaries in search of some kind of fulfillment. There are paradoxes of course, which we know. They in some way approach God through sin. It is the moral search of a lonely man that in Greene, as in Conrad, attracts me irresistibly." The interview can be found online on the website *CrimeReads*: crimereads.com/john-le-carre-and-the-most-interesting-author-interview-you-will-ever-see/ (accessed May 13, 2023).
3. See, for example, Robert Whitney's "The Architect of the Cuban State" for a discussion of the roots of the volatile mix of the authoritarian and the populist impetus in the era of Batista's leadership. In some important ways, including the setting of a Central American nation marked by a similar political dynamic, Greene's torch is clearly picked up and carried forward by le Carré.
4. Apart from Greene's novel, a passionate interest in the Caribbean is most discernible in Ian Fleming's fiction. There are two memorable and somewhat unusual James Bond short stories, "Quantum of Solace" and "The Hildebrand Rarity"; beyond that, of course, the novels with extensive Caribbean settings include *Live and Let Die* (1954), *Dr. No* (1958), and *Thunderball* (1961). Film adaptations of Fleming have returned again and again to the region.
5. There is something worth noting about the attraction of the Caribbean for all three British authors, Greene, Fleming, and then le Carré. The legacy of the slave trade and the sugar plantation converges with imperial nostalgia to create a semi-tropical arena now dominated by the United States, but one with a very different landscape (or seascape) of social and ethnic demographics from America's.
6. The notable resilience of Savile Row men's tailoring as both commercial enterprise and myth is given its implicit due in le Carré's novel. For a brief but informative note in the history, see the account by Christopher Breward at https://fashion-history.lovetoknow.com/fashion-history-eras/savile-row.
7. The corrupting interplay of governmental and corporate roles became a significant theme for le Carré from the late 1990s.
8. Lassner, *Espionage and Exile*, 208–9.
9. Lassner, *Espionage and Exile*, 190. The echoes of "spectral" not only emphasize Elsa Fennan's somewhat ghostly aura of resignation, but also conjure up the famous English translation of the opening sentence of *The Communist Manifesto* (1848): "A spectre is haunting Europe—the spectre of communism." This is often quoted as if it is approving the specter, but in fact Marx and Engels move quickly to assert that the scary figure making the continent nervous has little to do with the actual communist movement and more to do with the fears of established economic and political authorities.
10. West Germany underwent its own fraught confrontation with the Nazi past in a more public manner during the 1960s, when the first federal

prosecutions for war crimes and crimes against humanity took place. The East German authorities were always eager to point to former Nazi Party officials who had government positions or held political office in the Federal Republic of Germany, but over time it became obvious that the GDR also had a few similar skeletons in its closet, as many Nazi functionaries and military officers had been given safe harbor there provided they convincingly declared their loyalty to the Communist Party.

11. Conor McCarthy notes "vague suggestions of Irishness . . . of not-quite-belonging" in the portrayal of Alec Leamas (*Outlaws and Spies*, 111), although he does not explore further the extent to which this aspect of identity might add an extra dimension to his relationship with Liz Gold (nor does *The Spy*, to be fair); I do not want to suggest simplistic parallels between Irish and Jewish immigrant experience in Britain, but the connection seems to hang in the air. It is a little curious, too, that le Carré never set any of his novels in Ireland or Northern Ireland, but what his reservations were about this, we will probably never know.

12. Leamas explains the ruling consideration of expediency for intelligence agencies, in that famous exchange in the car in East Berlin; still, it remains an odd after-effect of *The Spy Who Came In from the Cold* that the violent deaths of both Jewish characters, Fiedler (not yet, but inevitably) and Gold, wrap up, in a sense, the operation both for London and for Mundt.

13. This very issue emerges in le Carré's *A Legacy of Spies* (2017), which returns to the events and characters of the 1963 novel.

14. See Hari Kunzru's introduction to the 2011 Penguin Modern Classics edition of *A Small Town in Germany* for a brief but informative discussion of the topic.

15. In West Germany there was always a small but distinctly more nationalist grouping within the primarily New Left and ecological camp represented by the Green Party, which became a serious political presence in the 1980s. Although this was not a significant feature of the student movement in the late 1960s, the notion of an independent path for Germany was attractive to some.

16. Toby Manning suggests that le Carré's project in this novel is to "associate the student movement with Nazi war criminals is quite a reversal of the political reality" (*John le Carré and the Cold War*, 104, n. 3). This is something of a misrepresentation of *A Small Town in Germany*, as Karfeld hides his past from his young followers, who regard the Movement as opening a path for an independent Germany free from American or Soviet direction—and, after all, there is some considerable distance from that idea to an actual rebirth of Nazism. To clarify that point, Sisman's biography shows that at that time le Carré, assigned to the British embassy, was very aware of the presence of former Nazi

officials in German political life, not in extra-parliamentary activism but rather in the Bonn corridors of power.
17. As Phyllis Lassner notes succinctly in her essay, le Carré "never releases [his] Jewish characters from the pain of the Holocaust" ("John le Carré's Jews," n.p.).
18. Lassner, *Espionage and Exile*, 186.
19. To include this novel changes the landscape of the argument about Jews in the European diaspora, admittedly, but part of the reason for doing so is that it is an early example of the problem I discuss in the final chapter, where authors wrestle with the nature of a conflict that includes both ethnic and religious dimensions.
20. The phrase is also used by le Carré in *The Pigeon Tunnel*, his collection of memoir pieces. In the essay entitled "Theatre of the Real: The Villa Brigitte," he describes his brief interview with a young German woman, identified only by her first name Brigitte, captured during a failed terrorist attack on an El Al passenger plane in Nairobi and held secretly in Israel. He finds himself in agreement with some of her beliefs, including that Palestinians are being made to compensate for Western crimes against Jews, but she has no interest in an exchange of views. Curiously, in his biography Adam Sisman uses the essay extensively (426–27) when describing le Carré's research for *Little Drummer Girl*, but adds Brigitte's surname Schulz, without explaining that she was held in Israel with another German, tried in a military court, and then released to West Germany in 1980—news which was widely reported and discussed in the German press at the time.
21. Le Carré's interest in Conrad raises the intriguing possibility of some connection to Kurtz in *Heart of Darkness*, even if he is in many ways the polar opposite of the character in *The Little Drummer Girl*.
22. Bruno Bauer (1809–82), philosopher and contemporary of Karl Marx, played a significant role in the "historical Jesus" controversies of the nineteenth century.
23. I realize that "natural" is a controversial choice of term, and that many influential authors such as Hannah Arendt deny that there was some kind of organic historical process that ended in the Holocaust. By using it here, I mean simply to suggest that there was a kind of menacing progression in which some of the European nationalisms of the nineteenth and early twentieth centuries found it both convenient and satisfying to identify Jews as the non-national Other. This in turn made even a mere passive acquiescence in the Final Solution seem acceptable.
24. For a British Jewish perspective on this, see Morris Beckman's *The 43 Group*, his memoir of the antifascist network organized by Jewish ex-servicemen in the late 1940s, as the Mosleyite movement attempted to restore its prewar strength (Beckman's is the only book-length history I'm aware of, but the topic is mentioned in memoirs and

briefer accounts, for example in celebrity hairdresser Vidal Sassoon's autobiography).
25. For a rich analysis of changes in the relationship during the 1970s between Arab societies, Europe, and the United States, and especially America's move to the center of that matrix, see Salim Yaqub's study *Imperfect Strangers* (2016).
26. Fagin, the stereotypically Jewish wheeler-and-dealer in Dickens's *Oliver Twist*; Harold Pinter (1930–2008), the influential and unapologetically outspoken playwright; Sid James (1913–76), the immensely popular actor and comedian, one of the stars of the *Carry On* series.
27. An "Englishness" not unlike that which gives Maugham's Ashenden his sense of purpose.

Chapter 5

The American Uncertainty: Genre and Borders in Charles McCarry and Don DeLillo

> "You Americans are almost incredibly romantic."
> "Of course we are. That's just what makes everything so nice for us."
>
> Henry James, *The Golden Bowl*

There is probably an entertaining dispute to be had over whether or not Charles McCarry's novel *The Miernik Dossier*, published in 1973, can lay claim to be the first if not the only modernist experiment in the genre of espionage fiction. On first consideration, it is difficult to think of any novel that might otherwise come into question. In the Anglophone cultural world in particular, modernist literature was broadly hostile to genre, seeing it as essentially a commercial publishing category aimed at satisfying mainstream audience expectations. This was precisely the kind of enjoyment that modernist authors desired to withhold from the average reader, a goal that the integration of difficulty as a significant aesthetic component of the reception experience was meant to achieve. Meaning and pleasure would come only after effort, in the modernist declaration of principles (implicit or explicit), and thus genre narratives were at least suspect and most likely indictable in that they offered satisfaction without struggle.[1]

And yet, even if that status were to be conceded to McCarry's first novel, there seems to be something immediately not quite right with this move. The date of publication, for instance: 1973. Even making the case for a generation's delay as the benefits of literary modernism finally made their way, in some cultural equivalent of the conservative "trickle-down" theory of economic prosperity, out to the suburban tracts of genre, it would still seem as if the whole premise is really unconvincingly late. To state the case, *The Miernik Dossier* is too unusual to be the end of anything.[2]

But is it perhaps pastiche, a literary sub-category not particularly common in Anglophone literary culture? Something that describes a semi-parodic reiteration of a more substantial form or model for a readership that either enjoys the parody or, more likely, enjoys the text without realizing that it is, in fact, parody (thus increasing the snooty pleasure of the joke)? Pastiche and the postmodern would also seem to be related in that the postmodern literary artifact is unconcerned with the struggles over artistic validity and the creative heroism that defined modernism.[3] Given that proposition, there could well be nothing more emblematic of that unconcern than an author cheerfully raiding the technique archive of modernism to produce his or her genre exercise.

The justification for raising this question is not a matter of painstaking categorization, but rather an attempt to explain why the question comes up at all in relation to *The Miernik Dossier*. The novel, set roughly in 1958 or 1959, recounts the mission assigned to Paul Christopher, a young Central Intelligence Agency (CIA) officer stationed in Geneva, involving an expatriate Polish scientist working with the World Research Organization, a fictional United Nations body located in that city. The scientist, Tadeusz Miernik, becomes a person of interest to several parties who wish to observe his activities. The story posits a joint road trip to Sub-Saharan Africa from which several individuals, representing various governments and other entities, file their reports. The novel is composed of their unmediated reports and, often, comments on those by higher authorities. The premise given at the very outset, in which an undefined "Committee" is presented with the material as a type of exemplary mission file, is that the readers of the dossier will be, or should be, able to work out connections and significances for themselves. Outside this compilation and minimal framing by the implied author of *The Miernik Dossier*, there is no single omniscient narrative presence.

One of the attractions of such a narrative mode is that it replicates the bureaucratic document flow of organizations that are key players within the fictions of spying: reports to intelligence and other government agencies; notes and commentaries analyzing such reports; memoranda revealing higher levels of knowledge or proposing courses of action that other players may follow without being aware of their significance.[4] There is a literary tradition, taking its cue from the traditional epistolary narrative and both predating and active within modernism broadly conceived, that involves using forms of narration that put a perceptual and cultural weight upon partial awareness of the action of the story. The presence of typewritten accounts of events in Bram Stoker's *Dracula* (1897), for example, representing a modern bureaucratic style set against Eastern European vampire folklore, would be one item of evidence; another might be the growth—in many national literatures—of police-procedural narratives that capture on the page the minutiae of investigation and inquiry, the reports, memoranda, and interview transcripts.[5] McCarry could have had the less ambitious intention, of course, of simply using a bureaucratic textual form to give a sense of institutional procedures that supply, in turn, a kind of distancing effect in the narrative: rather than introducing modernist or postmodern elements into *The Miernik Dossier*, he is simply enhancing the genre text with structural effects that are now no longer associated with difficulty in fictional works but rather with attractive rhetorical maneuvers that are interesting and a little quirky, but not intended to exclude by way of difficulty.

To that extent, it is both a technique and a central value of Charles McCarry's first novel that it foregrounds the question of narrative coherence if not quite the issue of form. In its movement through space and political geography, the novel proceeds from Switzerland through southern Europe and across the Mediterranean to Egypt and Sudan, but in its internal shifting of forces in terms of plot and character, the story becomes more complex.[6] Motives for joining the collective journey with the expensive American car are described and also interrogated, as the one or the other member of the group seeks to provide an analysis of the situation, a reading of their fellow travelers, and some speculation as to future developments.

In this matrix—the composition of narrative positionality—Paul Christopher's reports to the CIA station in Geneva are given a certain bonus of credibility (they are also somewhat more entertaining in the storytelling sense). By way of our assumptions about character and nationality, and in response to the tone of certain passages, we are nudged to see Christopher as our most likely informant and perhaps even something of a pragmatic or even ethical reference point. As we are left at the conclusion of the story with an enigma, however, he is no longer available in the matrix of accounts and assessments to give the reader a final word. The implication at the novel's conclusion is that there are certain things that Christopher (and by implication the reader) should not be privy to, that he has given the best that he can on this mission but has no final truth to offer.

One effect of the structure of the novel is to put the reader in the same position as other recipients of the communications flowing back from the trip and later from the Sudanese town in which the Amir of Khatar, father of one of the traveling group, is the ruler. The reader is, of course, in a somewhat better position to perceive the meaning of events, as they are in the same position as the "Committee," and thus have the full range of such communications available, not just one or two reports such as individual parties would actually receive. Even with that advantage, however, the story still remains an account of events that implies rather than explains. The format of *The Miernik Dossier* is one that invites the audience to connect the dots, or such dots as the text provides, into a more revealing graphic. Even after connection, however, there remains something inexplicable, something that seems to evade rational analysis, in the resolution of the broader narrative and, more specifically, the death of Tadeusz Miernik.

To deploy a form that both provides and withholds information from the reader, and mimics thereby the rhetoric and procedures of large institutions, is a literary project that risks losing some credibility as genre fiction while gaining no real compensatory value. As noted earlier, there is a touch of pastiche about this text, but in a certain way that pastiche itself acts as the justification for a narrative that is both framed by genre conventions and simultaneously pushing for a way to transcend them. McCarry is doing something unusual with the espionage novel here, and in doing that unusual thing he has permitted the text to act as if it is going through the motions of a genre exercise while seeking to break out from its formal constraints.[7] These constraints are not those of assigning virtue and malice (even of an ambiguous nature or along a spectrum of nuances) within the dynamic of the story, but rather those of the degree of explanatory resolution that the text is normally expected to deliver.

The Miernik Dossier seems to take a certain pleasure in failing to provide any particularly high degree of explanatory relief for the reader as it concludes. Even the penultimate document, a personal message from Jack, the CIA station chief, to Paul Christopher in which he lets his junior officer know a little more about the background and reassures him that he made the right decisions in the field, is something the reader at this stage might be a little skeptical of. It is not out of the question that Jack might feel the need to put his junior officer at ease to calm him down after a demanding assignment in which it was very difficult to establish who was doing what, and why. A bit of extra truth is not the whole truth, after all, and the novel as a totality gives every sign of being committed to an aesthetic of partial truth.

The argument here is that there is a way of looking at the American conspiracy text, or the fiction of conspiracy theory, not as a proposition of hidden forces beyond any individual, legal, or political control that determine one's fate (or the fate of the nation, or of the world), but as a fiction of partial truth. Thus the secret conspiracy text is not standing in direct opposition to the text of rational and democratic revelation, but rather obliquely and perhaps within hailing distance.[8] To put it another way, the knowledge that we are left in possession of at the end of *The Miernik Dossier* is not useless, merely proving once again how we are the powerless in the face of the administrative elite who determine what is said, what is implied, and what cannot be uttered. But we might not be able to exchange that knowledge for redemptive relief such as the American imagination is inclined to seek: rather, we might have to hang on to that knowledge, protect it, and wait for the opportunity to deploy it in the interest of the humanist cause. To that extent, we become then to some degree complicit in the management of conspiracy, or at least in accepting its presence (a little later I turn to McCarry's second novel, *The Tears of Autumn*, to show him addressing this issue with a very different type of narrative gambit). As the unlikely group of travelers moves from Europe across the Mediterranean into North Africa, the forces and institutions watching them, and attempting to glean what is happening, are in some ways all conspiracies, but it seems important to establish that they are not one conspiracy. *The Miernik Dossier* is not the tale of a seamless totality but rather the shuffled notes of one entity that includes indications as to what other entities—some allied, some neutral, some hostile—are engaged in at the same time.[9]

Thus even the motley crew bringing the Cadillac from Switzerland to Sudan, despite the existence of externally governed assignments for some of the participants, seems itself to be a kind of signal against totalizing explanations. These individuals are, without doubt, unmistakably themselves: the intensity of Miernik, the Polish intellectual; the cheerful arrogance of the Sudanese prince Kalash el-Khatar; the English calm of Nigel Collins; the vital energies of the two very different young women, Zofia Miernik and Ilona Bentley; and the analytic eye of Paul Christopher. Even the existence of covert as well as ostensible identities for several characters, Christopher and Collins as US and British intelligence operatives most obviously, does not necessarily shrink the narrative scope to a revelation of the real beneath the disguise or to a final clarification that two identities have been collapsed into one, so to speak. Rather, it seems to infuse the tension between the secret and the overt with a kind of personality of its own, as if the character of Nigel Collins were not only the United Nations civil servant by day or the British spy after dark, but both of those and the curious composite that such a double life brings forth: Collins as friend, lover, colleague, covert operative, all jostling for position as circumstances demand.[10]

The potential deus ex machina of *The Miernik Dossier* is the ALF, the Anointed Liberation Front, a Soviet-directed but locally recruited army of militants with an Islamist-inflected revolutionary message. Planning a series of terror attacks against both the Sudanese government and other regional rulers such as the Amir of Khatar, the ALF appears to be seeking some kind of spiritual leadership that will cast its political message within a more religious frame for the Sudanese Muslim peasantry.[11] As the group drive the Cadillac toward western Sudan, the reader becomes privy to intelligence reports in the file, primarily from American assets, that reveal internal matters within the ALF leadership (from the US agent codenamed Firecracker but also from decryptions of Soviet communications traffic) and discuss possible measures to be taken to neutralize the front.

Somewhat prescient in the setting of Sudan, which became a country in the news from the late 1990s onward, and more than somewhat imaginative in the creation of the ALF with its amalgam of Islamic millennialism and social revolution, the political situation sketched out in *The Miernik Dossier* is one in which the Cold War and the superpower conflict determine the outside frame of the action, but local actors are unpredictable. Between the measured plans of the intelligence agencies and the thousand contingencies on the ground are layers of human interaction, only some of which can really be predicted. Questions surface one after the other in the course of the novel, some being clarified by the availability of later information, others not. If Miernik's sister is a genuine student of art history in Warsaw, and extracting her from behind the Iron Curtain a risk worth taking, why is her name not to be found on the registration books for Warsaw University or any other Polish college, for example? Yet, when we meet Zofia, her personality and general style, as well as the affection between her and her brother, are undeniably convincing. But if Zofia's escape from Czechoslovakia was essentially approved by the KGB as well as Polish and Czech sister services as part of a larger operation, why was Zofia permitted to raise doubts about the legitimacy of her story by dropping out of college? If Miernik himself is the key to some long-term Polish or Soviet intelligence project, why was his personality so awkward and so seemingly designed to irritate people or put them off? Was making life difficult for himself part of his individual tradecraft, as Paul Christopher speculates, in Geneva and later, or almost conclusive evidence that his story is genuine? Was the decision by the deputy leader of the ALF, Qemal, otherwise the American asset Firecracker, to execute his superior Ahmed as soon as the indication came from the Soviets that he (Ahmed) might be a CIA mole made because he genuinely misunderstood the instruction or because he thought it might be his one chance to take over the organization?

As *The Miernik Dossier* enters the final phase of the narrative, several events take on the character of contingent accidents, or missed communications, rather than the unfolding of a well-conceived plot. The Sudanese government's intention to attack and obliterate the ALF militarily coincides with the arrival, announced by coded transmission to Qemal, of the Soviet operative known as Richard, who will carry instructions for the ALF. Tadeusz Miernik makes an apparently spontaneous trip with Kalash to see some ruins in the desert (Kalash plans to negotiate with Qemal, as they are related by family) and disappears. The gradual piling-up of various reports ultimately reveals the possible sequence of events that has led to Miernik being found crucified upside-down on an X-shaped wooden cross on a hilltop, a mode of execution favored by the ALF for its most hated enemies. His body is found by Paul Christopher, who has left the Amir's palace with Zofia Miernik in a Land Rover in an attempt to find her brother, dead or alive. Within the same period of a couple of days, Sudanese paratroopers mount an assault on the ALF camp headquarters, killing most of the group, including Kalash's cousin Qemal.

A report submitted by the Sudanese intelligence officer Aly Qasim (also a blood relative of Kalash's) reveals that the interrogation of an ALF survivor after the attack brought out some odd details about Miernik's death. In particular, Miernik seems to have been baffled that the group thought that he was the Soviet contact Richard. Seeking revenge for what they regard as the illicit Soviet order to kill Ahmad (they do not, of course, realize that Qemal is working for the CIA), they intend to show the Russians that they have no intention of being manipulated by them. Believing that Miernik is Richard, the Soviet representative, as he gives a rough version of the predetermined recognition phrase when they first confront him in the ruins, the ALF men kill him by crucifixion.

The grim irony is, of course, that Miernik seems to have been seeking some kind of retribution for himself, with his provocative victimhood, previously just a source of irritation for his friends, finally given bloody reality as he is mutilated and bleeds to death tied to a cross on a Sudanese desert hillside.[12] Was he Richard or not? Was he the key figure in a long-planned operation, a Polish intelligence operative who maintained for years the cover of an anti-communist and self-despising, but oddly persuasive, intellectual?

Paul Christopher's letter of disagreement to his case officer, challenging the assumptions now built into the evaluation of the Miernik operation, and his case officer's sympathetic but ultimately clear rejection of his arguments conclude the dossier and the novel, with the exception of a final extract from the debriefing interview with Zofia Miernik in which she describes the speedy termination of her romantic relationship with Christopher. Christopher makes the reasonable point that Tadeusz Miernik engaged in a number of actions and behaviors that make absolutely no sense if he was a Soviet agent carrying out an important mission involving the creation and nurturing of an armed Sudanese guerilla organization dedicated to bringing down the government in the name of Islam. He argues that the analytic procedures of intelligence organizations, although the people who work in them are convinced that their default posture is skepticism and that they look at only real evidence, are designed to ultimately justify speculation being relabeled as information: "To transform a supposition into a fact is the sweetest reward a desk man can know" (247). There is an unavoidable tendency to frame the analytic moment as a rational search for truth, so all the details that do not fit are often left out of the picture. As he says, in the case of Miernik, parallel to all the indicators, some quite strong, that he was a Soviet agent are the indicators that he was not. Christopher calls them "a second body of evidence, like a planet identical to Earth on the other side of the sun" (248). Unable to see this planet, and thus assuming it cannot be there, those who built the case against Miernik did so only on the observable astronomical readings, with any anomalies being ignored.

His case officer asks, among other comments, one question in return that has to be asked: if Miernik was not Richard, the KGB's and the Polish service's representative to the ALF, whose arrival was communicated to the ALF just before Miernik appeared in the ruins, then who was Richard? No other possibility seems to suggest itself. If Paul in his letter portrays a mode of analysis that is less objective than it appears because it looks closely only at the evidence that turns supposition into fact, then his case officer replies with a reading of Miernik's dossier and particularly of Miernik's journal (which he invites Paul to read in full to get a better grasp of how his mind operated) that says, more or less, that in the absence of other reasonable explanations, then the available one, even if unreasonable in parts, has to be true.[13] Thus *The Miernik Dossier* is not so much a narrative of certainties being rendered uncertain as a story of competing certainties. The dossier renders an implicit demand that one must adopt a particular certainty, if only to ensure a measure of stability in our minds and in the world.

If *The Miernik Dossier* is at least temporarily intriguing because of its use of a bureaucratic form of textual organization to invoke the sense of an objective review of the material of the narrative, then Charles McCarry's subsequent novel *The Tears of Autumn* (1974) substitutes an imaginative counterfactual premise within a traditional narrative format for the first novel's play with organizational files and data collection. Set in the immediate aftermath of the assassination of President John F. Kennedy in November 1963, the story once again has Paul Christopher as its protagonist, but in *The Tears of Autumn* he is more distinctly the central focus than he is in McCarry's first novel. *The Miernik Dossier* can be fairly accurately described as multi-focalized: that is, that while there is no first-person narrative voice, there is also no single protagonist who completely dominates the entire narrative fabric of the book. Christopher's reports and commentaries are given a certain extra dimension of importance, and readerly confidence is invited, but attention is also drawn independently to Tadeusz Miernik's journal entries, for example, and Nigel Collins's reports to London.

In *The Tears of Autumn* Paul Christopher bears the entire burden of the narrative and this is a demanding, perhaps even exhausting experience for him. The weight of the experience he undergoes in the course of the story seems to embody exactly the kind of master narrative that *The Miernik Dossier* avoids delivering. As his investigations bring him closer to the complex and dangerous underworld of powerful Vietnamese family networks, he seems often alone and without the organizational support and supervision that he might expect to be in place for such a mission. Furthermore, the assassination of a president was, in the immediate aftermath of the event at least, a traumatic experience for many Americans, and Christopher's mission is therefore overshadowed by the possibility of popular protest and a devastating loss of trust in the political system, a possibility far removed from the concerns of *The Miernik Dossier*. The momentary relief granted simply by the breaks between the different sections and components of the Miernik file—the comfort of its composite nature, one could say—is completely absent in this novel, which proceeds in unbroken narrative flow from start to finish.

Christopher's journey to the center of the mystery involves an original and even eccentric premise that would explain the Kennedy assassination in a very different way from those which have been advanced over the decades by almost any party, whether the Warren Commission's lone gunman theory or the advocates of various complex and multi-layered conspiratorial explanations. It has rarely been the case (I know of no other example, in fact) that even fictional stories have shown an interest in the possibility that the trigger for JFK's death was not to be found in Washington or Havana or Texas, but in the Republic of Vietnam, whose leader Ngo Dinh Diem was arrested in a coup, almost certainly with CIA involvement, on November 1, 1963. Diem and his brother were killed, probably by South Vietnamese military personnel, the following day. The officers' coup had its origins in a perception that Diem (who is generally referred to by his given name, as Vietnamese names are in reverse order from English ones) had departed from the official line that South Vietnam was a front-line state in the struggle with communism and wanted to explore the possibility that an independent or non-aligned path for the country was a viable option. It remains a murky point of historical record whether or not President Kennedy knew anything of the nuts and bolts of the plan to take down Diem, but it is probable that he did not. He had known of the coup in advance and thought that it should go ahead, however, presumably without being able to foresee what it would entail.[14]

Paul Christopher enters the story, then, in a moment subsequent to the assassination of two political leaders, the presidents of the Republic of Vietnam and the United States, respectively. His travels following the trail of conspiracy bring him to the conclusion that the commonly held assumptions about Dallas on November 22, 1963 are substantially wide of the mark. The conspiracy has different roots and certainly a more ominous aura of vengeance than even the stories about Fidel Castro wanting to exact revenge for the American plots against his life. It involves a direct act of retribution that would be difficult to explain in public except with reference to Diem's murder, and the news that JFK had taken a bullet in the head in Dallas in an act of regional score-settling or a clan honor killing could not be revealed to the American people without serious consequences.

This is what distinguishes *The Miernik Dossier* from *The Tears of Autumn*: whereas in the former, the materials in the archive are presented with the assumption that the narrative of events and its significance can be determined, even if questions remain open, by professional analysts (and with the related assumption that the actual reader is in something like the same position outside the fictional construct), in the latter the details are fully known to Paul Christopher alone. In this novel he is not one player among others, a significant one but possibly not entirely informed as to all issues, but in some senses the only player, the one who knows, and is haunted by that fact. It is an interesting side note that Christopher's poetry is mentioned several times in *The Tears of Autumn*, but only once in the earlier novel, as if poetry might be an escape from the prose of narrative accounts. The idea that Paul might require an emotional release that is in some way safer than sex or drugs or gambling, and that this release is literary, suggests that the actual form of this novel might be unsatisfactory but somehow pre-determined. One could easily imagine a counterfactual sequence that had *The Miernik Dossier* as a straight narrative about the operation and the enigma of the title character, and *The Tears of Autumn* more appropriately dismantled into its constituent parts, but we might suspect that it would be a curious swapping of narrative form and central premise: the facts of JFK's death might seem even stranger than those of Tadeusz Miernik's when put on paper as an exercise in dispassionate analysis and delivered to the archive.[15]

One could posit, then, that *The Tears of Autumn* is driven by circumstances to being the more conventional genre expression when the implications of its narrative are more threatening to a stable framework of constitutional politics. In contrast, *The Miernik Dossier* embodies an open aesthetic of choice, in which the reader is invited to follow the disassembled form of the text in order to exercise a right to self-organize, rather like the postmodernist experimental novels which invite the reader to essentially read in any sequence that pleases him or her, or in several.[16] Although *The Miernik Dossier* material is organized in a chronological sequence of events over roughly two and a half months, from early May to mid-July, some of the individual texts and entries go back and forth over a few days: the precise ordering is not so important, as the dates are given so that the reader can see, for instance, that a later account of an incident may not have more information than an earlier account simply by virtue of its date, because its author may lack information available to an earlier contribution to the master file.

In *The Tears of Autumn*, however, as Paul Christopher roves from Southeast Asia to Europe to Africa, gradually putting together the pieces of the conspiracy that led to the moment in Dallas when sighting and distance and the movement of the target were all optimal, the ominous implications of what he has discovered become more interwoven into a narrative that offers up Christopher as a kind of mythical hero for the era, as if James Bond had just reappeared with an interest in writing poetry and a sensitive way with his girlfriends. The problem that this novel opens up is that the structure of the heroic tale is at variance with the premise of the narrative. Christopher is simply too perfect a character to be the deliverer of bad news in the shape of an explanation for the death of the US president that is too disturbing to ever be brought to the public domain. The novel's investment in his foreign language, unarmed combat, and general covert operations skills is considerable, but what can the ideal spy (or the trained-to-the-nth-degree intelligence officer) do with information that even his own service does not really want to hear? Why would you, even with a strong sense of patriotic duty, risk your life to obtain intelligence that is really too embarrassing to report? As the senior White House official Trumbull says to Christopher at the end of the novel, "You've got to be careful who you let change history . . .[y]ou're sure that this is the only copy of this thing?" (268).

When one turns from Paul Christopher to the main characters populating Don DeLillo's 1982 novel *The Names*, one is to a certain extent liberated from wondering whether the genre identifiers borne by McCarry's fiction are aesthetic constraints, or perhaps some form of status indicator that might render the discussion of modernist or postmodernist classifications moot. DeLillo's career has taken in some interesting experiments with fictions on the cusp of genre, but largely his reputation as a "serious" novelist has permitted him to play on the borderlands of popular forms without being stranded in their neighborhood after dark. In *The Names* we are confronted with what might be described as a thriller with difficulty. The textual difficulties are a function of DeLillo's prose aesthetic in which a failure to communicate accurately plays the most significant role, and, even more strikingly, the novel ends with a precociously talented revisiting of one of its key characters, Owen Brademas, by James Axton's unusually gifted nine-year-old son Tap, who writes a story that is not exactly part of the narrative *per se*, but is formally a component (indeed the final component) of the novel itself. It is nonetheless surprising how committed DeLillo is to a more conventional narrative style in the longer run of his work, and some of the claims of difficulty and experimental writing in his earlier career seem a little overdone and more concerned with rescuing DeLillo from any suspicion of being an author too willing to devise a mode of narration that marries obliqueness with accessibility.

James Axton, the character-narrator of *The Names*, is an American consultant traveling in Greece and the eastern Mediterranean, working on risk analysis for various clients, mostly US-based corporations concerned with the safety of both the investments they are thinking of making and the staff they are sending into the region. What risk analysis actually involves is not entirely clear, but it obviously has to do with an evaluation of potential threats to American business travelers and, in the bigger picture, corporate operations in general: politics, attitudes, climate, communication, terrorism, ominous local particularities—all are grist to Axton's analytic mill. The narrator's own problems in life, especially in his marriage and his relationship with his son Tap, operate as an ironic parallel narrative that serves to undermine and render unconvincing his capacity for delivering reliable assessments. James Axton is at sea, too, in the particular region of the world in which he does his work. The political volatility, the multiple languages, the nuanced attitudes toward Americans from amiable to hostile, and similar features of the eastern Mediterranean seem often to be a little beyond his ken, as it were. Axton is invaded by psychic uncertainty, while marketing a product ranked by its reliability and expertise. The implication is that he is good at negotiating certain formal measures, filing reports that are supported by viable data, but his basic orientation in the world blinds him to a great deal that falls outside those parameters. As if truth will ensure both credibility and safety, he announces, "I am James. The risk analyst" (59).

There is a focus on languages and the nature of language itself in *The Names*: the desire to fix elements of reality in place and communicate the result requires the stability of language held in common, but not all languages are shared—especially by Anglophone Americans who are often disinclined to learn anything other than English—and the need to find that stability can be something like a signal of weakness.[17] Owen Brademas, a free-ranging archaeologist who has given Axton's wife Kathryn a section of his dig to work on and who also acts as a kind of philosophical sounding-board for James's doubts, paradoxes, and intuitions, is more obsessed with the stability of reality, but the novel raises parallel questions about the degree to which one can determine truth in language as against, for example, determining which country or government can be seen as safe or trustworthy if there is always information that eludes the analyst. An ostensible expert like Axton is paid to clarify risk and identify the places where it is lowest, but the fact remains that to make such an analysis is itself risky, as there will always be things you have not taken into account.[18]

One site of ignorance is James's awkward and frustrating relationship with his estranged wife and, to some extent, with his son.

His professional capabilities which reassure clients that he knows what he is talking about and that his product is reliable are not readily available for dealing with the family dynamics. In the domestic sphere, it is less a case of risks to be analyzed than one of a set of emotional situations which show that even intimate (or previously intimate) marriage partners can be operating on non-connecting planes that exist above or below each other so that communication is always heard with enough static and distortion to get it wrong, or to enable one party to act as if they got it wrong. Kathryn and Tap hear different things from Axton, and process them in ways that he often has little clue about.

This conceit of close but often non-communicating planes of existence is reflected in the larger context of Axton's work in the eastern Mediterranean. One country that looms large in this narrative is Greece, and Greece's relationship to the political West is implicitly in question in *The Names*. The country's membership of NATO and the legacy of the long history of Hellenic civilization, rendered of course within the languages and cultural inheritance of the wider Europe and Atlantic, are revealed to be somewhat shaky foundations for an assumption of common interests. Greece is also a society with a strong, even paranoid distrust of the United States among a large sector of the population after the American tolerance of a military dictatorship in Athens from the mid-1960s to the mid-1970s.[19] One might even posit that Greece is something like a genre itself, or at least a cultural trope. Axton is merely the latest in a long line of modern English and American visitors, from Patrick Leigh-Fermor and Lawrence Durrell to Barry Unsworth and Paul Theroux, who have tried, sometimes with modest success, to read the inner life of the country and its people.[20]

With the assistance of movies such as Jules Dassin's *Never on Sunday* (1960), J. Lee Thompson's *The Guns of Navarone* (1961), and Costa-Gavras's *Z* (1969) contributing to a particular vision of Greece throughout the 1960s, however, a certain type of freedom beckoned.[21] Not surprisingly, an attractive combination of sunshine, good food, cheap wine, and evocative ruins, as well as inspiring tales of Greek resistance during World War II, could make a very compelling alternative to a rainy Saturday afternoon in London or winter in Montreal. Carrying on an older tradition, innumerable students and educated tourists with an interest in archaeology and history made their way toward Greece, especially to Crete and the other islands.[22] To that extent, James Axton's career, which moves him back and forth across the region, takes place against a backdrop that is both exotic and yet familiar. The role and purpose of the genre of Greece are to embody that very combination, for example, in a language which has left an indispensable linguistic and conceptual legacy for all European languages but remains, with its initially frustrating Cyrillic script, disconcertingly Other.

Indeed, if the solution to the mysterious killings in *The Names* is one that seems to fly in the face of a humane, or at least civilized, commitment to rational justification for actions that involve the taking of life, then in one way that does, in fact, represent both the classical culture of Ancient Greece and the sense of the fragility of norms in the face of unexpected cosmic forces. Confronted by an explanation that Axton's risk-analysis procedures could not take into account ("Let's face it, the most interesting thing we do is kill," says one of the cult members [293]), he seems psychologically at a kind of terminus, and the assassins' network comes to embody something like a black box into which the stable parameters of normal life disappear.

The unpredictable and even terror-inducing convergence of religion and intellectual procedure at the end of DeLillo's novel brings us back across the boundaries of publishing categories to the end of McCarry's *The Miernik Dossier*, in which a finally inexplicable (or unclarifiable, at least) event—the Polish intellectual Tadeusz Miernik's crucifixion on the desert hilltop—casts a retrospective shadow of doubt on the objective nature of intelligence analysis at the height of the Cold War. One could make some fine distinctions here, particularly the role of Paul Christopher as a romantic intellectual hero of the espionage profession against James Axton as the purveyor of a suspect branch of commercial social science, but I would argue that that has less significance than it might have, especially in the context of *The Tears of Autumn*.

If *The Miernik Dossier* is the spy story that nobody wants to admit is also a late modernist or even postmodernist novel, and *The Names* is the postmodernist fiction that one hesitantly concedes is also a conspiracy thriller, then *The Tears of Autumn* is the genre exercise that has terminated in the politically unspeakable—not so much the Conradian "horror" or Adorno's demand for the end of poetry after Auschwitz as the poignant American confusion over why the world is more complicated than it need be, and why bad things happen to good folks. Christopher's positionality, that he knows the truth but cannot say the truth, has something akin to the prophet ignored in his own country—perhaps, given the Christopher family's early Massachusetts origins, a modern version of the Puritan Jeremiah, a prophetic figure reading out the ominous direction of the community but unable to make himself heard over the endless buzz of economic and political life.[23] The conundrum that Paul Christopher has to resolve in this novel places him in the company of modern protagonists like Joyce's Stephen Dedalus who seek to express an artistic truth on a global scale, but in contrast to them the American is bound to secrecy. With neither Paul Christopher nor James Axton able to pass on their knowledge to humanity, *The Tears of Autumn* appears as a transition point between the last possible stretch of the traditional genre musculature and the casual pick-up of the genre markers by the postmodernists. The espionage narrative turns out to be, in McCarry's second novel, a border crossing where people shuffle through in both directions.[24]

If one draws a line between the premises of these three novels, from the crucified Miernik in the Sudanese desert, through the imaginative solution of the still murky assassination mystery of the first (and until recently, the only) Catholic president of the United States, to the randomly contingent murders of the alphabet-obsessed cult in *The Names*, that line does not actually respect the property fences of genre or the cultural rankings that we in some ways still cling to, or at least not fully.[25] The line that we can draw does suggest, however, that in American fiction a touch of genre can help the medicine go down, the hard truth be digested, the difficult history get a word in edgewise.

In this chapter, my aim is to shift the focus from a notion of conspiracy as the field of cosmic plotting by one's beloved enemies or the key to all unsolved mysteries to the recognition that American literature has come to regard conspiracy as a reflection more of the difficulty of final explanation than of the resolving of an equation. And to live with the absence of a final explanation may be a sign of maturity, and it is interesting that such maturity can be seen at home in popular, sometimes disregarded, literary and dramatic forms as much as in the higher literary fiction whose claim to precedence is often based on some notion of the mature versus the callow and the easily consumed. But without the genre fiction that *The Names* milks covertly for its narrative energy, it wouldn't be able to achieve the peculiar effect it does, as a philosophical text on risk and stability;[26] likewise, the near presence of texts that claim a higher literary status are still useful for novels like McCarry's, in that they set a certain measure for espionage novels that they do not have to reach, but the measure helps sharpen the performance the genre has to deliver to keep itself relevant. In other words, the one provides material for narrative pleasure in the context of a higher cultural premise, while the other keeps popular fiction from becoming too lazy.

It is evidently the case that conspiratorial thinking, while now and then taking on dangerously paranoid forms in reality, can often have a certain poetic side to it. The feeling that there is something more to know, something beyond the quotidian to perceive, or something vicious behind the mask of virtue is not necessarily a more naïve posture than believing in the fact of contingency. There may even be a type of negative capability, in this case a romantic energy that seeks clarification, that lifts the intuition of conspiracy out of the swamp of persecution mania. It might be that, for example, novels such as *The Miernik Dossier*, *The Names*, and particularly *The Tears of Autumn* offer a way of dealing with the frustration of conspiracy without falling prey to its morbid seductiveness.[27]

And, to that extent, the placing of any one of those novels in the correct slot on the spectrum from genre thriller to postmodern novel is in fact a counterproductive exercise, as the question I posed at the opening of the chapter is not answered thereby: rather, it limits the reader and the critic to the problem of categorization when the reality is that categorization is only a predictable formal maneuver aimed at reducing the number of things one has to take seriously. If we step back from categories and rankings for a moment, then we might see that texts possess somewhat elastic attributes and qualities that cannot always be pinned down for the purposes of labeling and correct storage. To wonder at the fear and strangeness of Tadeusz Miernik's savage end in the wilderness is not to reveal thereby an inability to read fiction at a complex level, and to praise Don DeLillo's play with millennialist fantasies and murderous sects beyond law and social control while dismissing McCarry's dark speculation about President Kennedy's assassination is not to prove a higher level of cultural taste. Despite the assumptions of the American popular imagination, the inner contradictions of the Cold War and the other wars that grew, often unnoticed, in its shadow did not take on the shape of clearly delineated sides, intentions, and ideologies. Indeed, the very fact that they did not take on that shape was, ominously enough, the shape that they took on.

Notes

1. As I noted in my discussion of Jorge Semprun's novel in the introduction to this book, some elements of modernist techniques seem to have been more easily integrated into popular fiction in other languages; or perhaps the notion of a strict borderline between genre fiction and literary fiction has not been as authoritative beyond the Anglophone realm.

2. It might have been even a signpost of where the spy story could go. At the same time, *The Miernik Dossier* also reveals that odd combination of traditional and experimental elements we can identify in the founding generation of modernist fiction.
3. It has proven difficult to identify where modernism shades into postmodernism, but it seems uncontroversial to say that modernist literature had a sense of the high calling of the artist, and of the justification of art, that is generally absent from postmodernism.
4. See "Secret Intelligence" in Eva Horn's *The Secret War* for an analysis of the formative institutional structures of intelligence agencies, 101–13.
5. *Dracula* is a work that reveals some surprisingly twentieth-century literary techniques, despite the essentially Victorian gothic rhetorical style.
6. The novel also begins in a United Nations body, symbolic of world progress and international cooperation, and ends in a desert region dominated by family and autocratic power.
7. Genre expectations on the reader's part can be sometimes met in a creative way by the author, possibly even persuading, or nudging, the reader to be more flexible in their expectations.
8. This is the memorable argument set out by Richard Hofstadter in his essay "The Paranoid Style in American Politics" (1964).
9. See comments on the difference between emotion and affect by Pieter Vermeulen in his *Contemporary Literature and the End of the Novel*; the difference is a marker of the shift from realist fiction to a postmodern fiction of the artifice (7–8). However, I see McCarry's novel as also negotiating a rearrangement of affect and emotion, but for narrative rather than ideological purposes.
10. As Kwame Anthony Appiah has noted, "To create a life is to create a life out of the materials history has given you" (*Ethics of Identity*, 19); all members of the traveling group have to an extent done exactly that, but for a mix of purposes, mostly kept to themselves.
11. Two years after the creation of the Republic of Sudan in 1956, there was an army officers' coup, which would place the time of the visit in McCarry's novel roughly a year into the period of military rule. There has been a long history of tension between the Muslim north and the partly Christian, partly pantheistic south, resulting in the division of the country in 2011. It is not quite clear from the story whether the Soviet plan is to foment some kind of internal revolt, against either the Khartoum government or local leaders like Kalash's father, using a mix of communist and Islamic ideas. See Rolandsen and Daly, *A History of South Sudan* for a succinct background history, esp. chapter 4, "The Curse of Colonial Continuity, 1953–1963."
12. Miernik's desire for martyrdom, if indeed that was what it was, points to some intriguing questions about the novel: for example, would the

ALF be entirely uninterested in the presumably important differences between a Polish communist and a Polish Catholic?
13. Perhaps a description would be something like "Occam's qualified razor"?
14. It should also be noted, however, that Diem's increasingly violent persecution of Buddhist religious communities with the excuse of rooting out communists, and his corresponding elevation of the Catholic Church to a position of privilege, contributed to the US government seeing no viable future if he remained in power.
15. DeLillo's 1988 novel *Libra*, which also offers a relatively unusual explanation for JFK's assassination, contains a note by the author to the effect that "while drawing from the historical record, [he has] made no attempt to furnish factual answers to any questions"; quoted in Codebò, *Narrating from the Archive*, 141. In some respects, that might be McCarry's defense of the rights of fiction too.
16. There have been some experimental works of fiction that remove both plot sequence and page order from the text, such as B. S. Johnson's *The Unfortunates* (1969) and a recently republished novel by Edward Powys Mather, *Cain's Jawbone* (1934). The latter has become the subject of a social media craze over the last couple of years.
17. *The Names* is also a narrative in which people say things they don't quite mean, and mean things they don't quite say.
18. See Donovan, *Postmodern Counternarratives*, 64–69 for a probing discussion of *The Names*, and especially his reading of the novel as ultimately unable to integrate the world-views of both James Axton and Owen Brademas.
19. The 1964 military coup in Greece was carried out with some encouragement on the part of the CIA station in Athens.
20. Patrick Leigh-Fermor (1915–2011), travel writer and special forces veteran who fought in German-occupied Crete; Lawrence Durrell (1912–90), novelist and travel writer; Barry Unsworth (1930–2012), novelist; Paul Theroux (b. 1941), novelist and travel writer. Helen MacInnes, whom I discuss in Chapter 3, also reveals both a deep affection for Greece and a substantial knowledge of postwar Greek politics in *Decision at Delphi* (1960), although her more rigid political and moral framework impedes her own literary options in that as in other later novels.
21. Even in the context of an ominous political thriller like Z, with the right-wing coup victorious at the conclusion, Greece seems attractive in so many ways. The movie was actually shot in Algeria, however, as it obviously could not be made in Greece under the military regime.
22. The creative impetus that Greece and the islands gave songwriters and musicians in that era includes, for example, Joni Mitchell's experiences in Matala on the south coast of Crete (mentioned in her song "Carey") and Leonard Cohen's sojourn on the island of Hydra, where he met

Marianne Jensen, the woman he later named in the song, "So Long Marianne."
23. Sacvan Bercovitch's study *The American Jeremiad* recounts the long history of this religio-political form of public speaking for the New England colonies and the United States. Bercovitch shows the jeremiad as playing a role in both the Revolutionary War and the Civil War, and once one learns to recognize its key components, it becomes relatively easy to see it still alive and well in contemporary times. As a side note, Charles McCarry has also published an historical romance set in London and New England in the early seventeenth century, *The Bride of the Wilderness* (1988).
24. Christopher Donovan's astute comment that "DeLillo abandons the narrative at the interpretive crossroads" (*Postmodern Counternarratives*, 68) could apply to McCarry in *The Miernik Dossier* as much as to *The Names*.
25. Although a long tradition of JFK assassination stories—history, fiction, and much that comes in-between—has grown over sixty years, the religious aspect is not one that authors have been much interested in.
26. See Donovan's argument in his chapter "Evil Is the Movement toward Void" on DeLillo's early novels and their relationship to genre fiction; see also Kylie Regan's "'The jolly coverts'" on reading DeLillo's *Libra* as espionage fiction.
27. The Warren Commission investigated the assassination of John F. Kennedy and submitted its final report in September 1964. The central findings, that Lee Oswald had worked alone and killed the president with a rifle fired from an upper floor in the Texas Schoolbook Depository in Dallas, have been contested from the very beginning. Even if one discounts other theories of the actual shooting itself, repeated inquiries and reviews suggest that the commission was, at the very least, heavily focused on evidence that solidified the argument that Oswald had acted alone and there was a wider conspiracy to uncover. Whether or not that restricted their investigations is difficult to say.

Chapter 6

Race and Intelligence: African-Americans and the Secret Life

In John Stockwell's account of his career in the Central Intelligence Agency in the 1960s and 1970s, *In Search of Enemies: A CIA Story* (1978), he describes going through a list of available officers to see who would make the best recruits for his Angola task force. Using a pseudonym (his normal practice in the book), he mentions an African-American colleague whom he would like to have, if it were possible:

> Andy Anderson was also interested, and he would have been a good man for Angola. But he was black. His loyalty should have been beyond question, since he had originally been recruited to surveil and report on American black radicals as they traveled in North Africa, one of the agency's most explosively sensitive and closely held operations against Americans.[1]

Although *In Search of Enemies* is a memoir rather than a work of fiction, it has a confident and compelling narrative style and a way of suggesting further stories behind the immediate moment. The reader will inevitably become curious about all that remains unsaid about this encounter: what were the details of Anderson's mission, for example, and which Black Panther or other activists was he pursuing? The more complex question, however, and one that is of more interest for this chapter, is about the professional motivations and subjective attitudes of African-Americans working for US intelligence services and carrying out assignments that directly involved the more militant black radicalism of those decades. Nothing similar to Stockwell's book has been authored so far by an African-American after his or her career in the CIA, and the thematic range of American espionage fiction—where the political and personal conflicts of such a scenario could also be effectively explored—has proven itself to be somewhat thin and unsatisfactory in this area.[2] With regard to espionage fiction, however, it is not necessarily an unexpected discovery that African-American authors are mostly absent from a popular genre in which American authors in general have not been substantially present. While black writers have worked within, astride, and outside standard styles and forms, in all modes of literature and drama, they have been attracted to some genres and types more than to others.[3]

In the case of espionage fiction, a distinctively separate genre, there have been nevertheless a couple of authentic offerings, one of the most distinctive being Samuel E. (Sam) Greenlee's 1969 novel *The Spook Who Sat by the Door*. Sam Greenlee was a foreign service officer working with the US Information Agency at a time when there were only a handful of non-white personnel in such positions.[4] He served in Iraq, Pakistan, and Greece between 1957 and 1966, when he resigned from government service and returned to Chicago to begin a new career as a writer, radio journalist, and activist. His novel about the Iraqi military coup of 1958, *Baghdad Blues* (1976), is less well known than *The Spook Who Sat by the Door*, but is a fascinating fictional account both of the historical event and of the experience of being the only African-American in the social setting of the US embassy and the American foreign service in general.[5] *The Spook Who Sat by the Door* is both a compelling story and a spy novel with a number of very distinct implications for how a black writer might or might not be willing to use the genre characteristics. There are some intriguing parallels between Greenlee's fiction and the novels of Walter Mosley, writing some twenty years later, around the theme of black Americans' relationship to institutional authority. If part of the legacy of the hardboiled crime thriller anchored by the figure of the private investigator is the suspicion that in the United States the police are not a neutral agency or, at the very least, cannot be trusted in certain circumstances, then his protagonist Easy Rawlins as a (somewhat) cynical private detective in Los Angeles in the decades after World War II draws on that legacy to manage his relationship with the Los Angeles Police Department and the white political establishment.[6]

If Easy Rawlins has a tense relationship with law enforcement that is both a traditional strand in the private eye tale and also a function of the racial hierarchy in mid-twentieth-century California, then Sam Greenlee's protagonist Dan Freeman is not only the CIA's rogue graduate who takes his skills and uses them against the system of white supremacy but also, ironically, the man who wanted to join the CIA in the first place, before he is forced to realize that he is merely a kind of hood ornament to convince a few liberals in Congress that the agency takes diversity seriously. Ironically, however, his superiors' dismissal of Freeman's professional ambitions on racial grounds at the outset of the novel opens the door to the protagonist's subversive transformation and his inexorable journey toward the ultimate revolutionary confrontation.[7] This is not to dismiss the agenda, I should emphasize, but there is a set of assumptions about Freeman's inner motivations that, while being broadly sympathetic to the protagonist's attitudes and actions, tend to over-simplify this component of the narrative. This flattening of ideological development is noticeably absent from Greenlee's other novel, *Baghdad Blues*, published later than *The Spook Who Sat by the Door* but possibly written at an earlier stage.[8]

The other work that launches a similar exploration of race, identity, and the black relationship to the American state (in the sense of the federal government), but on a different scale and with a different set of cultural motifs, is John A. Williams's *The Man Who Cried I Am* (1967). The historical sweep, international setting, and existential psychological atmosphere of Williams's novel are all markers of an attempt to step outside, rather than burrow down within, the oppressive bonds of the United States' social, racial, and sexual configurations. The novel presents a range of locations and engagements that work to complicate the narrative of the black intellectual loner, walking the mean streets of the twentieth century. Max Reddick has military service in World War II in his past, which gives him a thin slice of American access to European history as well as a slight competitive edge in his relationship with his friend and older author colleague Harry Ames. In the movement of the narrative from the New York left milieu of the 1930s to the Cold War world of the early 1960s, Williams selects a path that other espionage writers have also taken. The question of the loyalties of one's youth becoming the burden of one's middle age took on a particular flavor in the United States in the early Cold War years, with the fear of being tarred with the communist brush having real grounds, since jobs, opportunities, grants, and even one's passport could be subject to refusal after an official glance into an individual's file.

The comparative reading of Greenlee and Williams is an interesting exercise in seeing whether the broader or narrower vision is the more effective for exploring the relationship of blacks to white (or white-supremacist) intellectual and political structures. For Greenlee, the return of his protagonist to Chicago is tantamount to the rejection of the possible futures that working for the federal government might offer. Chicago in *The Spook Who Sat by the Door* is not the home of Irish or Polish ethnic familiarity and blue-collar networking, but rather one of the most hostile environments for an African-American. Freeman is faced with a city in which the political establishment presents a kind of progressive-modernizing face to the outside world, but is in fact marked by rigid territorial and racial divisions and borders and where a kind of zero-sum political culture regards any advance by black residents as a loss for someone else.[9] In contrast, Williams's novel is marked by releases of tension as the narrative focus moves from New York to Amsterdam and Paris, or even from one part of New York City to another. The possibility of travel, change, and the challenge of new circumstances (even ones with a potentially bleak outcome) raises *The Man Who Cried I Am* to a level in which epic movements of history are not, as in the chilly and unbending Chicago that Dan Freeman faces, uniformly pressing everything down in a kind of urban chamber of oppression, but continually offering—but also withdrawing—openings that contain other futures. The United States itself is also a peculiar presence in Williams's novel, as it is not only the site of domestic racist maneuvering but also a large and significant entity in a global system where conflicts are not ostensibly about race and its particular meaning in the American social theater but predicated on ideas and ideologies than may well cross racial and national boundaries in a way that disrupts American certainties, including those held by black characters.[10]

Both Greenlee's and Williams's protagonists and their other key players have some kind of relationship to the United States, whether it be loyal, neutral, or hostile, or some fluid configuration of all three. In fact, that relationship may be more crucial to the narrative of these two novels than is often recognized. The concept of a "crucial" relationship does not, of course, mean that it is positive, productive, or mutually satisfactory, only that it plays an important role in how the characters have come to be who, where, and how they are. Greenlee's highly focused protagonist Dan Freeman has clearly wanted to join the CIA at some point, and while one reading could suggest that he initially applied for intelligence work under false pretenses, as it were, in order to gain training that was intended to serve some covert agenda or politically revolutionary goal, another might argue that it was recognizable personal and professional ambition, echoing the motives for Dave Burrell's decision to join the US Information Agency in Greenlee's *Baghdad Blues*.[11]

In a similar fashion, Max Reddick notices on his reporting mission to the Congo that the government officials in Elizabethville show more enthusiasm for engaging professionally and socially with the European and white American diplomats stationed there than with African-American officials, whom they tend to treat with an unmistakable lack of interest. Reddick suspects that the credit achieved by having at least an institutional equality of status with white diplomats is somehow drained off when meeting with black American officials. The officials of the newly independent state, he observes to himself, "were not terribly happy about the Negroes" (331). At the conclusion of the novel, Reddick discovers, too, that the participation of blacks in the system can go high. Not so high, of course, that they discover the true genocidal intentions of the *Alliance Blanc*, but enough to enable a superficial claim of equality of opportunity to be made.[12] The *Alliance Blanc* is, of course, a melodramatic conspiracy trope in an apocalyptic story, but the segregation practiced in the US Department of State in the 1950s and 1960s was quite real. In Michael Krenn's *Black Diplomacy*, for example, there is ample evidence of an array of small segregations and humiliations directed at African-American diplomats and consular staff, especially new recruits and trainees.[13]

The other dimension of *The Man Who Cried I Am* that marks it out as a novel of its era is the exploration of sexual dissatisfaction and paranoia. The former becomes somewhat of a repetitive state of mind shadowing the uncertainty and the sense of missed targets with which Max Reddick often struggles in regard to his writing and its purpose, and the latter seems to emerge from his haunted feeling that he cannot ever escape racial identification in his relationships with women, both white and black, American and European. The combination of admiration and envy that characterizes his relationship to his friend and mentor Harry Ames is also a source of frustration, and the convergence of the two men's lives at the conclusion of the narrative, with a terminally ill Max trying to carry out Harry's mission after his mentor's death, taps into the bleakest of scenarios to offer some resolution that might define their personal and professional comradeship.

For espionage fiction as a genre, it is useful to examine in what way it can be distinguished from crime fiction in general and from the broader thriller category as a kind of extended genre classification. I would posit here that the spy story requires what one might call a competitive sovereignty situation, a narrative setting that involves a conflict between politically sovereign bodies or between a sovereign body and a political force (whether individual or collective) that contests the legitimacy of that body. Certainly, there can be texts that evade this descriptive frame, perhaps by way of parody or a very specific metaphorical use of espionage fiction elements, but it would seem to be a workable measure for making some distinctions, as I discuss elsewhere in this book.

When we look at both Greenlee's and Williams's novels, then, as espionage fictions that in both cases open up an unusual set of perspectives on the plotting, characterization, and narrative tones associated with the genre, perspectives that have a great deal to do with the era the novels were published in, can we determine how the competitive sovereignty situation is presented? Although a long list is not by itself an explanation, it is undeniable that the mid- to late 1960s were a period marked by the apex of the original Civil Rights Movement, the arrival on the scene of militant student activism and the separatist politics of the Black Panthers, the murders of Martin Luther King, Jr., and Robert Kennedy, the continuing series of anticolonial struggles overseas, especially in Africa, communist-oriented revolutionary movements elsewhere in the Americas, and the United States' ever more costly involvement in the war in Vietnam. You did not have to be African-American, of course, to be drawn into the roiling political and social waters of the time, but if you were, and an author to boot, the drama offered some particular opportunities. If one takes the problem of competitive sovereignty in this historical context (and, indeed, in others going back to the Civil War and beyond), then it becomes an interesting conundrum for black Americans and their battle for genuine recognition of their citizenship: are there situations where sovereignty and its implications are not at all as clear as they might be for whites? To put it another way: does the aspiration of African-Americans for full and uncompromised legitimacy within the national political imaginary, especially in situations where there are local or state forces active in denying it, mean that the loyalty demanded by the US federal government must be rendered by a black individual? Does the desire for uncontested citizenship and recognition involve a kind of assumption of the appropriate loyalty or patriotism even if the citizenship or recognition is, at any particular moment, compromised and inadequate rather than valid and complete?[14] *The Spook Who Sat by the Door* argues the case one way, and *The Man Who Cried I Am* another, although both novels end with the gloomy assessment that this aspiration will never be met in America or, at least, not as currently constituted.

There is another dimension to both these texts, however, that bears upon my central thesis in this chapter, and that is whether the conditions of espionage fiction are simply less visible but nonetheless present in stories by black authors that lie outside the genre boundaries, but share some of its atmosphere. In other words, by over-focusing on the affective norms of the genre, we may miss those literary characteristics that, while embedded in very different types of narrative, point toward the spy and the ethic of secrecy. To take an example from a generation before Greenlee and Williams, Richard Wright's early short story "Big Boy Leaves Home," which appeared as the first piece in the 1938 collection *Uncle Tom's Children*, offers an ending in particular that seems to echo certain narrative conventions found in the espionage novel. After Big Boy's unintended killing of a white man who has shot two of his three friends after they are all accidentally seen swimming naked by a white woman who panics and calls the man for help, he has to flee the Southern town where they all live. The third friend, who has escaped from the scene with Big Boy, is found later and burned at the stake by a white mob. Big Boy's family succeed in arranging for him to get a ride north with a truck driver, and he is able to make the rendezvous and escape. What is striking, among other things, is the way in which his local area, which he and his friends know intimately, has become a dangerous and deadly place where his life is on the line. The escape in the truck has all the characteristics of a story of resistance in occupied Europe in World War II, or of Cold War-era spy novels, where crossing a frontier without being discovered made the difference between reaching freedom and being brought back for interrogation and possible execution.

There is an important dimension of territorial sovereignty in these and similar narratives that have their roots in the competitive sovereignty situation that obtained in the United States before the 1850s, where black escapees had to physically put themselves, often at great risk, beyond the reach of the slaveholding states by crossing the Mississippi or Ohio rivers or making it north of Maryland by some means. This situation was rendered even more challenging by the 1850 Fugitive Slave Act, which federalized slaveowner claims on refugees from slavery even if they were now residents of a free state. What is often an active "defamiliarization" on the Shklovsky model practiced by African-American writers in narratives like Wright's comes about because a white readership will be initially thrown by the narrative perspective of a story in which a part of the United States (or even the larger nation in some cases) manifests itself as foreign and dangerous, where the protagonist has to be ever on the alert as if they were an agent operating behind enemy lines.[15]

"Big Boy Leaves Home" is a story in which the flight of the slave in both nineteenth-century American history and popular culture is repeated in way that suggests that Marx's dictum from the Eighteenth Brumaire, that in the repetition of history the second time around is comic rather than tragic, may be inaccurate. The tragic does tend toward the comic in the sense that it is the racial paranoia of the white woman seeing the nudity of the teenagers at the swimming hole that triggers the series of violent events, as exaggerated fear where there is nothing to be scared of is indeed often comic. But it is difficult to parse the interwoven threads of racial horror and sexual projection that occur in this story. Clearly, Big Boy and his friends intend no harm to her or to anyone else, and in a normal environment it might just be a chance encounter that causes some brief mutual awkwardness. As the environment is only normal in the sense that it reflects the local norms of the South in the 1930s, however, they panic when they see her. The woman's reaction may be deliberately exaggerated so that she has some basis in her mind for calling her companion Jim to help. Is she worried that, if she didn't call for help, she was initiating some betrayal of the racial and social order in the South by perhaps admitting to a momentary interest in the young men? As the reader cannot be sure, it remains simply a fact that the mutual observation becomes the tripwire that, once touched, makes what seems like home to the four boys immediately a foreign country in which they are hunted down as interlopers and sexual predators. This cannot be a crime story, however, as the existence of some kind of legitimate field of law and legality, even if very distant from the action, is a *sine qua non* of that genre. Even if very elastic, that sense of a commonly viewed if not consensually accepted field of law is necessary to even initially define something as a crime and something else as not one. Richard Wright's purpose here in a story of the South is to explode the myth of equal citizenship for black and white Americans and reveal (as he went on to do for Chicago, the place that Big Boy speculatively escapes to, in his 1940 novel *Native Son*) a land of segregation and racial hierarchy through which black people must travel, ever compelled to be alert to every hint of danger.

In this way, too, the skills that African-Americans must learn within the frame of life in the Jim Crow South are those taught to covert operatives who are to be sent into the field. The psychological posture they must adopt behind enemy lines is one geared to not making an unplanned mistake, not making oneself more noticeable than one has to be, and not talking to the wrong people or talking to them at the wrong time. As for intelligence agents on a mission, it cannot be all fake, and some aspects have to be just personality, but at no time does it pay to be careless.

Indeed, the position of black figures on the hostile territory of white supremacy is one that cuts to the bone of the nature of the American political tradition, which aimed to establish itself as ethically opposed to the aristocratic and conspiratorial milieu of the monarchies of Europe. American political culture would be one of open access and transparent dealing, the Revolution asserted. Of course, this seems quite absurd against the background of the actual conduct of political life over the last couple of centuries, but the general assumptions upon which a national political culture is built never entirely lose their significance. Secrecy, at least in domestic policy, has been condemned and challenged, and constitutional protection for journalism has been a principle that every new type of media, from newspapers to the Internet, has invoked at one time or another. Indeed, to be against transparency has come to be regarded as morally suspect in the United States, as if confidentiality itself were an occasion of sin within a theological framework of public discourse. But the problem with the binary choice of secrecy or transparency is that of most binaries: it evades or disguises the reality that no behavior remains free of the values that structure and shape it. To be transparent in a social world that presupposes a robust equality, where no protocol is breached by, for example, one individual expressing their view candidly to another, is quite different from being transparent in a situation of manifest inequality and fixed racial hierarchy where candor from someone lower on that hierarchical scale can lead to grim, perhaps even fatal, consequences.[16] It should be obvious that the values of secrecy versus those of transparency are not simply transferable from a world in which political freedom is assumed to the world of state-enforced racial segregation and discrimination. The existence of meta-values of race and social segregation cannot be (and were not, of course) ignored because, even if they are obscured or their existence denied, they have done their job in shaping the consequences of the ostensibly free choice of transparency over secrecy.

To that extent, Richard Wright is a particularly interesting figure to think about in respect of this issue because his own political career, in its active phase from the 1930s onward, saw him become involved with the Communist Party of the USA (CPUSA) and then, years later, eventually break with the party and become a contributor to the best-known collection of conversion essays by former communists, *The God that Failed: A Confession* (1949). For much of its history in this era, the CPUSA had a strong covert and, often, illegal side that was directed by representatives from the Soviet-dominated Comintern, bypassing many of the regular organizational structures of the party.[17] Wright was not involved in this work, but there was a culture of confidentiality and compartmentalizing that went with active membership. The American Communist Party valued black membership, which it saw as a locus of real organizing strength, and won the loyalty of many African-Americans for its defense of black rights in the South. Black communists were also negotiating their way through its ranks just as the party was feeling its way toward the larger constituency of black Americans. The CPUSA wanted to show itself to be the most reliable political ally of African-Americans, a better longer-term bet than other political parties, but it also wanted black members to be disciplined party soldiers and to put their racial identity into second or third place if so ordered. Many did so, of course, but many suspected that the larger political interests for blacks (or even the working class as a whole) sometimes functioned as a convenient cover story to obscure personal or sub-group agendas in internal struggles. For black members, the sense of operating on foreign territory did not completely disappear, even within the context of a political force dedicated to overthrow of the American capitalist—and by obvious association, racist—order.

In another wrinkle, they might be also victims of betrayal sooner than whites, as in Wright's story "Bright and Morning Star," also from *Uncle Tom's Children*. In this narrative, a white communist, Booker, is revealed as the informer in an underground group of communists, and the distrust of white communists by black communists is openly discussed at an earlier point between two black characters, Sue and her son Johnny-Boy. This suspicion that whites might be the weaker comrades, or even actively working against the cause, snakes through many such texts right down to the present day, as we shall see. There is no initial agreement on this in "Bright and Morning Star," as in the conversation between Sue and Johnny-Boy, the latter arguing with feeling for not considering race as an issue among fellow communists. Set in the 1920s or 1930s, of course, this story is not a guideline for later political developments, as the Black Panthers, for example, turned their backs on the fiction of cross-racial solidarity within traditional left radicalism and operated on a view of the world that would be closer to Sue's than to Johnny-Boy's.[18] The notion that the informer will always be white, however, revealed itself in later history to be an unreliable principle. The upshot of this is only to say, first of all, that, by the 1960s, employment chances for black applicants for national security careers in the federal government had improved at least to the extent that penetrating groups such as the Black Panthers offered a particular career opportunity, and second, that African-Americans showed no greater propensity for militant anti-capitalist politics than any other demographic in the country. And this is indeed the problem at the core of *The Spook Who Sat by the Door*, a novel that in some ways, and not least in its Chicago setting, stands in direct line of inheritance from Wright's classic fiction of a generation earlier.

Both Greenlee's novels, *Baghdad Blues* and *The Spook Who Sat by the Door*, deal with the relationship that black Americans have, or could possibly have, to the structures of established governmental power: the former critical, although pragmatic, and at the end resolved by swapping diplomatic work for a writing career; the latter uncompromisingly oppositional and culminating in violence. *The Spook Who Sat by the Door* can be read as a tragedy of manipulated racial progress in which Freeman tries to bring the covert action skills from his US government training to bear upon the structures of racial oppression in Chicago, only to be eventually confronted by his childhood friend Dawson, a city police officer. Freeman and Dawson do not so much represent opposite ideologies as act as professionals who have come to different decisions. Although critical readings have not emphasized this, *The Spook Who Sat by the Door* is at least ambivalent about the prospects for armed rebellion on the United States to the extent that Dawson's arguments are given a considerable airing and, while Freeman's responses are dominant—and the novel's ending clear—they are not presented as convincing in every point.[19] Greenlee's fiction reaches for armed insurgency but suggests also that such a development may be hindered by black people doing their jobs, both in law enforcement and potentially (had Freeman been granted the career opportunity he had sought) in national security work.

With John A. Williams and *The Man Who Cried I Am*, we are already at that particular stage. The relationship to the state has proven attractive for at least a few of the characters, and as in Greenlee the divisions among African-Americans serve as a prescient note, looking forward to the rise in electoral victories and higher administrative posts on various levels in the United States that would begin to come to black candidates and applicants in the decades that followed, bearing fruit in, most dramatically, Barack Obama's national political breakthrough in the early twenty-first century. But it is still the case in Greenlee's and Williams's fiction that the senior positions remain closed to minority candidates, and performance is, at least to an extent, also measured by race. Here, fiction and real life concur. John Stockwell notes, for example, a case where a black CIA officer took over a dangerous field post in Vietnam in which a couple of white officers had given up because of nervous breakdowns. In a later review of the operation, writes Stockwell, all white personnel involved received medals, but the black officer only a commendation.[20] *The Man Who Cried I Am* is of course more of an apocalyptic narrative whose implications go far beyond American political culture alone, but at some level the issue of how the relationship of black citizens to the state has played out, or should play out, in military, political, and cultural fields remains central to this novel. There is in both Greenlee and Williams an ideological tension, rooted in the volatility of the era, that seems not to favor one side or the other, but holds black political energy in a force field between radical opposition and working within the system. This may be, in fact, precisely the reason why African-American writers were not attracted generally to the espionage genre. The genre is friendly to open, unresolved conclusions, and even to morally bleak implications, but it is not friendly to endings that slide out from under the competitive sovereignty situation, because if a text loses that framing stability, it ceases to be a spy story and becomes something else.[21] Williams's novel is a good example as it courts the danger of using espionage fiction as a kind of functional vehicle to deliver a payload that does not really have any interest in the genre it is being carried by. It achieves its goal, however, because once again the emotional affect of the espionage story is deployed to effectively translate, as it were, the racial, sexual, and creative *agon* into a different narrative environment.

Finally, for this set of issues, it is worth saying that both Greenlee's and Williams's novels are set in an era in which struggles over power, legitimacy, representation, and rights were going through a transition that would, some few years later, lead to a shift in American politics after which it was possible for black candidates for local political offices and state legislatures to be elected, and for black applicants for more senior administrative jobs to be considered serious candidates (and, to a more limited extent, in the corporate world also).[22] One should be cautious about interpreting this change too ambitiously, however, as there are some important aspects to consider, not least of which is whether the white establishment found it pragmatically useful to open the gates to ambitious African-Americans precisely at the point in modern American history when the long period of economic prosperity kicked off by the New Deal in the 1930s and fueled by the

United States' rise to global authority was fading. It is not especially conspiratorial to imagine that white politicians no longer had a great deal of enthusiasm for becoming mayors of cities, for example, that had been deserted by many of their former white residents and were now populated by racial and ethnic minorities who had discovered that the industrial economy that had made those cities good places to live for the white working class was on the point of departing. Be that as it may, the presence of black Americans in political office or governmental employment would no longer be, from the 1970s on, a peculiar sight.

If we change our perspective from black-authored fiction and the mid-twentieth century to the political and cultural landscape of today, then new circumstances obtain, but also unhappily familiar ones that reveal strikingly similar contours to those which I have discussed in this chapter. On the one hand, it is possible to say that the presence of black Americans in government, including in senior positions, is now part of the normal run of everyday life. Recent elections have shown, however, that there is a large constituency marked by political resentment still active in the United States, and deeper strains of racist and conspiratorial thinking have emerged. Not only, for example, does a certain percentage of Americans believe, for example, that President Obama favored black people, to the planned disadvantage of whites, during his period in office, but more recently Joe Biden's victory in the 2020 presidential election triggered groundless claims of fraud, with African-American polling clerks and elections administrators often a particular target of suspicion and hostility. To look at the role of black protagonists and black characters in espionage fictions over the last fifteen to twenty years is to see both the achievement that is a shadowy presence in the novels of Sam Greenlee and John A. Williams and the long echo of the struggles of the Civil Rights era and the 1960s upheavals.

This more recent era has coincided with the arrival of a number of black actors who have taken on roles in movies or television dramas with an espionage theme. A spy story can, of course, be embedded in an action movie aimed at the widest possible reception at home and abroad, or given a realistic setting and played for political nuance in an HBO or cable channel for a smaller audience to whom that kind of premise appeals, with many examples between those two poles. Indeed, "action movie" and "realistic espionage drama" are not necessarily mutually exclusive categories. Although not a US-originating production, the BBC series *Spooks* (renamed *MI-5* for American broadcast) ran for ten seasons from 2002 to 2011 and had Nigerian-British actor David Oyelowo in a leading role for three of them. Oyelowo went on to have an acting career in the United States, and played Martin Luther King, Jr., in the 2014 movie *Selma*. The option to cast a black British rather than an African-American actor in a distinctly American and historically significant role is obviously reflective of a more porous transatlantic hiring market for casting directors looking for a range of personalities and appearances, but it is interesting that one of the definitive American spy dramas on television, *Homeland*, first broadcast in 2011, had British actors in key roles: particularly, for the first three seasons, Damien Lewis as Nicholas Brody, and for the first two seasons David Harewood as David Estes, a black CIA officer who leads the agency's counter-terrorism center.[23]

David Estes is portrayed as a tough and uncompromising intelligence manager who pushes subordinates for results but in some ways seems to be more of an organization man than either of the two other principal characters, Saul Berenson or Carrie Mathison. His tussles with Carrie Mathison, in particular, are rooted both in her unorthodox and stubborn approach to the job and, more subtly, in what we are given to understand was a sexual relationship between the two at some point in the past. While Berenson's relationship with Carrie Mathison is more like that of an older professor and a gifted but wayward former student in the same field, Estes seems at times to be more worried about the potential effects on his own promotion chances if Carrie makes a serious mistake while he is her superior in the agency's chain of command. This is especially intense in the first part of *Homeland*'s opening season, when her suspicions about Sergeant Brody seem initially not only unfounded, but dangerously obsessive. There is no doubt that, at some level, Estes has a feeling that, as a black man in a senior national security position, he cannot afford to be over-confident about his future. When we see him once with his young son when Carrie calls at his house, for example, the audience becomes aware, not for the first time, that Estes is divorced; and Estes's earlier remark to Berenson that Carrie is the reason why "My wife lives in Palm Beach and I only see my kids twice a year" confirms that a fling with Carrie and the fate of his marriage were connected.[24] What makes a powerful dramatic performance, however, is Harewood's embodiment of the controlled focus and dedication that this man brings to his responsibilities. In a different way from Carrie Mathison, David Estes is nonetheless also driven by a demon or two—maybe not an uncommon complaint in the intelligence business.

But if Estes is an organization man, at some important level, is this because he always was, or because he had to become one? Is he a manifestation of some implicit protocol, like the old racial protocols of Jim Crow America, that says that African-Americans must always be loyal to the organization in a culture that tends to romanticize the loner who follows his or her gut instinct? It seems that he, at least, believes so. No matter how high he has managed to climb in his career at the agency, the bonus of American individualism will never quite outweigh the need to prove oneself a team player. This configuration is particularly interesting in *Homeland* because there is another character in the story whose role seems to hold traces of an earlier time when the image of black men as "driven" often had very different connotations.

Although with very little actual physical presence in the drama, Brody's Marine comrade and fellow prisoner Tom Walker plays a significant role in the first season of *Homeland*. Walker is reported by Brody to have been killed in Afghanistan, but Walker's widow gradually becomes convinced that he is, in fact, alive. When the real state of affairs is gradually (but only partly) revealed, it becomes obvious that, whatever the truth about Nicholas Brody, Tom Walker has been well and truly turned during his captivity and is committed to the mission they have been given by the senior al-Qaeda operative, Abu Nazir. In a confrontation in a Washington DC park at night, Brody shoots Walker on Abu Nazir's instructions. After hearing about the failed bomb attack on the US vice president, Walker has accused Brody of retreating from the mission now that he is back home, suggesting he has chickened out for personal reasons. The murder of Walker seems to be the result of Brody having convinced the al-Qaeda commander that he, Brody, can wreak more damage as a long-term penetration agent (he has, for example, been asked to run for Congress), and that Walker is a loose cannon who endangers this more sophisticated mission.

What seems implicit but undeniable in this scene and in the longer unfolding of Tom Walker's role is that Brody is, to an extent, correct. Walker is, if not a loose cannon, more openly fanatical about hitting back at the country that sent him to war than Brody is, and this fanaticism seems to be, at least in part, rooted in his blackness. Brody is engaged in a complex act of vengeance, but Walker is more infused with a kind of relentless fury. In one of those strange dramatic moves made by *Homeland* in its earlier years, Brody is made to seem sympathetic at that moment in the park, in contrast to the angry black man confronting him. That is, in part, because we have spent a great part of the time with Sergeant Brody as one of the major players in the drama, but I would argue that it is also because Brody is showcased counter-intuitively as the "rational" terrorist plant. Is this because he is white? We might be driven to endorse Brody and condemn Walker, in other words, because Brody's enigmatic presence is invested with more value than Walker's open fanaticism, even though the ultimate goal is one they both share.

The past seems to chase and slowly overtake the present as Tom Walker becomes as much a Black Panther guerilla of the late 1960s as a US Marine turned by the Islamist terrorists who have held him prisoner in the early twenty-first century. The irony is that, despite the fact that at that point we know—indeed we have seen in gripping detail—that Brody is the key figure in an ambitious al-Qaeda conspiracy, the implicit racial coding at work makes Brody seem less of a threat than Walker, although he is a greater one. The casual ordering of his death by Abu Nazir, and Brody's speedy follow-through in the tunnel in the park, suggest that Walker was ultimately a secondary figure in the plot, a useful tool fueled by his desire for revenge but also limited by it.[25]

There is no direct confrontation between counter-terrorism officer David Estes and armed militant Tom Walker in *Homeland*, but it does not take a great deal of imagination to see Estes and Walker as, respectively, the Pete Dawson and Dan Freeman from *The Spook Who Sat by the Door* reincarnated in the new, post-9/11 world, in which both characters have gotten a promotion and have, in a sense, shifted their roles around: Estes might be the contemporary Dawson, but he is also a Dave Freeman who had made a different choice, put his head down, and gritted his teeth for a few years at the CIA and eventually obtained a proper field assignment, and was able to work his way up the career ladder; Walker might be the Freeman who took his skills from the Marine Corps rather than the agency, but in a way he is also a Dawson who is a bit of an organization guy, not an original thinker, but this time he has swapped the Marine oath for a final redirection of loyalty to Abu Nazir, a step he is not going to reverse. This is not to say that there are only two options for African-Americans within the cultural drama of espionage narratives, but the resistant energies of former—and present—times seem to suppress possibilities that the one or the other white character, Carrie Mathison in particular, has at their fingertips.

So many black writers and artists have played with the idea of the covert, the notion that you cannot let whites see your real thoughts, that it has escaped attention that there is a place where that kind of secretiveness is part of everyday existence and not something that requires the premise of a particular institutional situation or historical setting. Or, to put it another way, black writers and their fictional protagonists have been dealing with the nature of the secret life for a long time, and much longer than the history of the espionage genre in Anglo-American popular literature. More than others, the value of secrecy and the contrasting and (to say the least) dubious advantages of transparency have been informing values of black fiction that have pushed the assumptions of the espionage genre into other fields of cultural identity beyond the model of competitive sovereignty.

To be a spy in one's own country, perhaps even the realization that that is precisely the existential reality offered by the society and the polity, is to live on a certain edge. No real trust can be risked, as Johnny-Boy discovers in "Bright and Morning Star," if the mission slides into territory where race can, and will, trump class solidarity. How to live, if the only homeland you can return and report to is an imagined future? For African-American literature in the twentieth century, race and intelligence have always been an indispensable alliance. That alliance can gradually morph into something more complicated, however, as the availability of opportunity and career in areas relating to intelligence in the institutional or governmental sense increases, as it has done in the United States since the end of the Civil Rights era. The complications, as *Homeland* lays out in its first two seasons (2011–13), are not, however, completely disconnected from the political choices presented in earlier narratives, Greenlee's and Williams's in particular. Indeed, the force of the roles of David Estes and Tom Walker, the sense of controlled violence that seems to link the director of the CIA counterterrorism center and the US Marine turned-al-Qaeda operative, emerges from the way in which the radical dissenting energies of *The Spook Who Sat by the Door* and *The Man Who Cried I Am* continue to flicker in the background.

The central argument in the first part of the chapter was that we need to understand that the question as to why black American authors have been slow to take up the espionage genre, or indeed have ignored it, can be answered, at least in part, by showing how African-American fiction has been in fact emotionally, atmospherically, and culturally bonded to the genre—even if invisibly—through particular historical struggles over rights, citizenship, and sovereignty. The discussion of *Homeland* in the second part is designed to change perspective sharply and examine black masculine characters within fully formed manifestations of the spy story in the contemporary American era. Often, a kind of default hostility to inspirational tales of black success within the middle-class ramifications of a capitalist United States can become blind to social shifts and changes of any type and come to embrace a kind of folklore of negativity, as if there is no journey that can be made where white supremacy does not get to the destination first and poison it in some way.[26] A one-dimensional understanding of progress and a flat and uninteresting concept of sovereignty are not, however, reliable guides to reading either classic novels of militant black opposition or the stories that, in their cultural rhetoric, represent a more plausible racial and ethnic landscape of American intelligence for the contemporary era. If there is a thread that links Johnny-Boy through Dan Freeman and Max Reddick to David Estes and Tom Walker, however, then it cannot be simply one in which Estes is the careerist sellout and Walker the embodiment of uncompromising militancy. Nevertheless, the way in which the configuration of race in *Homeland* is manifested reveals that the historical confrontations of earlier eras, both the 1930s and the 1960s, continue to operate within the dynamics of the present, and that the espionage story can never not be about the past.

Notes

1. Stockwell, *In Search of Enemies*, 75.
2. There is, however, a very interesting extended interview with Darrell M. Blocker, who retired from the agency in 2018 as one of its highest-ranking African-American officers, holding several posts including that of deputy director of the counter-terrorism center. It can be found online as a podcast at "Darrell M. Blocker—His Journey in the CIA as a Real Life 007 Secret Agent." *YouTube*, https://www.youtube.com/watch?v=n_Il35s7_IE (accessed June 8, 2023).
3. As regards African-American authors and genre fiction, revaluations of Octavia Butler (speculative and science fiction) and Frank Yerby (historical fiction) in particular have taken their place alongside studies of the longer history of black crime fiction and the thriller from the 1920s to the hip-hop era, e.g. Bailey, *African American Mystery Writers*. There is still an incomplete historical understanding, however, of the relationship between African-American writers and espionage fiction, and indeed this is reflected in the politics of black characterization in some modern and contemporary cinema and television drama, as I discuss later in the chapter.
4. The combination of a post-World War II need for manpower and the desegregation of the military in 1948 helped black applicants fill more federal positions, gaining access to stable incomes and benefits.

However, opportunity did not dispel segregationist practices, so most of these jobs were at the lower wage and salary scales, and when they were not, they were often token positions to comply with affirmative action policies. Greenlee's recruitment by the United States Information Agency has him belonging to a select few at the end of the 1950s.
5. See Griffin, "Dave Burrell's *Baghdad Blues*"; for a broader historical analysis of the presence of African-Americans in the State Department and related agencies, see Krenn, *Black Diplomacy*, especially chapters 4 and 5.
6. Mosley has written a revealing essay, "1926," on the hardboiled tradition in American writing, for the *New Literary History of America*. For a thorough discussion of Mosley's fiction and subsequent critical evaluations, see in particular English, "The Modern in the Postmodern."
7. That paradox of openings for ambitious black Americans within the expanding global presence of diplomacy and intelligence-gathering during the Cold War is given some probing analysis in an article by Adriane Lentz-Smith, "Passports to Adventure." Lentz-Smith argues that Greenlee never quite escaped from the contradiction between his years of faithful service to the United States abroad and his later commitment to radical black activism and cultural work.
8. Although published several years after *The Spook Who Sat by the Door*, *Baghdad Blues* reveals several characteristics in the text that strongly suggest earlier composition, not least of which is a more personal, less combative first-person narrative voice and posture.
9. Under the administration of Democratic mayor Richard J. Daley, Chicago during the 1960s looked like a seat of political power and social advancement, but it was also a city with intense segregation and police brutality. Redlining and the decline of manufacturing jobs displaced black citizens and decreased their economic prospects, and the impact of this is still noticeable today. Though Daley had benefited from support from the black community in several important elections, his mishandling of protests following the murder of Martin Luther King, Jr., revealed his readiness to choose force as the preferred option.
10. Although the United States, and especially the Kennedy and Johnson administrations, tried to appear progressive in its response to racial inequalities, the government's active participation in the struggles of newly independent African countries gave leaders and activists cause to criticize domestic as well as foreign policies. As Kevin Gaines notes in "The Civil Rights Movement in World Perspective," "[t]he conjuncture of the Cold War and America's aspirations for global hegemony, the U.S. civil rights movement, and the decolonization of Africa [was] . . . a momentous one" (58). Nonetheless, even remote and ostensibly non-racial battles over civil rights such as the early conflict in Northern Ireland at the end of the 1960s could reveal echoes of the Civil Rights Movement, with the widescale adoption of songs like "We Shall Not Be Moved" by the Catholic marchers.

11. As Penny von Eschen has argued in *Race against Empire*, there was a significant shift among African-American liberals in the course of the early 1950s toward a qualified support for the United States as a global leader in the struggle with communism (see esp. chapter 8, "No Exit: From Bandung to Ghana"); Greenlee's career in the United States Information Agency reflects this, at least in a pragmatic rather than an intellectual mode.
12. See Bailey, *African American Mystery Writers* on how a fictional conspiracy slid into the popular mind, and came to be held by some as a documentary truth (62).
13. See n. 5 above on Krenn.
14. In *Patriotism Black and White*, Nichole R. Phillips finds that national belonging corresponds with both religious practice and military performance. Through case studies within a Southern rural community, Phillips concludes that although "being American born was not enough to be a racial equalizer, service to the country, to the point of death, was" (217).
15. Viktor Shklovsky's influential 1917 essay "Art as Device," often called "Art as Technique," posited that originality in narrative or drama did not emerge from plots or characters in themselves, but rather from the perspective from which the story is recounted. A conventional plot becomes unconventional, in other words, if it is narrated from an unexpected angle or point of view. In this way, black writing is often disconcerting to white American readers precisely because it renders the familiar coordinates of American life unfamiliar: what are regarded as norms for whites are shown to be privileges or at least intermittent norms for African-Americans, upsetting the assumption of, for example, a fraternal bonding status between all citizens.
16. One might note also that there were other motives to be less than welcoming of transparency. As Gary Holcomb discusses in his book *Claude McKay, Code Name Sasha*, transgressive sexual orientation in an era of punitive enforcement of conventional behaviors could provide a powerful motive for secrecy and the preservation of a covert life whose revelation could be as damaging in many ways as political activism, if not more so. Sexuality, as well as radical anti-capitalist politics, was "forced into the shadows" (17).
17. Wright's membership (whether completely formalized or not) coincided with a rise in the popularity of the CPUSA, as enrollment numbers surged in the late 1930s and early 1940s. Around this time the party was strategically supporting civil rights campaigns and fielding candidates for local, state, and presidential elections. The electoral statistics for American Communist Party candidates in various elections from the 1920s to the 1940s have been estimated (for example, by the University of Washington's *Mapping American Social Movements Project*) but are an inaccurate guide to the party's often substantial influence outside its immediate ranks.

18. This history is dealt with extensively in Harold Cruse's iconic study from 1967, *The Crisis of the Negro Intellectual*. The consequences of the competition between interracial solidarity and national-ethnic group autonomy permeates Cruse's book, but for some discussion that focuses particularly on the period in which Wright's story is set, see the chapters entitled "1920s–1930s—West Indian Influence" and "Jews and Negroes in the Communist Party"; see also Cruse's commentary on Richard Wright (181–9).
19. Some scholarly attention has been given to the overall impact of *The Spook Who Sat by the Door* as a film, pointing to the cultural importance of the text overall more than the individual characters' ideologies. Examining Greenlee's purpose in the cinematic production of *Spook*, Elizabeth Reich argues that the project "reimagines marginalization as a position of potential power" and conveys a revolutionary philosophy ("A New Kind of Black Soldier," 327). In a similar vein, Samantha Sheppard believes that *Spook* was transformed into a protest film with an "enduring ethos of radicalness" ("Persistently Displaced," 74).
20. Stockwell, *In Search of Enemies*, 75.
21. This is an interesting question, as there are a couple of examples of a novel by an author working in the espionage genre that, without it being a spy story, stays within the fold in respect of central character or setting or even atmosphere: John le Carré's second novel *A Murder of Quality* (1962) succeeds in this, and enjoys a somewhat iconic status in le Carre's body of work. This may be due to George Smiley still being a protagonist under construction, so to speak, and to the fact that the English public school milieu in which *A Murder of Quality* takes place seems to overlap with le Carre's more commonly used social and professional settings, Whitehall being the obvious example. In any case, such examples seem to be the exceptions that prove the rule.
22. Between 1960 and 1970 Congress saw its first real shift in demographics, although the number of black legislators was still disproportionately low in comparison to the US population (as late as 1980, 94 percent of Congress was white, despite a national population figure of 80 percent white). The 1960s were also a time that marked a change in elections for mayors. While several cities elected black mayors between 1964 and 1966, 1967 was the first year in which two major American cities elected African-Americans: Carl Stokes was elected mayor of Cleveland, Ohio, and Richard Hatcher was elected mayor of Gary, Indiana.
23. I discuss *Homeland* with a different focus in Chapter 8.
24. *Homeland*, season 1, episode 1, broadcast October 2011.
25. One might see Tom Walker as a figure framed by a new racial neoliberalism, as described in David Theo Goldberg's *The Thread of Race*, especially in chapter 3 and the discussion of what he terms "Racial Americanization." Although a hierarchy of race is embodied in the

relationship of power between the two Marines, the dominance of a post-civil-rights neoliberal ideology makes it appear that it is merely an accident of fate that one is black and the other is white. Although playing a role in the story, as it were, it plays no role in the story.

26. For example, when the two-term presidency of Barack Obama, hailed as national progress toward a post-racial America, was followed by the vitriolic and divisive first term of Donald Trump, it was often seen as proof of this at the highest and most visible level. Even more recently, the high-profile controversy and conclusion surrounding the attempt in 2021 to hire the journalist Nikole Hannah-Jones, editor of the *New York Times* feature "The 1619 Project," at the University of North Carolina has garnered some cynicism about black intellectual celebrity and actual social progress (on this last point, see Jason England's essay "The Pernicious Fantasy of the Nikole Hannah-Jones Saga").

Chapter 7

The Soldier's Song: Britain's Irish War in Gerald Seymour's Trilogy

> Friendly young Englishman: So what's going on in Northern Ireland? What's all the bombing and violence about?
> Friendly young Irish woman: I don't know. It's supposed to be *your* country, so you tell me.
>
> Conversation on a flight to Dublin, early 1990s

The term often used for the thirty-year armed conflict between Irish nationalist paramilitaries, the British and Northern Ireland security forces, and armed Ulster unionist militants is provocative by virtue of its euphemistic nature. "The Troubles" is, like most euphemisms, both a side-stepping of something ugly or distasteful and a way of moving on in a conversation rather than getting bogged down in heavily contested terminology.[1] What the term covered was a contained civil war of a kind, a largely underground conflict that, while nothing like as deadly as some other modern inter-community clashes, marked three decades of life in a very small place with terror, hatred, and violence. In the imaginative realm of espionage fiction, therefore, Northern Ireland provides none of the exotic pleasures of almost any other location in the world, including the corridors of Whitehall. Indeed, the northeastern corner of Ireland, the last holding of British territorial sovereignty on the island, might be the ground zero for the spy novel, the place where it arrives shorn of all its romantic ambience and performative ideological jousting—retaining not even those of the bleakest corners of the Cold War. In the novels of Gerald Seymour, his loose trilogy comprising the titles *Harry's Game* (1975), *Field of Blood* (1985), and *The Journeyman Tailor* (1992), the process of disillusionment is unrelenting. With a decade separating the first and second novels and another decade separating the second and third, the stages that the war passes through define in their own way each of the three narratives, seeming to reach an impasse in the final volume in the sequence where both the British intelligence services and the Provisional Irish Republican Army (Provisional IRA) appear to have exhausted themselves, psychologically and morally, in the almost twenty years of war since *Harry's Game*.

The war in the province of Northern Ireland was further complicated by geography and international relations. Divided by water from the rest of the United Kingdom, Northern Ireland also shares a three-hundred-mile land border with the neighboring Republic of Ireland, a legacy of the Irish struggle for national independence a century ago. The Anglo-Irish Treaty of 1922 contained a crude solution to the problem of different majority loyalties in the northeast of the island of Ireland: known as Partition, the separation of the six northeastern counties left a Catholic and mostly Irish nationalist minority in a province dominated by a Protestant (Anglican and Presbyterian) and mostly unionist and loyalist population.[2] A possibly temporary but increasingly permanent state of affairs was copper-fastened in the decades that followed as the new Irish Free State (a republic since 1949) became a seamlessly Catholic and socially highly conservative society, mirroring the conservative Protestant ethos that imbued Northern Ireland with its own sense of the appropriate moral and political order.[3]

In the late 1960s, peaceful attempts to reform the province's structural discrimination against Catholics led to a hardline response on the part of the authorities and deadly attacks on Catholics by loyalist mobs in the main cities, Derry and Belfast.[4] The eventual crisis brought down the provincial government, and the British government suspended the parliament at Stormont and replaced it with direct rule from London. Some two years after this, in 1971, militant Northern Irish republicans broke from their larger all-Ireland organization over the question of armed resistance; with that the Provisional IRA was born and the war against the British Crown and, unavoidably, against the Protestant and loyalist community also, begun.[5]

As the Provisionals' campaign moved quickly from armed attacks on British army personnel and the police—the Royal Ulster Constabulary (RUC)—within the province to the bombing of both governmental and civilian targets on mainland Britain, the security threat was aggressive and unpredictable. The authorities' response was a multi-agency network involving the RUC, whose task was to supply local knowledge, the British army's own intelligence-gathering mechanisms as part of its official role of providing assistance to the civil power, and at the cutting edge the development of a Northern Ireland mission by the Security Service, known by its older title of MI5. The province being part of the United Kingdom, MI5 claimed jurisdiction, while any intelligence operations in the Republic of Ireland were within the remit of the Secret Intelligence Service (SIS), or MI6. The government of the Republic also considered the Provisional IRA a major security headache, and moved to make IRA membership, regardless of any particular crime in which an individual might be complicit, an indictable offense.[6] Finally, the existence of fringe nationalist grouplets such as the Irish National Liberation Army, which had a revolutionary socialist agenda, and loyalist paramilitary groups operating independently of any official structures, complicated the picture.[7]

The underground intelligence war that soon developed in Northern Ireland was grim and merciless. For the British security forces, especially MI5 and the RUC's counter-terrorism branch, it became the primary goal to find potential informers and agents within the ranks of militant republicans, especially within active IRA circles. For the Provisionals, it was crucial to both identify and neutralize informers and create an aura of fear that anyone guilty of informing the authorities would suffer an immediate and potentially terminal punishment.[8]

Expressed in that way, the landscape of the war was no different from what could be found in many other countries that were a theater for anticolonial struggles. What made it different, however, was the peculiar status of Northern Ireland in relation to the United Kingdom and its inexact, but also unavoidable, reflection of the larger history of Ireland's relationship with its more powerful neighbor. In the web of oddities and ironies that mark Irish history in its narrative of independence lost and won, national identity dissolved and reborn, and loyalties simple and complex, Northern Ireland is both an anomaly and a crystallization of the historical norm. It is the only part of the United Kingdom where religion and voting are connected in such an obsessional way; it was, until Stormont with its legislative authority was abolished in 1969, the only region of the United Kingdom that had a devolved parliament, decades before the Scottish or Welsh assemblies became reality; it was not, however, a political autonomy built on—as the Scottish and Welsh variants are—a general if not universally supported movement for regional independence, but rather one that underlined its loyalty to the British Crown by using its authority to suppress its Catholic and mostly Irish nationalist minority community.

To that extent, with the exception of the cities of Glasgow (Scotland) and Liverpool (northwest England), marked as they were over generations by fluctuating tensions between Catholics and Protestants, often reflected in loyalty to specific football teams, the modern British political reality had evolved so far away from that of Northern Ireland that it was difficult for many in the mainland United Kingdom to interpret the situation when the crisis erupted in the late 1960s and early 1970s. For the population of the Republic, in contrast, there was a spectrum that ranged from passionate support for the militant nationalist cause to a contempt for the Provisional IRA as a terrorist organization that, with some fudging here and there, denied the legitimacy of the Republic itself and its institutions.[9] At the very least, there was a consensus south of the border that Northern Ireland was a poisonous and unresolved dimension of modern Irish history that Britain bore a significant responsibility for, and a responsibility for resolving. Beyond the war and the political consequences, however, there was also a cultural dimension that was clear to all, or to most.

Culture, as many have found to their cost, can be a confusing thing. For everyone who arrives in another country from outside looking for a certain kind of authenticity, there is at least one inhabitant of that country who is tired of being assigned the job of delivering that authenticity. For every member of a community who values the coherence and familiarity supplied by their surroundings, there is someone else who feels constrained, and looks to the outside world for something new, something that does not necessarily arrive with the stamp of approval from one's own milieu.[10] Around the corner from every enthusiastic invocation of the specific qualities of a culture, and the need for its autonomy, there is the reality of borrowing, sharing, and pirating to create a fabric that is difficult to disentangle in order to inspect particular strands for their purity.

Which is to say, among other things, that the streets of working-class areas of Northern Ireland looked uncomfortably like the streets of working-class areas in Glasgow, Leeds, Birmingham, or Cardiff. The slight cognitive dissonance that was associated with the familiarity of the urban setting in particular was a standard accompaniment to the years of the Troubles, and became a common perception as a result of the television coverage of the conflict, especially in its early years during the 1970s. Although some Catholic and Protestant neighborhoods in Belfast and Derry were (and, to an extent, are still) distinguishable by the Irish nationalist or British unionist iconography on walls and gable-ends, the ordinary habits of life apart from religious practice were identical. Clothing, food, leisure activities, music, television preferences, and the like were largely uniform across the community divide, as they were and are, to a lesser degree, across Ireland and the United Kingdom. The one exception to this working-class cultural norming was the commitment to an older type of cultural politics among nationalists, especially involving the Irish language and sports such as hurling and Gaelic football, traditionally seen as expressing a national identity freed of the corrupting effects of British colonial rule. This nurturing of language and leisure as part of the political struggle had its roots in the Gaelic League and the Gaelic Athletic Association, or GAA, two organizations that grew quickly as part of the new Irish nationalist movement at the turn of the twentieth century.[11] Small but bitter skirmishes over leisure time and lifestyle habits marked Northern Ireland's history, such as unionist-run municipal councils refusing to open sports facilities for GAA teams on Sunday afternoons, as Protestants disapproved of Catholics playing organized games on the Lord's Day.

A more subtle reading of culture will, of course, reveal nuances, emphases, and areas of evasion that live below the surface of social activity and ostensibly common lifestyles. Even in the somewhat more muffled environment of the middle and professional classes, a name or a stray reference would reveal a Catholic or Protestant identity even if a speaker was not openly making any such declaration. And tribal belonging did not itself, at any point, completely dictate individual lives: Catholics served in the British armed forces (although rarely in Northern Ireland itself) or the RUC, or simply emigrated to mainland Britain where they were, for the vast majority of English people, indistinguishable from their Protestant counterparts doing the same.[12] Indeed, in the longer historical arc, Irish nationalist tendencies were not unknown among Protestants either, as even a brief acquaintanceship with the story of Irish independence will reveal. Romances, relationships and marriages between Catholics and Protestants in Northern Ireland also took place, although for many such couples the question of how tolerant, or not, each partner's family and community were going to be was a roll of the dice. For the outsider, much of this might be invisible; for the insider, it was a thick web of signals and recognitions and warnings, made all the more dangerous by the years of hostility and violence. In *Harry's Game*, Gerald Seymour's first novel to be set in Northern Ireland, the protagonist Harry Brown re-enters the web in the treacherous years of the early 1970s.

With the cover identity of Harry McEvoy, a local boy who has returned to Belfast after twenty years in the merchant navy, MI5 sends Brown, a British army officer stationed in West Berlin, married with two young sons, to Northern Ireland to track down and, if possible, kill Billy Downes. Downes is an IRA operative who has carried out the assassination of a former British cabinet minister in London. Brown's mission is an interesting variant on the classic story of the agent in enemy territory, as Harry Brown is, of course, still on the territory of the United Kingdom, and indeed it is his current status rather than his origin *per se* that is an invention. He has been chosen not only because he is from Northern Ireland, although not from Belfast, but because of a successful intelligence-gathering mission he performed earlier in his career during the anticolonial war in Aden in the 1960s. In Belfast, he will be returning to his origins in ways that are noteworthy for being almost in perfect step with his story rather than diverging from it. He has to pretend successfully to be something that he isn't (an ex-sailor) but also something that he is (a local returning home). His accent and vocal patterns eventually become a matter of curiosity to the Belfast IRA's intelligence section, with senior members of the organization trying to figure out whether he is genuine or not or, at least, which aspects are genuine. As the mission proceeds, Harry Brown becomes more familiar, more intimately involved with his new environment, mainly through his brief relationship with Josephine Laverty, a young Catholic woman who works at his boarding house, but he also becomes more vulnerable as clues as to his real identity begin to accumulate.

In Belfast's Falls Road, a nationalist enclave, everything is close by and people's lives are inevitably crossing each other with high frequency. One of the early set pieces in Seymour's novel is the Saturday night in the shebeen, or illegal drinking club. A British army patrol raids the club, and one of the soldiers recognizes Harry, but manages to control his reaction and not reveal anything (114). Although Brown has no idea of this, his target Billy Downes is also among the patrons in the shebeen that evening. The configuration in the club is suggestive: Harry Brown, the soldier who is recognized; Billy Downes, the IRA operative who is not recognized. When they are juxtaposed in that way, the slightly oppressive similarity of the protagonist's and antagonist's names, Brown and Downes, tightens the circle around them. Neither name is particularly Irish, in fact, and both names can be found in every corner of the Anglophone world. The accidental connections between Brown and Downes will draw the two men closer until the burst of violence and situational irony that brings *Harry's Game* to a close. The skills that Harry Brown has at his disposal are ultimately more effective than the skills Billy Downes has put at the service of the IRA in its strategy of bringing the war out of Northern Ireland to the streets of London, but they are not all-powerful.

The narrative offers some distinctive sketches of the characters in the militant nationalist milieu of the Falls, and avoids the twin traps of romanticizing the Provisionals and painting them as the mindless killers beloved of the British popular media, then and now.[13] This is itself a thorny path to negotiate and certainly is part of the explanation for the very sparse representation of the Northern Ireland conflict in literature, television drama, and film.[14] Hardly any drama, in any mode, retains much interest if a simplistic assignment of good and evil blocks the audience's investment in potential complexities of self or situation. The danger of appearing to humanize and therefore, apparently, justify an enemy such as the Provisional IRA arose out of two sources of ambiguity, one of which—the similarities between Northern Irish working-class culture and environment and those of their English counterparts—has already been discussed; the second source of ambiguity was the relatively neutral attitude on the British mainland in respect of the first battle for Irish independence a century ago. The closeness of social and family connections between the two countries provided a kind of continuing balance to compensate for the political separation in 1922, and the re-emergence of violent action by the IRA in the early 1940s and mid-1950s had been sporadic and ineffective on both sides of the Irish Sea.

Perspectives upon Ireland and its historical relationship with England are, of course, many and varied. Citizens of the United Kingdom with an Irish background (with, for example, parents who emigrated to Britain some decades ago) usually have a high level of information; in contrast, people who are less well informed may harbor any number of confused notions, from believing that all of Ireland is still part of the United Kingdom to being convinced that no part of it is.[15] In large part, however, the War of Independence between 1919 and 1921 has not been an enduring historical sore in the relationship, despite that fact that the IRA and the British forces (regular military, the police, the paramilitary Black and Tans) killed each other, and often civilians, with a dedicated passion. This was the conflict that produced Michael Collins, whose intelligence and assassination operations in Dublin, always one move ahead of the British authorities in Dublin Castle, became a textbook example of successful urban guerilla warfare in the twentieth century.

But Collins also went to London as head of the Irish nationalist negotiating team in 1921 and sat across the table from the British prime minister, David Lloyd George, and he brought home the Anglo-Irish Treaty with the clause on the separation of the six northeastern, majority-Protestant counties. Eventually Collins himself became the targeted victim of the republican rejectionist forces who would not accept the result, despite its endorsement by the Irish electorate in the twenty-six counties in the summer of 1922. Some of this history is active in Irish memory, far less so in British memory, but Partition would be the blocking agent that prevented it all from sliding into the shadowy past.

Almost fifty years after the Northern Ireland statelet was created, the relationship between Britain and Ireland, which by the 1960s had settled into a placid if sometimes prickly neighborliness, was put under considerable strain by the crisis in the North.[16] The Republic was determined both that the Catholic population in the six counties be protected from loyalist violence, and that the Provisional IRA not be permitted to simply capture the credibility and authority of the Irish nationalist cause; the British wanted to defeat the IRA, but also in such a way as to not damage the relationship with the Republic, essentially a close ally.[17] It was also clear that the wider international audience tended to view the conflict, mistakenly or not, as a classic anticolonial war against an imperial overlord.[18]

In terms of the cultural politics of that era, therefore, there was a kind of joint Anglo-Irish fear of both demonizing the militant republican movement and, at the other extreme, domesticating it by showing its leaders, for example, to be more like calculating strategists with a graspable cause than fanatics or psychopaths. This accounts, at least in part, for the fact that one of the noticeable things about *Harry's Game*, and in particular its British television adaptation in 1982, is the way it stood out as a somewhat isolated production. The theme music by the Irish traditional group Clannad, which became an international success for the band, was itself a significant contribution to the adaptation.[19] It embodies beautifully the mesh of contradictions that haunt popular storytelling about the Northern Ireland conflict: a narrative in which an Irishman in the British army is sent to Belfast to hunt down the killer of a senior British politician, written by an English reporter-turned-novelist and later filmed by a British television company, is given its sharpest cultural edge by a song sung in Gaelic by one of the most high-profile groups working in Irish folk and traditional music at the time. And yet the grim resolution of the story of *Harry's Game*, both novel and adaptation, is marked by irony, contingency, and the sense that the "game" of the title is a kind of trap where losing and winning are pointlessly entangled. The price that Harry Brown pays to terminate Billy Downes and his potential future missions is delivered by soldiers in a British army observation post watching the Falls Road who fail to understand what they are seeing take place. The haunting notes and vocals of the Clannad song that closes the drama are a lament for a situation more than anything.

In Seymour's next novel about Ireland, *Field of Blood*, which appeared a decade after *Harry's Game*, the political and emotional landscapes of the war have both been altered. While the first novel portrayed the early 1970s, an era in which the conflict was new, the sides to some degree not completely fixed in place, *Field of Blood* is a setting marked by a mechanical process into which both the IRA and the British forces have slid: knowing the enemy's weak spots, maintaining the moral and operational viability of one's own side, and seeking even a small edge to exploit in the day-by-day procedures of low-intensity warfare in urban and rural communities.

The protagonists in this novel form a parallel of sorts to Harry Brown and Billy Downes in *Harry's Game*, but the divergences from their forerunners are noticeable. Harry Brown was a special forces soldier, while David Ferris is a junior regular army officer who has, so far, failed to be accepted into the Special Air Service (SAS). On the other side of the fence is Sean "Gingy" McAnally, who is, in contrast to the risk-taking Billy Downes, a technician with weapons rather than a romantic republican fighter, and seems to have settled into a dull and listless routine in the Republic of Ireland when he is recalled by the IRA's Belfast command to carry out a special task. The consequences of this mission will include, among other things, a long and awkward relationship between Sean McAnally and David Ferris as the latter tries to protect and encourage the former on his journey to testify in court against his republican comrades.

For this is now the era of the "supergrass." By the early 1980s, British intelligence efforts in Northern Ireland and on the British mainland, spearheaded by the Security Service, had succeeded in penetrating the IRA up to relatively senior levels via an array of methods: sometimes money; sometimes a guarantee of no prosecution for offenses; sometimes pressures relating to family or personal life; sometimes probing doubts about the armed struggle itself; often a combination of all four. Although the primary purpose was intelligence gathering, the possibility of large-scale prosecutions in court and the conviction of groups of defendants was tempting for the British government. For one, it would degrade the morale of the Provisional IRA to know that its ranks had been undermined from the inside; for another, it was an opportunity to show that the war in Northern Ireland was actually against criminals, terrorists who could be arraigned in court, and not an army of freedom fighters as they liked to view themselves. For this purpose, a knowledgeable witness who could plausibly testify against a number of IRA suspects, who would have an insider's facts and dates at his fingertips, and who could explain the movement's command structures and operational habits, was required. Such a figure became known as a supergrass.[20]

A significant mythology, some of which still surfaces today, surrounds the history of MI5's and the RUC Special Branch's penetration of senior republican circles including the Provisionals' military chain of command. Conspiracy theories concerning the road toward the Good Friday Agreement of 1999, which officially ended hostilities, wove suspicions around senior IRA and Sinn Féin leaders, even such well-known and politically active figures as Martin McGuinness and Gerry Adams, suggesting that they themselves were agents of the British for shorter or longer periods during the conflict.[21] As far as the factual accuracy goes, the question is not a theme for this study, but I would argue that *Field of Blood* presents a close-up of the most sensitive issue that affected the republican movement over thirty years, and still resonates today.

Thus, as happened with many armed and even peaceful anti-colonial movements in various parts of the world, the vision of a dedicated, idealistic cadre of volunteers committed to the cause of the nation was often disrupted by the reality of informers in the ranks, moved by either personal gain, hope for better treatment by the authorities, or even some ideological wavering. The novel's central character, Sean McAnally, represents at least the first two of these considerations as they play out over the course of the narrative. The man who becomes his protector, Captain David Ferris, is a British army officer but one who is not closed to trying to understand McAnally's motivations. Gingy McAnally is, however, a somewhat confused mixture of the average sensual man, a working-class Catholic also attuned to the hostility and discrimination he grew up with in Northern Ireland in the 1950s and 1960s, and a good weapons technician, something like a capable NCO to have running a small armored unit, who doesn't overthink the politics and follows the orders he is given.

Indeed, in contrast to *Harry's Game*, which has to some extent the atmosphere of a situation still evolving, the world of *Field of*

Blood is locked in place and geared to procedure. Nobody has to particularly believe in anything: people just have to do their jobs. Where this meets its limits, however, is within the family and the smaller community that surrounds it. McAnally's wife Roisin, mother of their three children, becomes the human battleground upon which this conflict-within-a-conflict unfolds. As the operation to protect McAnally from the Provisional IRA, who now realize he has gone over to the other side, is built up, Roisin and the children are brought to a safe house to be with him. Eventually, however, she cannot bear the confusion of feelings she has toward him and the increasing alienation from both their families and her neighborhood. Gingy McAnally has become, of course, a traitor not only to his organization but also to the wider nationalist community. While there is an old joke in Ireland about no political organization being complete without its informer, no crime in militant nationalist circles was ever treated with more horror and detestation than informing on one's comrades to the authorities (whether British or, after independence, Irish). The literary treatment of the theme in the modern era begins with Liam O'Flaherty's 1925 novel *The Informer*, in which a slow-witted member of a revolutionary group betrays his comrades for a confused mix of motives, including money, but money used to pay for his girlfriend to leave Ireland for the United States.

That a set of small, interacting motives might be the driver of the decision to testify against former comrades, rather than one overriding or even idealistic motive, is something that *Field of Blood*, at a couple of removes, inherits from O'Flaherty's novel of two generations earlier. Of course, the British MI5, the RUC Special Branch, and various other players at the fringes of the operation all have an interest in the outcome and therefore an interest in nurturing whichever strand within the mesh of motives Gingy is feeling particularly strongly on any given day. Money on a long-term basis, a future for Roisin and the kids, a new identity, a kind of grudging respect from the British enemy who have to recognize his importance—all of these cycle through his mind as potential justifications for the act of betrayal, an act that he knows is considered by his own community to be below contempt. David Ferris alone seems to be interested in finding a deeper or more ethically subtle dimension to McAnally's path toward the courtroom as he "gushed his recollections to his interrogators" (117).

Ferris, who will pay the price for protecting and nurturing his supergrass, is himself increasingly filled with doubts as to the efficacy and ultimate sense of the British military campaign in Northern

Ireland. Searching for something going on inside McAnally, he discovers more and more going on inside himself: he questions his role as an army officer and how committed he is to any future the service might offer him. Like Harry Brown in *Harry's Game*, Ferris is ultimately a counter moved around the board of the Troubles by larger, more distant players, and the very success of their gambit will lead to him being simply taken off the board, as it were, when his luck runs out. Mourned by few beyond his parents and fiancée in England, although possibly by Gingy McAnally, David Ferris will never have truly departed the field.

In the third novel of the sequence, *The Journeyman Tailor*, Seymour re-enters the theater of endless hostility that Northern Ireland has become over the twenty-odd years since the political and security crisis emerged in the late 1960s. While *Harry's Game* plays out in Belfast's Falls Road, and *Field of Blood* in various safe houses and other interiors, *The Journeyman Tailor* is set among the hills and small towns of rural County Tyrone, a landscape where an icy patina of politeness barely hides the fear and the inter-community hostility that define the social and cultural map of the area. The local Catholics mostly detest the British forces; the British army, MI5, and the RUC see this as essentially enemy territory; the IRA has active but also much passive support, from people who don't want to get into trouble; local Protestants, all unionists, dislike and fear the militant nationalists but want to avoid becoming IRA targets themselves.

Again, Gerald Seymour represents a minority of authors in bringing his espionage fiction into play against the background of this war. It can be underlined once more that the place where guerilla units, armed military, MI5, and a militarized local police force conduct their activities is the territory of the United Kingdom: in other words, home, and yet not quite home. A resilient mix of national identity, cultural belonging, and religious community feeling has sunk into the groundwater of the conflict, made all the more painful because of the fact that the place is home to not only the two main traditions, nationalist and unionist, but also to those who step onto treacherous ground by trying to escape the clutches of either, or both. *The Journeyman Tailor* is perhaps the singular item of evidence that the reason why espionage fiction has been relatively unconcerned with Northern Ireland is that there is nothing much to mine there—no "Great Game" with global significance, no complex missions, no exotic locations, nothing much except the same streets, pubs, and fields as back across the Irish Sea.

The narrative line of *The Journeyman Tailor* is traced by the unfolding psychological education of Gary Brenner, delivered as a series of shocks to his moral sensibility. A junior and inexperienced intelligence officer who insists on being called Bren, he is posted to Belfast at short notice to work with a key figure in the Northern Ireland station called Parker. Parker is spoken of in admiring terms by the senior MI5 managers, and Brenner assumes that he is going to meet a tough operations veteran with a reputation for both ruthlessness and results. He prepares himself to be reviewed critically when he gets to his new duty station.

The Journeyman Tailor is a narrative of covert achievements, and of the price paid for such achievements which may be so high as to blur, at least, the distinction between success and failure. The novel is structured around a movement back and forth between opposing and hostile worlds: the universe of the British intelligence operations in the province of Northern Ireland, with their matrix of supposedly efficiently interlocking systems, the army, the SAS, the police, and MI5, organizations that are in reality often deeply at odds over how to prosecute the war against the Provisional IRA; the opposing cosmos of the IRA and its local chain of command, at home in the lanes and hills and farms of East Tyrone and the Catholic community on Altmore Mountain; between them the delicate operation to penetrate and undermine the IRA by way of the high-level informer Song Bird, the source of crucial intelligence from inside the leadership of the Provisionals' East Tyrone Brigade.

The dominant focalizing characters in the novel are Brenner and Mossie Nugent, both, though in different senses, dependent upon Parker, Bren for his approval to London as a Security Service officer qualified to operate in Northern Ireland, Song Bird for his money and his safety: their perspectives are essential to the map of each milieu that the reader is given. Bren is on the one hand used to covering his real identity and creating a new personality for himself, and on the other hand his hidden insecurities mark him as an odd man out who continually makes missteps when he arrives in Belfast. A working-class boy who made it to one of the better universities, he had created a new self:

> he had let it be known that anyone who cared to speak to him that his name was "Bren." "Gary" was buried, a terraced house in Filton went down the drain, a father who worked as a minibus driver for British Aerospace and a mother who loaded the dishwasher in the canteen were off limits. (40)

Unsure why exactly he has been selected for the assignment to what his superior calls "that dreadful country" (17), Bren embraces the opportunity and arrives in Northern Ireland fired up by a desire to prove himself, although he is notably unprepared for the social and operational environment into which he is suddenly plunged.[22]

Upon arrival at Aldergrove airport, Brenner is surprised to discover that the capable and experienced Parker he is expecting is in fact a young woman, Cathy Parker. She makes it clear immediately that Bren, already recovering from confusion due to his first mistaken assumption, has now landed in a territory he has little knowledge about, and in which he is vulnerable to making dangerous errors of judgment. Keeping a firearm within arm's reach as they drive out of the car park, she explains that the Provisionals have people who keep an eye out for passengers arriving from London who might not be what they seem. It is Bren's first lesson that the fact that Belfast is in the United Kingdom does not necessarily make it familiar in any meaningful sense he might imagine.

Mossie Nugent's overriding challenge involves more immediate dangers: above all, he has to compartmentalize his two identities as the intelligence officer for the active service unit of the IRA East Tyrone Brigade, and as Song Bird, an informant paid and protected by MI5 who provides the British with regular information on IRA planning and prospective targets. He knows that the risks involved in this activity are existential: the Provisionals are determined to seek out and remove informers, and suspicions can be easily raised. Torture and a gunshot to the head are the consequence if the IRA believes it has found a "tout." The body at the side of the road can be the result of a mistake or misdirection, however, as the fate of the young Patsy Riordan, a low-level and somewhat dimwitted IRA volunteer, reveals: a mixture of cluelessness on the boy's part and the well-timed manipulation of suspicions inside the brigade by Mossie Nugent lead to Patsy's interrogation and eventual execution by the IRA's own counter-intelligence section.

In contrast to the unrelenting pressure that accompanies Song Bird each day, always on the cusp of a mistake that can cost him his life, Bren's ability to find himself in awkward situations is often the stuff of social comedy rather than guerilla warfare. In his first few days in Northern Ireland, he is assigned a room in a shared house in Belfast maintained for MI5 and other covert operations staff. Discovering he has no coffee in his quarters, he knocks on a neighboring door and is greeted by a disheveled man with a beard and long hair, looking as if he belongs in a homeless shelter, in a room containing mud-stained clothes and a rifle with a night-sight. He treats Bren's nervous request for coffee with an expression of disbelief but finds a tin to give him. When the man mentions Parker, Bren makes another faux pas when he comments that he hadn't expected to find a woman doing this kind of work, which provokes a scornful reply:

> "I don't know who you are, squire, and I don't know what you know, but I'll tell you something. There's men here who would go through walls for that woman, got me?"
> "Yes, I only meant . . ."
> "And go through fire . . . Do you know *Henry IV, Part 2*?"
> "No."
> "Me neither, so be a good fellow and piss off and let me get into it." (84)

Dispatched with a snippy cultural gesture toward Shakespeare and English history by an SAS officer who has immediately wrong-footed him and judged him as potentially inadequate, Bren feels that he is creating impression upon negative impression, and contributing to what he is afraid might be a highly critical evaluation of his capabilities.

He also discovers that what is demanded of him is not only operational expertise but also a strong stomach for ruthless decisions that go beyond the limits he intuitively feels are to be observed even in the kind of covert warfare that the struggle in Northern Ireland demands. Early in the narrative, he describes himself as "a junior Executive Officer of the Security Service" (56) and feels himself to be someone special, not just another passenger disembarking from the plane at Aldergrove. A paragraph or two later, Bren finds the identical thought returning: "he was different, because he was a junior Executive Officer of Five" and he feels "the gush of pleasured excitement" (57). The repetition of his self-directed reassurance is, in an obvious way, not reassuring, as if he is aware both of the privilege of his position and yet also of its potential fragility. A little later, he is given the file with the policy and tactics for running the intelligence operation on Altmore Mountain and begins to sense the nature of the mission: "The place had terrified him, and all he had done was read" (80).

Bren's actual experience fills out his premonitions: meeting Song Bird for the first time, he is somewhat in awe of Cathy's ability to toggle back and forth between cajoling and encouraging her source, and instructing him clearly as to the fact that she is in charge of everything, including any decision to release him from his contract, but also of Song Bird's almost superhuman ability to compartmentalize his roles as IRA officer and informer for the enemy. At one point, he asks her "how does he stand it?" and Cathy replies that she doesn't know or care, that she is only interested in what he can deliver (96). What Song Bird can deliver, and what he ultimately succeeds in doing, is organizing the return to Northern Ireland of the Provisional IRA's best asset on the British mainland, Jon Jo Donnelly, whose expertise with explosives and weapons has enabled a string of bombings and attempted assassinations, including a recent bomb at Marylebone Station in London that killed several commuters waiting for their trains. If Bren and Mossie are in a curious way each other's opposite in their dependent relationship on Cathy Parker, then her opposite is Jon Jo Donnelly, whose single-minded and merciless dedication to the mission mirrors hers. In a striking moment, Cathy lays out from Bren an analysis, if not an indictment, of the peculiar asymmetry built into their situation as combatants in the struggle. Noting the Provisionals' lack of technology and organizational substance when set against the vast array of tools available to the British government, she says:

> "God knows what the percentage is of people over here who are just *indexing* the war. You can't index war and keep up with it, any more than you can index fog. I don't suppose Clausewitz said that, but if he'd been in Northern bloody Ireland he'd have said it alright." (303)

In her own way, Cathy has produced the now classic assessment of the potential for a guerilla warfare campaign to succeed against ostensibly massive odds: not only can you not index the fog, but fighting it also poses immense difficulties. The classic counter-insurgency praxis involves actions like the army's invasive search of Attracta Donnelly's house and farm, essentially punishing her for being married to her husband and guaranteed to further alienate the Catholic community on Altmore. Cathy Parker and the Security Service's alternative path—nurturing informers inside the IRA—leads to the deadly paradox, however, of permitting a particular Provisional operation to go ahead in order to protect the credibility of the source, sometimes with a fatal outcome for one or both sides.

The Journeyman Tailor is not only a novel of covert achievements, whatever their price, but also one of intimacy, whatever price that too may exact. The rediscovered intimacy between Mossie and his wife Siobhan follows Siobhan's discovery of the hidden bank book with the regular payments and the emergency alert device that Mossie can use if he is in sudden danger. Trying to calculate her husband's importance to the British authorities and the chances the extra income could offer the family against his role as a hated and despised informer, she finds herself drawn closer to him for the immense burden of secrecy that he lives and works under. The one night on which Cathy and Bren sleep together is in many ways less intimate than their long hours lying pressed together in the tiny camouflaged observation post next to a hedge out on the mountain, including having to use a metal bowl with a foil covering as a toilet and making sure to carry away all waste with them when they leave.[23] When Siobhan Nugent approaches Cathy Parker directly to talk about the danger Mossie is in, Cathy wins her over, achieving a woman-to-woman intimacy with the time-honored method of admiring her family: "Super children, Siobhan, you must be very proud. No worries now, I'll see you're safe" (162).

In this as in other novels, Seymour reveals his ability to use free indirect discourse to create a space for an understanding of mutually hostile world-views. Extended representation without narrator commentary of the flow of thoughts and feelings within different characters creates new frameworks for grasping motive and perspective, giving increased depth to characters across the lines of the conflict. Through this window, the reader glimpses Mossie Nugent's memories and resentments as he thinks about how he got into a difficult situation with the police after a drinking-and-driving incident in England and was rescued by Cathy Parker, and how he was persuaded and induced to return to Northern Ireland, reconnect with his Provisional IRA comrades, and eventually become Song Bird. Through the window we also accompany Siobhan Nugent's struggle to balance her new respect for her husband with her instinctive certainty that they have breached a basic principle of the nationalist community that can have fatal consequences, consequences that have already led to the death of the wrongly suspected Patsy Riordan.

To glimpse the existence of deeply rooted but alien beliefs is at least, however, to be compelled to recognize their reality if not their validity. The binding power of nationalist memory is also manifest in the episodic tale of the patriotic hero Shane Bearnagh Donnelly, whose legend from two centuries ago makes him implicitly a forebear of Jon Jo, that Attracta Donnelly tells her son Kevin each night before he goes to sleep. The story within a story, a tale of a noble cause and a heroic figure from romantic history, is set in ironic juxtaposition to the bombing of civilian targets, the ruthlessness of the intelligence war, and other sordid aspects of the contemporary British war in Ireland.

At the conclusion, after Jon Jo Donnelly has been wounded by Bren and finished off by an SAS man, the reader is left with Bren's moral exhaustion. And now certain that Mossie is the tout even before he leads Jon Jo into the trap, the IRA team call at his house and lift him, taking Siobhan with them after she tries to physically drag her husband from the car. As Cathy, Bren, and a British army unit inspect the Nugents' house the next morning, a report comes in stating that two bodies have been found further south, near the border with the Republic. Bren sees as if in a vision Cathy's encounter with the consequences of her work: "When the bags had been cut away from the heads of the bodies she would look down into the faces of her Song Bird and her Song Bird's woman" (361). His own decision is to request early termination of his posting and a return to London, so that he can go home before he is "destroyed," in his own words (360). She accepts this, expressing some regret and noting that he is probably undermining his own career prospects in the service. "But," she says, "you'll have thought that through" (360).

In the mirroring and doubling that mark Gerald Seymour's narratives of the Troubles, the relationships and interactions become more complex and more traumatic. Harry Brown and Billy Downes are relatively distinct as they move along the tracks that will ultimately converge in violence. Gingy McAnally and Captain David Ferris in *Field of Blood* have a more frustrating connection, entangled in failure to escape the clutches of the war, and only one of them surviving to, in a literal sense, testify. In *The Journeyman Tailor*, Northern Ireland is both home and not-home, British and Irish, elements of familiarity hiding implacable difference. The strategy in the covert war is divide and rule, but divides can rule in other ways: Bren's status as MI5 officer subverted by his hidden working-class past that he is in some way ashamed of, and ashamed that he is ashamed; Mossie Nugent's split consciousness as senior IRA volunteer in the East Tyrone Brigade and simultaneously invaluable British agent; Cathy Parker and Jon Jo Donnelly, for whom the mission is everything, rendering all ethical limits inactive; Jon Jo's innocent victims in the bombing of Marylebone Station and the heroic folktale of his eighteenth-century namesake.

Is the war in Northern Ireland "terrifying," as the narrator comments, "because it was incomprehensible in its brutality and its apparent irrelevance to the twentieth century" (56)? In a literary work, as J. Hillis Miller notes, the reality we experience as readers is a fictional creation of language, so the work cannot be inspected or evaluated merely as to its equivalence to the facts of history or the nature of the contemporary world.[24] In fact, the aim of Seymour's novels appears to be far more to create the possibility of empathetic understanding of otherwise incompatible positions, political and ethical judgments that would be very difficult to reconcile in lived reality. In *The Journeyman Tailor*, however, the twentieth-century espionage novel may have reached something of a cul-de-sac, or a ground zero, as it fictionalizes the kind of struggle that is confused and rendered insoluble by the shared territory of hostility and familiarity that the parties to that conflict both occupy.

Notes

1. Although it is an older and more general euphemism for conflict, "Troubles" has become identified with the political divisions and armed violence in Northern Ireland between 1967 and the late 1990s. The term suggests something beyond civil unrest but short of outright war.
2. The Anglo-Irish Treaty of 1922 created the new Irish Free State but carved out the six northeastern counties which had a distinct Protestant and unionist majority; they would stay part of the United Kingdom. It was unclear then for how long this solution would be in existence, and remains so.
3. The confessional nature of Northern Ireland was made clear in 1934 by its first prime minister James Craig when he boasted that unionists had secured "a Protestant parliament and a Protestant state"; the Irish Free State was, in contrast, nominally free of any institutional religious discrimination, but the 1937 Constitution, strongly favored by Taoiseach (Prime Minister) Eamon de Valera, legitimized the actual power and influence of the Catholic Church, giving it significant authority in education and social policy, and thus deepened the cultural as well as the national divide.
4. Discrimination in housing allocation was one of the primary drivers of the Northern Ireland Civil Rights Association, founded in 1967. For an account of growing up as a Catholic boy in Derry in the late 1940s and 1950s, see Eamonn McCann's *War and an Irish Town*, 65–82; written with analytic energy and much humor, McCann's book is a Marxist analysis of Northern Ireland like no other.
5. In this chapter, I use "nationalist" and "republican" interchangeably, and likewise "unionist" and "loyalist"; "Catholic" and "Protestant" appear where required; and "Irish" and "British" are used as general labels that should be clear from the relevant context (so Northern loyalists are Irish in the sense of being born on the island of Ireland, but British by citizenship and ideological choice).

6. Among other policies, the Irish government invoked Section 31 of the Broadcasting Act to ban interviews and statements from members of the IRA or its political party Sinn Féin on national television and radio. The censorship rule was active from 1968 until 1994, and was tougher than even the British government's policy as it blocked statements on any topic at all, not just on Northern Ireland.
7. It was the consensus that armed loyalist organizations such as the Ulster Freedom Fighters were particularly given to targeting and killing individual Catholics who were innocent of any connection to the Provisionals or the Irish National Liberation Army; however, in recent years it has become clearer that the IRA also targeted individuals in both communities with little or no justification other than suspicion or a drive for tribal revenge.
8. The term "informer" could be applied generously, and being suspected of sympathizing with the authorities or engaging in behavior seen as hostile (for example, a romantic attachment to a policeman or British soldier) could bring ostracization, if not worse.
9. One of the complexities of the Irish national history can be gauged by the fact that militant republicans contest the legitimacy of the Irish Republic as declared by the government in 1949. Both Northern Ireland republicans and Northern Ireland loyalists had specific terminology for denigrating the Republic: republicans would continually refer to "the Free State," the entity that existed from 1922 to 1949, implying that the 1949 declaration was invalid; loyalists would talk about "the Dublin government," underlining that it exercised no authority in the Six Counties.
10. Perhaps the real proportion is more like ten to one? But the larger point is that "community" is a term often misused to indicate a group of people who are assumed to have no disagreements on significant issues. In reporting on Northern Ireland, the media reinforced the notion of entrenched attitudes (which was a reasonable perspective) but failed to explain the more complicated history of Ireland and England (which offered too much detail for a media narrative), so the war appeared to be simply an endless cycle of dueling resentments.
11. The Gaelic Athletic Association was founded in 1884, and the Gaelic League (oriented toward language and culture) in 1893. Both organizations still exist today.
12. Kenneth Branagh's successful semi-autobiographical film *Belfast* (2021) makes a noticeable effort to emphasize a common social environment in which religion was the only major difference, but some critical voices have argued that he makes it seem as if the civil violence was a result of misunderstandings rather than deeply opposed experiences and attitudes.
13. Even a superficial review of the British popular press during those decades will discover a basic narrative that fanatical extremism was the only thing that could explain the IRA's actions; in fact, in certain ways,

its strategy for violence was controlled and sometimes highly selective in its targeting. In his book *Fiction and the Northern Ireland Troubles since 1969*, Elmer Kennedy-Andrews comments that the "conservativism of *Harry's Game* is easily discernable" (55), but this assessment seems to ignore the extent to which the nationalist perspective is illuminated in the novel. Curiously, Elmer Kennedy-Andrews believes Harry Brown comes from a Catholic background (53), whereas Aaron Kelly in *The Thriller in Northern Ireland* thinks he's a Protestant (49).

14. In more recent times there have been feature films, both fictional and historical, such as *'71* (2014; dir. Yann Demange) and *Bloody Sunday* (2002; dir. Paul Greengrass), that have begun to fill in the gaps.

15. The persistent use of the now somewhat rare "Éire" as the preferred name of the country (which was more common during the years of the Irish Free State between 1922 and 1949) among an older generation in Britain suggests the somewhat awkward relationship between the two countries in the years following independence, when the studied use of that name could mean anything from an attempt at courtesy to unspoken hostility.

16. The Irish Constitution contained clauses (Articles 2 and 3) that asserted the de jure claim to the whole island of Ireland, but this remained, for almost all parties, an idealist goal with no likelihood of achievement in the foreseeable future. It did provide, however, a certain abstract legitimacy to the campaign by the Provisional IRA and its political wing Sinn Féin. Articles 2 and 3 were amended in 1999 as a result of the Good Friday Agreement and the referendum held in both parts of Ireland the previous year. Notwithstanding this, Sinn Féin has made major gains in political strength, in both Northern Ireland and the Republic, over the last twenty years.

17. It is often overlooked in accounts of the Troubles that the historical legacy of Ireland's connection to the United Kingdom includes many special reciprocal arrangements such as travel, residency, and voting rights, most of which are more generous than what usually obtains between two neighboring countries. Both Ireland and the United Kingdom joined the European Union (then the EEC) in 1973, although the United Kingdom has now withdrawn as a consequence of the Brexit referendum in 2016.

18. Not only on the political left, of course, as American support for the IRA (via the active and well-funded network NORAID) was not really ideologically in tune with militant Irish nationalism in the modern era, which has been distinctively a socialist movement as regards economic theory, and has seen itself as allied with armed revolutionary movements worldwide.

19. *Harry's Game* (1982; Yorkshire Television). The song by Clannad is available on CD and online: www.youtube.com/watch?v=4zHTcxVjX0I (accessed May 14, 2023).

20. The term is not particularly Irish: "grassing" or "to grass someone up" means to inform on someone to the police, with the implication of insider knowledge. Television and crime fiction in the 1970s brought the word into more popular usage. The word "tout" remained the more common term for informer in nationalist circles. See Steven Greer, *Supergrasses*, for a succinct history of this policy and its impact, especially chapter 2, "Origins of the Supergrass System: 1969–1982."
21. There is a large body of commentary and analysis, online and in print, going into the possibility of Martin McGuinness having been a British intelligence asset; before his death in 2017 McGuinness always denied this charge, but it remains a fact that senior figures in the IRA were proven to have been supplying intelligence to the security forces.
22. Aaron Kelly argues that "enlightened English civility" is emphasized by "the projection of Northern Ireland as an atavistic backwater" in the novel (45, n. 32); the question is a little more complex, however, because if Bren is the character vehicle for this cultural mode, he is shown as a somewhat weak figure, partly because his own class-rooted insecurities make his civility defensive rather than enlightened.
23. Cathy's rueful apology that she ate "too many sausages" at breakfast and has to use the metal dish inside the hideout (148) might make Gerald Seymour the unchallenged kitchen-sink realist of the espionage fiction tradition.
24. In his essay in *Others* on Conrad's story "The Secret Sharer," Miller argues that the question of evidence for the reality of literary realism is a difficult one, "since a work of fiction proves nothing about the historical existence of the things it names" (140). To that extent, it is somewhat of a secular leap of faith to accept that Seymour's fiction captures more complex and indeed more emotionally compelling dimensions of the war in Northern Ireland than many documentary accounts. I admit to making that leap, in any case.

Chapter 8

Espionage Fiction and the Lost Adversary: Carlyle and Mathison

The story of Judith of Bethulia and the Assyrian king Holofernes is narrated in the biblical Book of Judith, a deuterocanonical text accepted by the Catholic and Eastern Orthodox churches but not included in the Hebrew Canon and generally considered by Protestants to belong to the Apocrypha. In the story of Judith's successful penetration of the enemy camp, and her seduction and beheading of Holofernes, there are some resonances with the more contemporary history of women and espionage. The Judith author goes to some lengths to emphasize that, whatever happened when the wealthy and beautiful widow Judith and the gullible sensualist Holofernes were alone together in his tent, Judith remained pure and untainted by the experience. She carried out her self-determined mission to save the Jewish population of Bethulia as a sacred duty to God. For a number of reasons, including perhaps the distinctly courageous and resourceful character of the main protagonist, creative artists over the centuries have been intrigued by Judith and have speculated about details and aspects of the biblical account that may be lurking between the lines of the text.

The poem "Judith of Bethulia" by the American poet John Crowe Ransom, for example, probes the post-conflict situation with the elders of the city as they worry about the implications of both Judith's actions to save the city and her apparent disinterest in remarrying, as it is now several years since her husband died. As the speaker of the poem notes, "a wandering beauty is a blade out of its scabbard," and even the military success her mission brought the Hebrew community cannot dispel the mix of prurient curiosity and disapproving fascination that follows her around. Judith went, the speaker reassures himself, recalling some official communiqué, "reluctant to that orgy," but he cannot help but notice that the men, young and old, are endlessly given to imagining—even if they won't admit it—what went on in the tent that night.[1] The central implication of Ransom's poem is that, from a male perspective, a woman cannot be imagined to have used her femininity and her sexuality for a tactical political or strategic purpose without the suspicion among her own people that she might either have enjoyed it too much or, more worryingly, be using those assets now. The long history of concern over the appropriate fields of competition and conflict for women has not necessarily come to its end merely because we now have contemporary bureaucratic institutions dedicated to gender equity. The female protagonists Liz Carlyle in Stella Rimington's novel *At Risk* and Carrie Mathison in the television series *Homeland*, in their different ways, confront the persistence of assumptions and mount a struggle with tradition in the realm of the espionage narrative. In this sense, content and convention are as force and inertia within the equilibrium of the work, staging the social and ideological drama of changing values within and between systems.

The figure of the adversary in espionage fiction in the twentieth century has often represented the hostile power with whom one does not want to go to war in the traditional manner. It is noticeable that during the Cold War a central justification for expenditures on intelligence gathering and covert operations of one kind or another was that these efforts were exactly what could prevent actual war from breaking out. In the age of the razor-edge nuclear standoff, focused intelligence work could identify and potentially neutralize conflicts that might, in some circumstances, grow into something more menacing. And, even if they could not be neutralized, they might be contained in a way that reflected the global ideological struggle between the West and the communist world—hence satisfying the need for political lines in the sand—without endangering the rest of humanity. As a frustrated Alec Leamas says to Liz Gold at the end of *The Spy Who Came In from the Cold*, the espionage war is "graphic and unpleasant" because it takes place on such a small and intimate scale, "But it's nothing, nothing at all beside other wars—the last or the next" (204).

Many parts of the world from Southeast Asia to central Europe became the arenas for these subordinated conflicts. In what has come to be called the Global South, however, political divisions could slide into paramilitary or, occasionally, more traditional military confrontation, often too in circumstances where a large section of the population was hesitant to be recruited into the ideological struggles of modernity – or, more accurately perhaps, where there was an authentic battle of ideas taking place in one or other nation or region, but one often defined by local frameworks within which it could be better understood and even potentially resolved. To that extent, the Vietnam wars in their unfolding over the years from the Japanese occupation of the colonial territory of French Indochina in World War II to the collapse of the Republic of South Vietnam in 1975 were understood by the more acute observers to be a struggle over independence: not over the principle of national autonomy itself, but rather about the character of the postcolonial nation that Vietnam would become. In the late 1940s the Viet Minh was a broad-based nationalist movement operating with the goal of removing French colonial rule from its country. Its bourgeois and communist strands co-existed, uneasily but pragmatically, with an old Vietnamese suspicion of China (and the Soviet relationship with communist China before the split made even Vietnamese communists a bit cautious) and a willingness to put victory over the French before other ideological goals.[2]

For the United States and particularly its military and foreign policy establishment, however, the notion of the struggle in Indochina as essentially an anticolonial war followed by a civil conflict over the type of society that the liberated nation would build was both naïve and dangerous: naïve, because it ignored the evidence of communist expansion under the guise of nationalist movements, and dangerous because to accept the idea of local conflicts having their own dynamic, not necessarily locked into the machinery of the Cold War, would be to weaken the justification for political involvement and military intervention. As this perspective put down increasingly deep and unshakeable roots in the political culture of the era, many other crisis points across the world began to have an outline or silhouette noticeably similar to that of the Vietnam War.

The eruption of the Iranian Islamist revolution onto the world stage in 1979 was one of the major signals of a new turn in modern history that, among other effects, significantly confounded categories that had become comfortably recognizable and usable since World War II. With its rejection of both democratic liberal capitalism and Soviet or Chinese communism, the new fundamentalist leadership drew a different map of ideological loyalty and identity across both the region and, to the large extent, the greater global neighborhood, which already during the late 1980s was marked by the presence of the vast, encompassing networks of communication and information that are part of normality in the early twenty-first century.

Although the full extent of the transformation was not on show until the collapse of the Soviet Union and the end of the Cold War, the fact of the ideological crumbling of that system was felt in the world of espionage fiction as it was in reality. Indeed, it was not entirely a welcome development: a department of literary culture that had, at is best, probed the subtleties of the post-1945 world order with some balance and sensitivity had not been prepared to be suddenly confronted with the rise of religious dogma as a central driver of global conflict. In some ways, the emergence of a new theater of political and ideological struggle of this kind seemed to threaten to push the spy story back toward the gauche orientalism of its earliest phase of development in the Indian summer of European imperialism and the menacing specter of international anarchism.[3] The very secularity of the genre mirrored the Cold War as a conflict between two modes of the rational exercise of political power in a desacralized social environment. Neither communism nor capitalist democracy promised a redemptive moment outside history and human time; religious faith in the West was mostly, even in very Catholic countries, a private matter; and if ever Soviet communism had harbored a millenarian vision for the future of humanity, it had certainly long since been numbed or eradicated by bureaucratic proceduralism.

There are some exceptions. The Middle East and the Israel–Palestine conflict represented a situation located, to an extent, outside the classic framework of Cold War narratives, and a small number of authors had found this to be fertile ground for espionage fiction well before the 1990s.[4] John le Carré had explored this setting and the kind of drama it gave rise to in *The Little Drummer Girl* (1983), but it is perhaps the striking individuality of this novel that shows up the absence of competitors.[5] In addition, for much of the late twentieth century, the central Middle East conflict was regarded from the outside, at least, as one of competing nationalisms, a concept easily grasped within the historical arms of modern political theory. The question of religious belief seemed more a matter of demographic analysis than of theological consequence. In this connection, however, the 1987 novel *Agents of Innocence* by David Ignatius is worth a brief discussion here, despite its more conventional male protagonist.

In *Agents of Innocence*, the Middle East conflict is a framework in which the basic dynamic of the Cold War has been, if not neutralized, at least marginalized. The novel's protagonist Tom Rogers, a young Kennedy-esque Central Intelligence Agency officer, takes over a slot in the Beirut station in 1969, and the story follows his attempts to find intelligence sources within the Palestinian leadership who are willing to work with the United States, in particular to identify and suppress random terrorist acts that do nothing for the broader national cause. *Agents of Innocence* terminates in 1984, when the situation in Lebanon has become more chaotic and destructive, and the possibility of an American–Palestinian understanding has been rendered next to impossible, not only because of a more militant approach to the conflict by both the Palestine Liberation Organization (PLO) and the more aggressive Popular Front for the Liberation of Palestine, but also as a result of Israeli influence at the higher levels of US intelligence. The 1980s are no place for the breezy confidence with which Rogers took up his work fifteen years earlier. He is no longer the pragmatic optimist who in 1969 tells the Fatah official and prospective CIA agent Jamal Ramwali that together they can work to suppress terrorism and also advance the Palestinian cause toward a positive end.[6]

The crucial and unresolved issues of this novel foreshadow, however, the political and conceptual problem that espionage fiction has confronted over the last twenty years, and that has become manifest in some well-known works of fiction, including film and television. It is very possible that Ignatius's story, in which the premise of an American attempt to create multiple connections (if not quite alliances) in the region is presented as a failed ideal, would be regarded by many partisans for the Palestinian cause as even more objectionable than a tale in which the United States was uniformly and seamlessly on the side of the Israelis.[7] In *Agents of Innocence* the project is to make the narrative complex enough to carry the reader's expectations that the novel itself is exploring nuance, ambiguity, and irony, thereby fulfilling a more sophisticated set of criteria than, say, mainstream Hollywood cinema about the Middle East (few and far between though such productions might have been[8]). Ignatius is attempting to make the intuitive architecture of the sophisticated Cold War espionage narrative function in the context of a very different kind of conflict.

Such a fictional architecture requires some limitations on the nature of the political struggle to make sense. To put the issue in a somewhat more polemical way, the liberal problem is, at the same time, the fiction problem: the requirement in fiction that the characters are subject to some kind of change as a result of experiences undergone is difficult to meet if the elements of positional irony (where stability of perception is relative rather than absolute) are neutralized by the presence of inflexible dogma. While it was possible in the fictional world for the intelligence professional from a Western service to explore and even appreciate the ideological thinking of, say, a Soviet-era opponent, and also possible for a KGB officer to have a sophisticated and nuanced attitude toward the oddities of a liberal democracy that was supposed to be his British or American counterpart's guiding light, that exchange becomes substantially more difficult if an assumed secular context is displaced by religious conviction.

In the earlier period before World War II, of course, a presumption of racial superiority was fairly common in the narratives of European imperialist competition. While one might have a certain wariness regarding the colonial ambitions of other civilized nations, as it were, the idea of colonies or protectorates being returned to the indigenous peoples and, beyond that, of those countries becoming sovereign interlocutors of the imperial powers was either a threat to be immediately suppressed or an occasion for ridicule. What makes *Agents of Innocence* such an interesting novel is that Ignatius sketches the possibility that the United States, in the character of Tom Rogers, can in some way transcend the legacy of white colonial intrusion in the Middle East by way of an American posture that combines progressive racial and ethnic sensitivity with pragmatic governance within constitutional norms—a premise grounded, in fact, in actual history.[9] The project fails, at least in part because Rogers's approach is ultimately less effective than either the CIA leadership's clumsy manipulation behind his back that undermines his Palestinian gambit or the more fanatical elements of the Lebanese political underworld who see rational political goals as a betrayal of their unassailable truth; unassailable, because Rogers makes the classic error of assuming that an argument from *logos* will only be countered by a similar type of counter-argument rather than by the assertion of a measure of value higher than the discourse of reason. Indeed, the response will embody not only that assertion but also the belief that the Western approach is itself not secular and open to people of all faiths, but is rather a form of Christian imperialist rhetoric fraudulently offering an equality of access that is not, in fact, available.

Agents of Innocence does, of course, in its very title signal and also problematize the notion of innocence as a factor in foreign policy: the novel embodies that innocence in the character of Tom Rogers and in its narrative arc from 1960s possibility to 1980s ethno-religious hatred, from the sunny prospects of Rogers's first months in Lebanon to the grim paranoia of his last visit to Beirut. The promise that Rogers, and behind him the United States, appears to make is that new paradigms of politics and of nationhood are possible, and even the central conflict of the age in that part of the world, between Israel and the Arabs, might be subject to enlightened treatment. In a certain way, *Agents of Innocence* is asking the question as to whether the secular dynamic of Western political cultures can take root in the Middle East, and whether the United States, as a country ostensibly detached from the colonial histories of Britain and France, is in a position to act as a model and mentor.[10] But the conclusion of the novel is more doubtful than its opening, which may in some ways be its achievement: to admit that the sale of American political ideas may be a more difficult mission than Rogers believes when he first arrives in Beirut, and for reasons he himself may not entirely understand even at the story's end.

The question of whether secularity is indeed free of religious or sacred influences or whether it has to be understood as something else was the theme of an extended debate a few years ago among philosophers and theologians Judith Butler, Talal Asad, Wendy Brown, and Saba Mahmood, published under the title *Is Critique Secular?* In this volume of positions and responses, the various scholars argue about the legitimacy of the assumption that the Western mode of critique, the continuing interrogation of the social ideologies of capitalist postmodernity from locations sited mostly in the humanities, is free of Western and Christian philosophical structures and assumptions.[11] This debate has as a background some of the most controversial and sensitive moments of conflict between Western social and cultural *mores* and Islamic religious beliefs (or ethnic or national behaviors weighted by theological justification) encountered in recent times. They include the Danish cartoon controversy in which the Prophet Mohammed was pictured in caricature in a daily paper, the ban on religious clothing and costume jewelry in France, and most dramatically, in what now seems the memory of a much earlier era, the global announcement by the Ayatollah Khomeini of a monetary reward for killing the British-Indian author Salman Rushdie for purported sacrilege in his 1988 novel *The Satanic Verses*. Not all such controversies led to terrorism or violent action by any particular party, but some did.[12]

The debate in *Is Critique Secular?* has some bearing upon espionage fiction, pointing to the question as to whether critique is an objective challenge to the political assumptions of the West or more of a transposition or oblique displacement of an older perspective in which a Christian and Eurocentric intellectual frame captures the world and renders it thereupon in its own, often subtly hostile terms. 'The world' in this sense would be the Near and Middle East, and other Arab or Muslim regions—complicated by the religious diversity of the area—with a history of the widening influence and the complicated effects of the European expansion and its postcolonial aftermath. If, in this book, I have been trying to tease out the political and cultural mesh of the twentieth century that the espionage narrative has both embodied and in a certain way defined, then this final chapter is an account of how that project may have met with a configuration it cannot (or cannot easily) deconstruct. If the rational discourse of the spy story rooted in the Cold War was sometimes rewarded by real-world shifts in the US–Soviet relationship (for example, accounts of moderate responses in crisis moments that showed that ideology did not always trump pragmatic assessment), then the new landscape of the so-called global war on terror seemed less inviting.

Against this historical background, however, another shift was taking place at a slow but steady pace: the increasing recruitment of women to intelligence and security services in Western countries. The implications of this development for both field operations and intelligence analysis have been the object of academic study and analysis.[13] A clear signal that this was not simply a minor shift in workplace demographics came in 1994, when a career MI5 officer, Stella Rimington, was announced in Prime Minister John Major's statement to the House of Commons as the new director-general of the Security Service. This was obviously a notable historical moment, not only because of her gender but also because Rimington was the first appointee to have her real name made public as the new intelligence chief.[14]

Upon her retirement, Stella Rimington turned to writing. Unsurprisingly, the author's professional career tended to overshadow her status as a fiction writer, and she found herself essentially trapped by the same type of misdirected commentary that has dogged other writers with employment experience in intelligence: reviewers tended to focus on her biography rather than her creative work.[15] Her first novel *At Risk* (2004) introduces Rimington's main protagonist, an MI5 field officer called Liz Carlyle, who becomes the vehicle for the representation of women as a relatively unremarkable presence in the world of intelligence and threat analysis, and a figure at the intersection of the espionage story as a narrative form and the pressures of a changing international order.

At Risk follows the investigation of a jihadist plan to commit a significant act of violence on United Kingdom soil.[16] Indications of the terrorist group's intentions begin to accrue, from a fake British driver's license sold in Hamburg to an informer's tip about a people-smuggling operation on the Norfolk coast ending unexpectedly in violence. The novel is structured as a series of focalized chapters centering on Liz Carlyle, whose narrative runs across the registers from professional efficiency to worry about unresolved issues in her personal life, and on the initially mysterious personality of the woman who is the British contact and mission partner for the Tajik operative Faraj Mansoor. The mind of Liz Carlyle and that of the woman who begins under a fake identity and is also Asimat (the Islamic name she has adopted, after the wife of Saladin[17]), but eventually becomes Jean d'Aubigny, are engaging both with and against each other. One is working to identify the actual target of the planned attack as the couple move across the landscape of southeast England trying to avoid capture and complete their mission on a specific day. Jean d'Aubigny senses somehow that the hunt for her and Mansoor is being led by a woman. "I can feel her shadow," Asimat informs her partner, who responds with "What kind of stupid talk is that?" (332). Faraj's reprimand is ambiguous, of course, as he could mean that her speculation seems unlikely, or perhaps that one should attach no importance to whether their enemy is female or male. That it might be a woman, however, means something to d'Aubigny, as if it alters the state of affairs in some identifiable way.

The narrative form of the novel moves sharply back and forth between short chapters focalized alternately through Carlyle and d'Aubigny. The partially omniscient narrator devotes the larger part of *At Risk* to the actions and extended thoughts of the two characters in such a way as to place the landscapes of their psychological and spiritual interiority at the center of the novel. Although there are no crude parallels drawn, it is obvious that Liz Carlyle's character is being tested both professionally and personally by the events in ways that mirror the journey of endurance, both physical and mental, that Jean d'Aubigny has embarked on. The former is troubled by the negative effect her job has on her relationships as well as by the patronizing attitude and obscure motives of Bruno Mackay, her MI6 liaison; the latter is continually trying to repress memories of her family and the ordinary English life she has left behind. Both are aware of unspoken doubts that men might harbor regarding their qualifications and fitness for the tasks they must carry out.

After the positive identification, Liz looks at Jean's photo in the file with something akin to sympathy (286). Asked for her assessment of what will happen when the security forces find and confront Mansoor and d'Aubigny, she says, "I don't think she'll come out with her hands up, put it like that. I think she'll want to be a martyr" (285). The statement recognizes the intensity of Jean d'Aubigny's commitment to her cause, and also that Liz's ability to grasp the nature of the other woman's cast of mind is one of her weapons. She quotes Felix Dzerzhinsky, the founder of the Soviet intelligence apparatus, in a jocular tone to Mackay when she says, "In any campaign, the first stronghold that you have to occupy is your enemy's consciousness" (303). She denies admiring d'Aubigny in any way, but the narrator's voice probes into the path she has taken to her present status as an officer of the Security Service:

> She was the right person in the right job. The Service's recruiters had known her better than she knew herself. They had recognized that her quiet sage-green gaze masked an unflinching determination. A hunger for the fierce, close-focused engagement of the chase. (177)

Within the Western framework of values an unflinching determination and a hunger for the chase are not the same as fanatical dedication and a willingness to accept martyrdom. It is worth asking, however, just how near they may come to each other and whether there is often an area of overlap. Martyrdom is a concept entirely familiar to the Christian tradition, and a willingness to sacrifice oneself for a great cause is not in all cases an undesirable trait. Whether or not Liz Carlyle admires Jean d'Aubigny is, for the implicit perspective that informs narrative of *At Risk*, of less significance than the novelty of the composite picture they create together as the story moves toward its conclusion.

That implicit perspective is what gives Rimington's first novel its striking emotional focus, as she makes notable use of what narrative theorist Dorrit Cohn has termed "narrated monologue" (a category invented to provide an interim mode between subjective first-person narration and what Cohn calls quoted monologue), in which there is "identification but not identity" with the character on the part of the narrator:[18] d'Aubigny's thinking is not rendered within the type of critical framing that opens a character to immediate and frequently negative moral assessment, but with a distinct feeling of understanding tempered by distance. It is the terrorist act that is beyond of borderline of legitimacy, but not the nature of the personality which led her to it, as it could have led her to a less absolute and fatal decision. As Cohn puts it, a narrative that sets "the language of a subjective mind into the grammar of objective narration" will transmit emotional conviction, but also "throw into ironic relief all false notes struck by a figural mind."[19] The narrator's reading of Carlyle's and d'Aubigny's interiority embraces both their differences and their likeness, with both difference and likeness acting together as a brake on easy assumptions.

For Jean d'Aubigny, the embrace of the Muslim faith and later of its passionately militant and fundamentalist wing has been the antidote for spiritual emptiness of her upbringing in a middle-class academic family. But the irony is that she is not alone, in the sense that Liz Carlyle has also felt that she wanted a life, a profession, that demanded more dedication and commitment than might be gained from another career or from the kind of marriage to a pleasant young man from a similar background that her mother is openly hoping for. She realizes that being "unable to compromise her independence [and] denying her own emotional needs" (177) does not come without a cost, and is ready to accept a certain loneliness as the price. To some degree, both women have voluntarily entered upon a life in which traditional pressures to align oneself with the society's expectations for domesticity and reproduction can be closed off—in the one case partially, in the other absolutely. In their radically different but strangely parallel moves to break the mold, Liz Carlyle and Jean d'Aubigny find themselves as duelists in the murky arena of political violence and national security, with the knowledge that only one of them will emerge intact.

In recent years the most high-profile television drama to address the conflict between the United States and revolutionary Islamism has been *Homeland*, which began in 2011 and concluded in 2020. I will deal primarily with the first two seasons here, as they embody with most clarity the elements of the crisis of espionage narrative as it appears today. The premise of *Homeland*, originating in an Israeli television drama, is that a Marine Corps sergeant, Nicholas Brody, who has disappeared for several years in Afghanistan, is rescued by friendly forces and returns to the United States. The personal and political implications of his coming back home after being essentially presumed dead are the central narrative threads of the drama. Questions as to his experiences in captivity, his true loyalties including a new religious faith, and his intentions beyond picking up his life again are what bring him into contact with a CIA officer, Carrie Mathison.[20]

Carrie Mathison is haunted by a bipolar psychological condition that is both her injury and her power. Given to periods of aggressive, manic activity and sharp insight, she is also prone to depression and the kind of lax attitude that has sometimes made her superiors doubt her suitability for intelligence work. Involved in the review of Sergeant Brody's captivity and release, she becomes both sexually attracted to him and also suspicious that he has returned with a mission hostile to the United States, as a result of either brainwashing or simply a complete shift in his loyalties from an American soldier to an al-Qaeda-directed terrorist. The notion that Brody may in some peculiar way be both a genuine repatriated prisoner and a man on a hostile mission aimed at his own country mirrors Carrie Mathison's own double character as a gifted intelligence officer and a directionless manic-depressive drawn to over-consumption of alcohol and casual pick-ups in bars.

If Nicholas Brody is seeking redemption of some kind, possibly for the actions of his own government in the war in which he was lost and then found, then something a little closer to visionary knowledge is what marks out the protagonist of *Homeland*. Carrie—and something about the verbal and visual text of the series puts us on first-name terms with her—is driven by conviction and is prepared to risk a great deal in her commitment to an analysis that does not always convince or please the senior ranks at Langley. Her belief that Brody has something to hide is held with an almost religious intensity, one that is ironically reflected in the fact that Brody's newfound Muslim faith is one important thing that he wishes to keep secret from everyone, including his wife and children with whom he is attempting, with difficulty, to reconnect. Her illegal and unauthorized electronic surveillance of Brody at his home is a mirror image of his own behavior with reversed polarity, as it were: circling each other both professionally and sexually, they embody opposite but mutual desires to express attraction and to stay under cover, to probe for the truth and to evade capture.

To put it in a slightly more hyperbolic way, in a global conflict with an opponent whose driving motivation eludes an array of Western secular and strategic tools by way of a promise of an eternal afterlife, the only counter-measures that will be effective must operate outside the secular limitations of the West's governing instrumental rationality. The extremism of the radical Islamist vision can be met, in this analysis, only by the blessedly mad who are on our side. This is of course a somewhat sensitive proposition, redolent of the conundrum presented during the Cold War by those dedicated opponents of communism who had to know it intimately to fight it. That intimate knowledge could potentially draw an individual away from their original belief system toward an identification with communism's ultimate goal. The visionary may see too much, and sympathetic understanding of the adversary's true circumstances can make one rethink one's basic loyalties. If a saintly madness—Carrie Mathison's troubling psychiatric issues, for example—should turn out to be the weapon needed to battle an opponent who values martyrdom as the superior tactic of war, can that madness ultimately become less saintly than morbid? If the visionary sees so clearly, through and around obscurity, she runs the danger of either being seduced by her vision or being damaged by it. The central narrative tension of *Homeland* is generated by the inability on Carrie's part to determine whether her sexual relationship with Brody (which leads ultimately to her pregnancy) is an authentic expression of desire or an operational move to investigate a serious terrorist conspiracy, the latter being the repeated justification offered to Saul Berenson and David Estes, her immediate CIA line managers.

Maybe "determine" is, however, exactly what Carrie Mathison does not wish to do. As *Homeland* has continually sought to push back any conclusive moment of resolution and even redemptive catharsis, so does Nicholas Brody, in the third season, leave the world of the drama—executed by the Iranian authorities—without any sense that we the audience have glimpsed the essential truth about him. Soldier, captive, traitor; father, husband, lover; terrorist, refugee, redeemed spy: all attempts to provide a "realistic" reading of character within a rational framework seem inappropriate because *Homeland* at some level recognizes that the fictions it puts to work have slipped the moorings of traditional narrative logic. If it is not magical realism, as that term is usually understood, then *Homeland* in its narrative mode has gambled on a certain willingness among its audience to accept delayed resolution, ontological instability as to character and motivation, and inconsistencies in story and progression while its focus on the politics of terror and counter-terror remained emotionally charged by events in the real world from the war in Afghanistan to the shifting ideological map of Washington's political culture. Washington's architectural landscape has been much deployed in the visual composition of *Homeland*, always evoking a bifurcated sense of familiarity and strangeness.

Indeed, one curious incident in the wider history of *Homeland* as a television drama product provides a window onto the question of the show's relationship with the political conditions it appropriates for its aesthetic purpose. At the beginning of the fifth season, there was a covert and inventive protest by Arabic translators who had been hired to provide realistic graffiti on walls and doors for an episode set in Beirut.[21] In one particular scene, Carrie Mathison arrives to assist in negotiating a hostage release from a battered-looking and war-torn neighborhood of the city, and a number of slogans are visible sprayed on the wall in a nearby alley. The sprayed graffiti in the scene is clearly meant to enhance a visual atmosphere of volatile, angry political passions to mirror the narrative of kidnapping and violence in Lebanon.

As the scene unfolded in the broadcast, however, it was revealed to any Arabic-speaking viewers that something unusual had happened. The graffiti did not consist of fictional slogans referring to Middle Eastern politics or Lebanese militias such as Hizbollah, but acerbic comments attacking *Homeland* itself, the television drama that had commissioned the wall as part of its scene-setting. The new language accused *Homeland* of being racist, and criticized the writers and producers for portraying characters of Arabic ethnicity or Islamic faith as only terrorists or CIA officers, as if those were the only two choices offered. The production leadership of *Homeland* appeared to respond to this unexpected and jarring maneuver with good grace, although they had no other real choice, and claimed that the very protest itself argued for both the relevance of the show's storylines and the authentic feelings of criticism or support that they aroused. They essentially tried to integrate the subversive graffiti protest into the *Homeland* mythology by claiming that its subversive energy had been ultimately enabled by *Homeland* itself. This is at least a defensible thesis, as the unexpected breaching of the fourth television wall seems not to have worked against the show in any way since then.

There is, however, another aspect of this incident worth examining, as it seems to offer exactly that useful access to the problem of liberal ideology and the difficulties faced by post-Cold War espionage fiction. The idea of the protest and the accusation of ethno-religious stereotyping are hard to imagine only a couple of decades ago when the conflict between the West and the Soviet Union dominated the international stage. It would have been quite strange to have encountered any similar kind of political subversion of a television drama such as, for example, Russian translators engaging in a similar gesture in order to register a protest against Russian stereotyping in British or American spy stories. Not only does it seem unlikely to have taken place, but the mere factual existence of such stereotyping (which was undeniable) would have been met by the response that in a story of conflict in a popular genre the opposing party is naturally represented as embodying an Otherness, a set of identity markers that reveal an explicit divergence from the familiar style of one's own tribe.

During the Cold War, a citizen of France, Britain, or the United States who was also a communist might well legitimately complain that the subtle nuances of ideology and position were never communicated in Western popular media, but only caricatured. Such complaints were registered in various contexts, to be sure, but the complaint opens up complicated questions involving the nature of fictional worlds, the requirements of genre, the constraints of narrative economy, and the concurrence of stereotype and reality. Those questions remain for *Homeland*, of course, but there is no doubt that the deployment of ethnic Arab or Muslim characters is a more sensitive matter for an espionage drama on American television in the early twenty-first century. The reasons are manifold: the presence of Muslim fellow citizens; the secular democratic principle that religious faith should be neither privileged nor denigrated; the ethic of diversity, treating cultures as having equal value to each other; the implications of a slanted playing field which forces Muslim citizens to continually prove they are not hostile to their own particular nations or even the West in general. It was rare to have such issues manifest themselves in earlier fictions of the Cold War era, and that was to a significant extent due to two factors. One was the mutual recognition of the struggle between Soviet communism and Western liberal democracy—nobody on any side denied that it was an actual political reality—and the second was the overlap of secular world-views between democracy and communism.[22]

The fact that there appears no such overlap when it comes to the relationship of Islamist and non-Muslim perspectives triggers a curious type of political and cultural abrasiveness, a mutual irritability rather than an overlaying of world-views, divergent but stemming from the same ideological and historical roots. Islam in a broader perspective has had, of course, its own discourses of secularity. Historical examples from Kemal Attaturk in 1920 to the Arab Spring in 2010 refute the notion of a religious monolith immune to ideas of a secular and independent civic and cultural life within a broad religious framework. But something at work in the interactions of post-Christian secularity with certain nodes of Islamic political formations in the West as well as in the Middle East and Southeast Asia has enabled a series of confrontations (sometimes with remote parties, sometimes with parties in proximity) that have given new authority to voices prophesying war—even if the "war" is often largely hyperbole.

It is not surprising that those writers who work, steadily or intermittently, in the field of espionage fiction have taken up the theme of a new kind of global political struggle and explored what it can offer for narratives of suspense that deal with intelligence and counter-terrorism. It is also not surprising that, like Stella Rimington and the writers of *Homeland*, they have wrestled with the problem posed by religious conviction and eschatological visions significantly different from the ideology that represented the threat to liberal capitalist democracy (and to its many non-democratic or authoritarian allies, of course) for a large part of the twentieth century.[23] Few people want to occupy the extreme position of declaring religious faith to be *per se* an existential threat to society, but in writing about fundamentalist Islamism within the espionage genre some version of that will emerge almost as an unpreventable chemical reaction between the elements of narrative. It would seem that the only way out is to find a region of interaction in which the truculence of politico-religious fundamentalism does not discover the bland assumptions of secular post-modernity to be its only available interlocutor.[24]

Thinking about both Liz Carlyle and Carrie Mathison as representative figures for espionage narratives, therefore, leads one to the recognition that the sociological context for contemporary espionage stories presents a paradox. There is a distinct irony in the fact that the arrival of fundamentalist Islamism as a principal adversary for the West has coincided with the entry, in relatively large numbers, of female recruits into the intelligence and security services, some of them attaining high-ranking positions that would have been inconceivable only forty years ago. This curious juxtaposition of progressive gender politics on one side with a combative misogyny on the other is of course complicated by the actions of mostly young women, some of them converts to Islam, who have joined militant jihadist organizations and even carried out armed assaults including suicide bombings. As with Jean d'Aubigny and Liz Carlyle in *At Risk*, the presence of two women, each dedicated to their cause, at the leading edge of the two hostile entities in counter-terrorism signals something of a sea-change in the gender assumptions of espionage fiction as it has developed over the twentieth and early twenty-first centuries.

The nature of fiction can mean, of course, that the intriguing new paradigm can quickly become the stereotypical format. A stereotype is not uniformly or always unproductive, however, and variations on a theme can be many and offer themselves over time as the real-world context shifts, and some variations are inseparable from the necessary defining and re-defining of our political and social systems—the systems that we in any case live within, or under. The notion of an intelligence apparatus with a more diverse workforce, for example, with more staff from ethnic or racial minorities and with more women, is not necessarily welcomed by the conservative right in, say, the United States or some European countries. But if the work of espionage fiction is, as I have argued, presenting a mode of imagining national and international political landscapes in both an individual and a collective dimension, recent narratives suggest a world in which the roles of immigrant experiences, varied religious identities, cultural sensitivity, and sexual equality will pose important and unavoidable questions for the profession of intelligence and national security. One might posit that espionage fiction is in certain ways not only a genre of fiction but also something like a sub-genre of international relations theory and analysis. It enfolds in the fabric of narrative invention the understanding of national and international conflicts over power, influence, and ideological legitimacy.

The work of espionage fiction means also the individual literary or dramatic text, its cohesion and aesthetic credibility. Reading espionage fiction, the guiding practice of this book, requires the exercise of critical judgment that both understands the nature of a popular form and avoids reductive assumptions about genre. The journey from Maugham's Ashenden to *Homeland*'s Mathison and Rimington's Carlyle is as much a literary tradition that explored its own creative possibilities as it is a map of twentieth-century political and ideological history. But who would deny that political and ideological history also needs its poetry, its symbolic narratives, and its ethical imaginary? Commitment and conflict, the push and pull of complicated political and personal loyalties in modernity, needed a cultural form that could both enlighten and entertain, and espionage fiction has attempted to carry out that mission. It has done so with too-easy denouements and too-satisfactory resolutions, undeniably, but often with a more mature perception, an awareness not only of the nature of political and personal commitments but also that they take place—to borrow Helen MacInnes's phrase from *I and My True Love*—where ragged edges overlap.

Notes

1. Ransom, *Selected Poems*, 30–31.
2. Of course, Vietnam was not the only country that fought an anticolonial war and found its political map fatally dividing after the original shared goal of defeating the colonial authority had been achieved.
3. The first appearance of a distinctively modern style of political violence can be found in the actions of the international anarchist movement

at the turn of the twentieth century, the most sensational being the assassinations of Empress Elizabeth of Austria-Hungary (1898), King Umberto I of Italy (1900), and US President McKinley (1901).

4. I should be cautious here: Reeva S. Simon's *Spies and Holy Wars* counts hundreds of novels up to the 1980s that use the background of the Middle East (68); it is a little curious, nevertheless, that le Carré's *The Little Drummer Girl* receives an extremely brief commentary (one paragraph) and David Ignatius, whose *Agents of Innocence* is one of the more subtle and informed works of espionage fiction with that setting, gets a single casual mention in the introduction. Simon is clearly more interested in a large-scale historical overview than in individual works.
5. Similar to the relative absence of espionage fiction focused on the Northern Ireland conflict, as I discuss in Chapter 7.
6. Ignatius, *Agents of Innocence*, 126.
7. For example, this author assigned the novel in an undergraduate class in espionage fiction a few years ago, and some disagreement emerged in class discussions and student papers. I presented *Agents of Innocence* as a subtle deployment of the espionage story exploring the counterfactual of an American posture toward the Israel–Palestine conflict that actually tries to explore how the Palestinian nationalist goals might potentially be incorporated into foreign policy and whether that might have ultimately benefited all major players in the region, including the United States. A couple of students regarded it, however, as Ignatius simply working to legitimize American pro-Israeli interference in the Middle East and setting up a romanticized character straight out of Kennedy's "New Frontier" to suggest the existence of a more progressive, anticolonialist strategy than is actually warranted by history.
8. *Syriana* (2005; dir. Stephen Gaghan) deserves mention as a compelling story that gets to grips with the indivisible complex of politics and fossil fuels.
9. See Hugh Wilford's preface to *America's Great Game*, in which he notes that CIA policy in the Middle East until the early 1960s was "a lost world of secret American Arabism" (xx) caught between "two contradictory influences: the British imperial legacy and the American missionary tradition" (xx).
10. The "settler-colonial" critique which is now widespread would have meant little or nothing in the 1960s, or indeed in the 1980s to someone like Rogers. For some interesting aspects of this issue, see Busbridge, "Israel-Palestine and the Settler Colonial 'Turn.'"
11. The various authors in the volume do not come to any consensus on the key questions, but the degree to which secular assumptions are challenged suggests a pressure for a significant re-orientation of basic positions within the academic left.
12. Since I first drafted this note about what I had thought was ancient history, Rushdie was attacked on August 12, 2022 by an assailant with

a knife at a reading in Chautauqua, New York. He sustained significant injuries, but survived.
13. Phoebe Godfrey's essay on a veteran of the Iraq war, "'I was one the better interrogators,'" looks at female recruits to US military intelligence rather than civilian agencies, but the basic dilemma of what one is supposed to bring to intelligence work as a woman remains noticeably active for fictional characters such as Liz Carlyle and Carrie Mathison.
14. As Rimington herself has noted, the actual release of her name came later than the news of the appointment; the notion of "a woman getting a man's job" drove the print media into a frenzy, and some papers were able to identify her and even her home address, at a time when she would have been a potential IRA target.
15. The professional experience is something that, just to take two examples from different times, Somerset Maugham and Charles McCarry (who admired Maugham's Ashenden stories) have in common. That does not mean, of course, that their fiction is disguised memoir. There appears to be a kind of inner resistance in some readers and reviewers to accepting that even after a career in intelligence work, one can write works of the imagination.
16. See Sedgwick, "Jihadism, Narrow and Wide" in *Perspectives on Terrorism* for a useful discussion of the term.
17. The Kingdom of Jerusalem, ruled by the Crusaders, surrendered to the Muslim commander Saladin in 1187.
18. Cohn, *Transparent Minds*, 112.
19. Cohn, *Transparent Minds*, 117.
20. It should be noted that the CIA has no operational authority inside the United States. Counter-terrorism as a significant mission for the FBI has also grown over the last twenty years. It is probable that the convenience of dramatic configuration and plot development came before strict authenticity, and in reality Carrie Mathison's rogue surveillance activities would have been even more provocative if they had been treading on FBI turf.
21. *Homeland*, season 7, episode 3.
22. There is also an argument that the relative equivalence of the nation-states of the Soviet Union and the United States created a separate dimension for the Cold War, one that involved a more traditional type of competition for global influence than the original politico-philosophical conflict between liberalism and communism as divergent projects for the social construction of modernity, both born of the Enlightenment.
23. It is also important not to define a stereotypical Western perspective as the only one worth thinking about (see n. 24 on Abdoh). Doyle Calhoun's essay "Dead Narrators, Queer Terrorists" in *New Literary History*, on a French-Moroccan novel by Mahi Binebine on the nature of suicide bombing, is both challenging and problematic, but without

any doubt looks down the line to fictions that will inevitably refuse to conform to established political and cultural norms about the justification for violence and the distinction between legitimate and illegitimate modes of warfare. But espionage fiction may also evade the revolutionary script as well as the state script.

24. One anomalous and intriguing example of a different "region of interaction" is Salar Abdoh's 2000 novel *The Poet Game*. Set in New York City, the story traces the efforts of an Iranian with binational parentage, Sami Amir, to prevent a terror attack by radical Islamist forces aimed at the Christmas celebrations in the city. Son of an American mother and an Iranian father, Amir works for an obscure office in the national security apparatus which has a different vision from that of the Revolutionary Guard and the more aggressive global ambitions of the Iranian political system. In particular, Sami Amir's controller, the Colonel, suspects that a terrorist attack to provoke an American over-reaction is the aim of radical circles within the Tehran intelligence establishment. Although the Shi'a–Sunni theological division adds a layer of complexity and difficulty to Iran's relationship with violent Islamist organizations, there is often enough convergence of purposes to warrant the Revolutionary Guard offering support for particular actions overseas. Thus, *The Poet Game* offers one relative novelty in the genre: if all parties are Muslim, however they interpret that identity, then the confrontation between Islam and the West is neutralized and becomes a shadowy element in the background rather than primary trigger in the narrative.

Works Cited

Primary Texts

Quotations from primary texts are referenced with parenthetical page numbers within the chapters.

Ambler, Eric. *A Coffin for Dimitrios*. 1939. Vintage-Random House, 2001.
DeLillo, Don. *The Names*. 1982. Vintage Books, 1989.
Garve, Andrew. *The Ashes of Loda*. 1964. Harper & Row, 1978.
Greenlee, Samuel E. *The Spook Who Sat by the Door*. 1969. Wayne State UP, 1990.
Homeland. Television series, seasons 1–8, Showtime, 2011–20.
Le Carré, John. *Call for the Dead*. 1961. Penguin, 2012.
———. *The Little Drummer Girl*. 1983. With an introduction by the author, Scribner, 2004.
———. *A Murder of Quality*. 1962. Penguin, 2012.
———. *A Small Town in Germany*. 1968. Introduction by Hari Kunzru. Penguin, 2011.
———. *The Spy Who Came In from the Cold*. 1963. Simon & Schuster, 2001.
———. *The Tailor of Panama*. Ballantine Books, 1996.
———. "Theatre of the Real: The Villa Brigitte." *The Pigeon Tunnel: Stories from my Life*, Viking, 2016, pp. 98–103.
MacInnes, Helen. *I and My True Love*. 1953. Titan Books, 2013.
MacNeice, Louis. *Autumn Journal*. 1939. Faber and Faber, 2012.
Maugham, W. Somerset. *Collected Short Stories*, vol 3. 1928 (as *Ashenden; or The British Agent*). Penguin, 1977.
McCarry, Charles. *The Miernik Dossier*. 1973. Overlook-Duckworth, 2007.
———. *The Tears of Autumn*. 1974. Overlook-Duckworth, 2007.
Rimington, Stella. *At Risk*. Vintage Crime, 2006.
Semprun, Jorge. *The Second Death of Ramón Mercader*. Translated by Len Ortzen, Grove Press, 1973.
Seymour, Gerald. *Field of Blood*. 1985. Hodder & Stoughton, 2014.
———. *Harry's Game*. 1975. Hodder & Stoughton, 2013.

———. *The Journeyman Tailor*. 1992. Hodder & Stoughton, 2013.
Williams, John A. *The Man Who Cried I Am*. 1967. Thunder's Mouth Press, 1985.
Wright, Richard. "Big Boy Leaves Town." 1938. *Uncle Tom's Children*, Harper Perennial, 2008, pp. 16–61.
———. "Bright and Morning Star." 1940. *Uncle Tom's Children*, Harper Perennial, 2008, pp. 221–63.

Secondary, Associated, and Critical Texts

Abdoh, Salar. *The Poet Game: A Novel*. Picador, 2000.
Appiah, Kwame Anthony. *The Ethics of Identity*. Princeton UP, 2005.
Asad, Talal, et al. *Is Critique Secular? Blasphemy, Injury, and Free Speech*. Fordham UP, 2013.
Bailey, Frankie Y. *African American Mystery Writers: A Historical and Thematic Study*. McFarland, Inc., 2008.
Barnard, F. M. *Herder on Nationality, Humanity, and History*. McGill-Queen's UP, 2003.
Beckman, Morris. *The 43 Group: Battling with Mosley's Blackshirts*. The History Press, 2013.
Belfast. Written and directed by Kenneth Branagh. TKBC; Northern Ireland Screen, 2021.
Bercovitch, Sacvan. *The American Jeremiad*. University of Wisconsin Press, 1978.
Bluemel, Kristin. "Introduction." *Intermodernism: Literary Culture in Mid-Twentieth-Century Britain*, edited by Kristin Bluemel, Edinburgh UP, 2009, pp. 1–18.
Boxall, Peter. *The Value of the Novel*. Cambridge UP, 2015.
Breward, Christopher. "Savile Row." fashion-history.lovetoknow.com/fashion-history-eras/savile-row n.d. Accessed April 20, 2022.
Brooks, Peter. *Reading for the Plot: Design and Intention in Narrative*. Alfred A. Knopf, 1984.
Buchan, John. *Greenmantle*. Edited with an introduction by Kate MacDonald, Oxford UP, 1993.
Busbridge, Rachel. "Israel-Palestine and the Settler Colonial 'Turn': From Interpretation to Decolonization." *Theory, Culture, & Society*, vol. 35, no. 1, 2018, pp. 91–115.
Calder, Angus. *The People's War: Britain 1939–1945*. Pantheon Books, 1969.
Calder, Robert. *Willie: The Life of W. Somerset Maugham*. Heinemann, 1989.
Calhoun, Doyle. "Dead Narrators, Queer Terrorists: On Suicide Bombing and Literature." *New Literary History*, vol. 53, no. 2, Spring 2022, pp. 285–304.

Cawelti, John G., and Bruce A. Rosenberg. *The Spy Story*. University of Chicago Press, 1987.
Cinema Journal, vol. 54, no. 4 (Summer 2015).
Codebò, Marco. *Narrating from the Archive: Novels, Records, and Bureaucrats in the Modern Age*. Fairleigh Dickinson UP, 2010.
Cohn, Dorrit. *Transparent Minds: Narrative Modes for Representing Consciousness in Fiction*. Princeton UP, 1978.
Conrad, Joseph. *Under Western Eyes*. Edited by Roger Osborne and Paul Eggert, Cambridge UP, 2013.
Cruse, Harold. *The Crisis of the Negro Intellectual: A Historical Analysis of the Failure of Black Leadership*. Introduction by Stanley Crouch, New York Review of Books, 2005.
Denning, Michael. *Cover Stories: Narrative and Ideology in the British Spy Thriller*. Routledge and Kegan Paul, 1987.
Donovan, Christopher. *Postmodern Counternarratives: Irony and Audience in the Novels of Paul Auster, Don DeLillo, Charles Johnson, and Tim O'Brien*. Routledge, 2005.
Eagleton, Terry. "Nationalism: Irony and Commitment." *Nationalism, Colonialism, and Literature*, University of Minnesota Press, 1990, pp. 23–39.
England, Jason. "The Pernicious Fantasy of the Nikole Hannah-Jones Saga: Her Success Is Not a Collective Victory for Black Academics." *The Chronicle of Higher Education*, vol. 68, no. 2 (July 21, 2021). www.chronicle.com/article/the-pernicious-fantasy-of-the-nikole-hannah-jones-saga. Accessed October 30, 2021.
English, Daylanne K. "The Modern in the Postmodern: Walter Mosley, Barbara Neely, and the Politics of the Contemporary African-American Detective Novel." *American Literary History*, vol. 18, no. 4, 2006, pp. 772–96.
Felski, Rita. "Identifying with Characters." *Character: Three Inquiries in Literary Studies*, University of Chicago Press, 2019, pp. 77–126.
Fernandez, James W., and May Taylor Huber, editors. *Irony in Action: Anthropology, Practice, and the Moral Imagination*. University of Chicago Press, 2001.
Fleming, Ian. "Quantum of Solace." *Quantum of Solace: The Complete James Bond Short Stories*, Penguin, 2008, pp. 79–103.
Gaines, Kevin. "The Civil Rights Movement in World Perspective." *OAH Magazine of History*, vol. 21, no. 1, 2007, pp. 57–64.
Gelder, Ken. *Popular Literature: The Logics and Practices of a Literary Field*. Routledge, 2004.
Godfrey, Phoebe C. "'I was one of the better interrogators': Gender Performativity, Identity Transformation and the Female Military Intelligence Officer in the Iraq War." *Gender and Conflict Since 1914*, edited by Ana Carden-Coyne, Palgrave Macmillan, 2012, pp. 154–70.

Goldberg, David Theo. *The Threat of Race: Reflections on Racial Neoliberalism.* Wiley Blackwell, 2009.
Greene, Graham. *Our Man in Havana.* Penguin, 2007.
Greenlee, Samuel E. *Baghdad Blues.* Kayode Publications, 1991.
Greer, Steven. *Supergrasses: A Study in Anti-Terrorist Law Enforcement in Northern Ireland.* Clarendon Press, 1995.
Griffin, Martin. "Dave Burrell's *Baghdad Blues*: Fiction, Race, and History in 1950s Iraq." *Stories of Nation: Fictions, Politics, and the American Experience*, edited by Martin Griffin and Christopher Hebert, University of Tennessee Press, 2017, pp. 225–42.
Hepburn, Allan. *Intrigue: Espionage and Culture.* Yale UP, 2005.
Hitchens, Christopher. *Blood, Class, and Empire: The Enduring Anglo-American Relationship.* Nation Books, 2004.
Hofstadter, Richard. *The Paranoid Style in American Politics and Other Essays.* Alfred A. Knopf, 1965.
Holcomb, Gary M. *Claude McKay, Code Name Sasha: Queer Black Marxism and the Harlem Renaissance.* UP of Florida, 2007.
Hollander, John. *Reflections on Espionage: The Question of Cupcake.* With introduction and notes, Yale UP, 1999.
Horn, Eva. *The Secret War: Treason, Espionage, and Modern Fiction.* Translated from the German and with an introduction by Geoffrey Winthrop-Young, Northwestern UP, 2013.
Ignatius, David. *Agents of Innocence.* W. W. Norton, 1997.
James, Henry. *The Golden Bowl.* 1904. Edited with an introduction and notes by Virginia Llewellen Smith. Oxford University Press, 2009.
Jelavich, Barbara. *History of the Balkans*, vol. 2, *Twentieth Century.* Cambridge UP, 1983.
Judge, Edward H., and John W. Langdon, editors. *The Cold War through Documents: A Global History.* 3rd ed, Rowman and Littlefield, 2017.
Judt, Tony. "The Past Is Another Country: Myth and Memory in Postwar Europe." *Daedalus*, vol. 121, no. 4, 1992, pp. 83–118.
Kelly, Aaron. *The Thriller and Northern Ireland since 1969: Utterly Resigned Terror.* Ashgate, 2005.
Kennedy-Andrews, Elmer. *Fiction and the Northern Ireland Troubles since 1969: (De-) constructing the North.* Four Courts Press, 2003.
Kipling, Rudyard. *Kim.* Edited with an introduction by Edward W. Said, Penguin, 1987.
———. "Tommy." www.kiplingsociety.co.uk/poems_tommy.htm.
Krenn, Michael L. *Black Diplomacy: African-Americans and the State Department, 1945–1969.* M. E. Sharpe, 1999.
Lassner, Phyllis. *Espionage and Exile: Fascism and Anti-Fascism in British Spy Fiction and Film.* Edinburgh UP, 2016.
———. "John le Carré's Jews." www.jewthink.org, December 18, 2020. Accessed March 1, 2021.

Lentz-Smith, Adriane. "Passports to Adventure: African Americans and the US Security Project." *American Quarterly*, vol. 68, no. 3, 2016, pp. 537–43.

Macdonald, Dwight. 1960. "Masscult and Midcult." *Masscult and Midcult: Essays Against the American Grain*. Introduction by Louis Menand, New York Review of Books, 2011, pp. 3–71.

MacInnes, Helen. *Decision at Delphi*. Titan Books, 2012.

McCann, Eamonn. *War and an Irish Town*, New updated ed., Pluto Press, 1993.

McCarthy, Conor. *Outlaws and Spies: Legal Exclusion in Law and Literature*. Edinburgh UP, 2020.

Manning, Toby. *John le Carré and the Cold War*. Bloomsbury Academic, 2017.

Mapping American Social Movements Project. Civil Rights and Labor History Consortium, University of Washington, 2015–present. depts.washington.edu/moves/CP_map-votes.shtml. Accessed November 10, 2021.

Marías, Javier. *Your Face Tomorrow* [1: *Fever and Spear*; 2: *Dancer and Dream*; 3: *Poison, Shadow and Farewell*]. Translated by Margaret Jull Costa, New Directions, 2005–09.

Maslen, Elizabeth. "A Cassandra with Clout: Storm Jameson, Little Englander and Good European." *Intermodernism: Literary Culture in Mid-Twentieth-Century Britain*, edited by Kristin Bluemel, Edinburgh UP, 2009, pp. 21–37.

Maxwell, Glyn. "Turn and Turn Against: The Case of *Autumn Journal*." *Incorrigibly Plural: Louis MacNeice and His Legacy*, edited by Fran Brearton and Edna Longley, Carcanet Press, 2012, pp. 171–89.

Melancon, Michael. *The Socialist Revolutionaries and the Russian Anti-War Movement, 1914–1917*. Ohio State UP, 1990.

MI-5 (aka *Spooks*). Television series, seasons 1–10, BBC, 2002–11.

Miller, J. Hillis. *Others*. Princeton UP, 2001.

———. *Reading Narrative*. University of Oklahoma Press, 1998.

Moi, Toril. "Rethinking Character." *Character: Three Inquiries in Literary Studies*, University of Chicago Press, 2019, pp. 27–75.

Moore-Gilbert, Bart. "Kipling and Postcolonial Literature." *The Cambridge Companion to Rudyard Kipling*, edited by Howard J. Booth, Cambridge UP, 2011, pp. 155–68.

Mosley, Walter. "The Art of Fiction." Interview in *Paris Review*, no. 220, Spring 2017, pp. 242–67.

———. "1926: Hardboiled." *A New Literary History of America*, edited by Greil Marcus and Werner Sollors, Belknap Press of Harvard UP, 2009, pp. 598–602.

Myers, Jeffrey. *Somerset Maugham: A Life*. Alfred A. Knopf, 2004.

Neilson, Keith. "Tsars and Commissars: W. Somerset Maugham, *Ashenden*, and Images of Russia in British Adventure Fiction, 1890–1930." *Canadian Journal of History*, vol. 27, no. 3, 1992, pp. 475–500.

Nussbaum, Martha. *Poetic Justice: The Literary Imagination and Public Life*. Beacon Press, 1995.
O'Flaherty, Liam. *The Informer*. With a preface by Denis Donoghue, Harcourt Brace & Company, 1980.
Palumbo, Antonino, and Alan Scott. "Weber, Durkheim, and the Sociology of the Modern State." *The Cambridge History of Twentieth-Century Political Thought*, edited by Terence Ball and Richard Bellamy, Cambridge UP, 2003, pp. 368–91.
Phillips, Nichole R. *Patriotism Black and White: The Color of American Exceptionalism*. Baylor UP, 2018.
Ransom, John Crowe. *Selected Poems*. Alfred A. Knopf, 1969.
Regan, Kylie. "'The jolly coverts': DeLillo's *Libra* as Espionage Fiction." *Critique: Studies in Contemporary Fiction*, vol. 59, no. 5, 2018, pp. 624–36.
Reich, Elizabeth. "A New Kind of Black Soldier: Performing Revolution in *The Spook Who Sat by the Door*." *African American Review*, vol. 45, no. 3, 2012, pp. 325–39.
Rolandsen, Østeyn H., and M. W. Daly. *A History of South Sudan: From Slavery to Independence*. Cambridge UP, 2018.
Sawyer, Benjamin. "Manufacturing Germans: Singer Manufacturing Company and American Capitalism in the Russian Imagination during World War I." *Enterprise & Society*, vol. 17, no. 2, 2016, pp. 301–23.
Sedgwick, Mark. "Jihadism, Narrow and Wide: The Dangers of Loose Use of an Important Term." *Perspectives on Terrorism*, vol. 9, no. 2, April 2015, pp. 34–41.
Sheppard, Samantha N. "Persistently Displaced: Situated Knowledges and Interrelated Histories in *The Spook Who Sat by the Door*." *Cinema Journal*, vol. 52, no. 2, 2013, pp. 71–92.
Shklovsky, Viktor. "Art as Device." *Theory of Prose*, translated by Benjamin Sher, Dalkey Archive Press, 1991, pp. 1–14.
Signorile, Michelangelo. *Queer in America: Sex, Media, and the Closets of Power*. University of Wisconsin Press, 2003.
Simon, Reeva S. *Spies and Holy Wars: The Middle East in 20th Century Crime Fiction*. University of Texas Press, 2010.
Sisman, Adam. *John le Carré: The Biography*. HarperCollins, 2015.
Skilling, H. Gordon. *Communism National and International: Eastern Europe after Stalin*. University of Toronto Press, 1964.
Snyder, Robert Lance. *The Art of Indirection in British Espionage Fiction: A Critical Study of Six Novelists*. McFarland, 2011.
———. *Eric Ambler's Novels: Critiquing Modernity*. Lexington Books, 2020.
Snyder, Timothy D. *Bloodlands: Europe between Hitler and Stalin*. Basic Books, 2010.
The Spook Who Sat by the Door. Directed by Ivan Dickson. Bokari, 1973.
Stockwell, John. *In Search of Enemies: A CIA Story*. W. W. Norton, 1978.

Stoker, Bram. *Dracula*. Penguin, 2003.
Tanner, Tony. *The American Mystery: American Literature from Emerson to DeLillo*. Foreword by Edward Said. Cambridge UP, 2000.
The 39 Steps. Directed by Alfred Hitchcock. Gaumont Corporation, 1935.
Thompson, Jon. *Fiction, Crime, and Empire: Clues to Modernity and Postmodernism*. University of Illinois Press, 1993.
Trivadi, Harish. "Reading Kipling in India." *The Cambridge Companion to Rudyard Kipling*, edited by Howard J. Booth, Cambridge UP, 2011, pp. 187–99.
Vermeulen, Pieter. *Contemporary Literature and the End of the Novel: Creature, Affect, Form*. Palgrave Macmillan, 2015.
Von Eschen, Penny M. *Race against Empire: Black Americans and Anticolonialism, 1937–1957*. Cornell UP, 1997.
Wark, Wesley K. "Introduction: Fictions of History." *Spy Fiction, Spy Films, and Real Intelligence*, edited by Wesley K. Wark, Routledge, 1991, pp. 1–16.
Whitney, Robert. "The Architect of the Cuban State: Fulgencio Batista and Populism in Cuba, 1937–1940." *Journal of Latin American Studies*, vol. 32, no. 2, 2000, pp. 435–59.
Wigginton, Chris. *Modernism from the Margins. The 1930s Poetry of Louis MacNeice and Dylan Thomas*. University of Wales Press, 2007.
Wilford, Hugh. *America's Great Game: The CIA's Secret Arabists and the Shaping of the Modern Middle East*. Basic Books, 2013.
Woods, Brett F. *Neutral Ground: A Political History of Espionage Fiction*. Algora Publishing, 2007.
Xin, Wendy Veronica. "Reading for the Plotters." *New Literary History*, vol. 49, no. 1, Winter 2018, pp. 93–118.
Yaqub, Salim. *Imperfect Strangers: Americans, Arabs, and U.S.–Middle East Relations in the 1970s*. Cornell UP, 2016.
Yeats, William Butler. "The Second Coming." *The Yeats Reader: A Portable Compendium of Poetry, Drama, and Prose*, rev. ed., edited by Richard J. Finneran, Scribners, 2002, p. 80. https://www.poetryfoundation.org/poems/43290/the-second-coming. Accessed June 10, 2023.

Index

Afghanistan, 169
Africa, 114, 117, 118, 131n
  Sub-Saharan, 94
  Sudan, 96, 97, 98, 99, 110n, 111–12n
African-Americans, 121–2, and espionage fiction, 11, 124
al-Qaeda, 127–8
Ambler, Eric
  A Coffin for Dimitrios, 34–5, 36, 37, 41–2, 44, 49
  cultural ranking order, 37
  Latimer as narrator, 36–7, 44
  Smyrna massacre, 41
American South, 119–20
antifascism, 9, 44

Boxhall, Peter, 4
British Palestine Mandate, 87
Brooks, Peter, 6
Buchan, John, 15–17

Carré, John le *see* le Carré, John
Central Intelligence Agency, 95, 111n, 113, 116, 126–7, 162
character, 7–8
Chicago, 114, 116, 131n
Civil Rights Movement, 118, 124
Cold War, 53, 56–7, 65, 68
  German Democratic Republic and, 77, 89–90n
Communist parties
  American (CPUSA), 121–2, 132n
  British, 78
  Czechoslovak (KSČ), 54, 57
  East German, 78, 80–1

conspiracy, and conspiracy theories, 10, 97, 102, 108–9
culture, 138–9, 142–3, 146

Delillo, Don, 104, 109, 111n
  The Names, 104–7, 108, 109
Denning, Michael, 9, 37
Diem, Ngo Dinh, 102

Eagleton, Terry, 15

Felski, Rita, 8
Fleming, Ian, 31n

Garve, Andrew, *The Ashes of Loda*, 60–8
gender assumptions, 12, 157–8
genre, 1, 10, 93, 94–5, 96, 103, 104, 107–8, 109, 110n, 114, 117–19, 124, 130n, 133n, 135, 156n, 158, 161, 163–4, 170, 172–3
Germany, SPD and CDU coalition government in, 82
Greece, 39, 48, 106–7, 111n
Greene, Graham, 71
  Our Man in Havana, 71–2, 74
Greenlee, Sam E., 114, 115–16, 123–4, 131n

Hepburn, Allen, 5
Herder, Johann Gottfried, 27
  and national traits, 27–8
Hillis Miller, J., 5–7
Hitchcock, Afred, 16–17
Homeland, 12, 126–30, 158, 167–72
homosexuality, 58–9

Ignatius, David, *Agents of Innocence,* 160, 174n
inevitability of war in the 1930s, 37
intermodernism, 34
irony, 15
Israel and the British left, 87
Israeli-Palestinian conflict, 84, 87

Kennedy, John F., 102–3
Kipling, Rudyard, 15–16, 43
Korean War, 55
"Kultur" (German concept), 23–4

Lassner, Phyllis, 75
le Carré, John, 133n, 160
  Call for the Dead, 75–8
  Jewish characters in, 75, 79–81
  The Little Drummer Girl, 84–7
  A Small Town in Germany, 81–4
  The Spy Who Came In from the Cold, 78–81, 86
  The Tailor of Panama, 71–5, 87
Lowell, James Russell, 43

McCarry, Charles
  The Miernik Dossier, 93, 95, 96, 97, 107
  The Tears of Autumn, 101, 102–4, 107–8
MacInnes, Helen, *I and My True Love,* 53–60
MacNeice, Louis, 35–6, 43–4
  Autumn Journal, 35–6, 43
  cultural ranking order of, 37
  distinct poetic identity of, 43
  geographies of, 47
  Ireland and, 36, 40
  Journal speaker/narrator, 36–7, 38
  modernism and form, 35–6, 41
  prophecy, 36, 38, 49
Marx, Karl, and the "Jewish Question," 86
Maugham, W. Somerset
  and Ashenden stories, 18–19
  Ashenden as collection, 20–1
  and naturalism, 17
  decline of reputation, 17–18
  "Miss King," 21–2
  "Mr. Harrington's Washing," 24–9
  "The Traitor," 22–4

Mediterranean, 105
M15 (Security Service), 137, 144, 148
M16 (Secret Intelligence Service), 137
Middle East, 31n, 87, 160, 161–2, 169–70, 174n
modernism and modernity, 158–9
  elements of, 93–5, 104, 107–8, 110n
Moi, Toril, 7
Moscow, 63
Mosely, Walter, 114, 131n
Mossad, 85

narrative, 113, 116, 118, 147, 152, 161, 165, 166–7, 169
  and memory, 66, 67
  characterization, 98–9, 103–4, 105–6, 107
  defamiliarization, 119
  focus, 101
  form, 94–6, 101, 102–3, 104,
  free indirect discourse, 2–3, 151
  irony, 140–1, 142–3, 151
  story, 8
  theme, 114–15
  trope, 127–8
national communism, 57
national exceptionalism, exposure of, 29
neutrality, 20
Noriega, Manuel, 72
Northern Ireland, 11, 135–7, 138, 140, 142, 146, 148, 152–3
Nussbaum, Martha, 8

Palestinian Liberation Organization (PLO), 85
plot, 5–8
popular fiction, 4, 65
postmodernity, 163
  elements of, 94, 104, 107–8, 109, 110n
prophetic stance in 1930s, three approaches, 45–7
Provisional IRA, 136, 138, 141, 145, 149
  supergrasses, 143–4, 145, 156n

racial prejudice, 113–15, 117, 119–20, 122–3, 127–8, 162

Ransom, John Crowe, 157
  "Judith of Bethulia," 157–8
religion, 107, 110n, 111n, 138–9, 142, 146, 153n, 157, 162–3, 167, 168, 171–2
  religious vs secular beliefs, 12, 159–60
Rimington, Stella, 158, 164
  At Risk, 158, 164–7, 172
Roosevelt, Franklin D., 53
Russia, 63, 66
Russian Revolution, 24–5

Savile Row, 73, 75
Semprun, Jorge, 2, 3
  The Second Death of Ramón Mercader, 2–5
Seymour, Gerald, 135–6, 151
  Harry's Game, 136–43, 146,
  Field of Blood, 143–6
  The Journeyman Tailor, 146–53
Snyder, Robert Lance, 31n, 42
Snyder, Timothy, 66–7

Soviet Union, 159–60
Stalinism, 57
Switzerland, 97
  Geneva, 94, 95

trauma, 76
Trotsky, Leon, 2

Ukraine, 65
United Kingdom, 141–2, 164–5

Vietnam, 102, 159

Wark, Wesley K., 21, 32n
Williams, John A., *The Man Who Cried I Am,* 115, 116–18, 123–4
World War II, 47, 68, 76–7, 159, 162
Wright, Richard, 11, 132n
  "Big Boy Leaves Home," 119–22
  "Bright and Morning Star," 122

Yeats, William Butler, 42

EU representative:
Easy Access System Europe
Mustamäe tee 50, 10621 Tallinn, Estonia
Gpsr.requests@easproject.com

www.ingramcontent.com/pod-product-compliance
Lightning Source LLC
Chambersburg PA
CBHW051126160426
43195CB00014B/2367